W9-AKA-793

FISKE NEW SAT INSIDER'S GUIDE

EDWARD B. FISKE & BRUCE G. HAMMOND

SOURCEBOOKS, INC.
NAPERVILLE, ILLINOIS

CPL YA

DISCARD

Copyright © 2004 by Edward B. Fiske and Bruce G. Hammond
Cover and internal design © 2004 by Sourcebooks, Inc.
Sourcebooks and the colophon are registered trademarks of Sourcebooks, Inc.

All rights reserved. No part of this book may be reproduced in any form or by any electronic or mechanical means including information storage and retrieval systems—except in the case of brief quotations embodied in critical articles or reviews—without permission in writing from its publisher, Sourcebooks, Inc.

This publication is designed to provide accurate and authoritative information in regard to the subject matter covered. It is sold with the understanding that the publisher is not engaged in rendering legal, accounting, or other professional service. If legal advice or other expert assistance is required, the services of a competent professional person should be sought.—*From a Declaration of Principles Jointly Adopted by a Committee of the American Bar Association and a Committee of Publishers and Associations*

All brand names and product names used in this book are trademarks, registered trademarks, or trade names of their respective holders. Sourcebooks, Inc., is not associated with any product or vendor in this book.

SAT is a registered trademark of the College Board, which was not involved in the production of, and does not endorse, this product.

SAT test directions contained herein have been selected from *Taking the SAT I Reasoning Test, 2003–2004, Taking the SAT II Reasoning Test, 2003–2004, The New SAT® and Your School, and How the New SAT® Essay Will Be Scored.* Copyright © 2003 by College Entrance Examination Board. Reprinted with permission. All rights reserved. www.collegeboard.com.

SAT Program Handbook, 2003–2004. Copyright © 2003 by College Entrance Examination Board. Reprinted with permission. All rights reserved. www.collegeboard.com.

Excerpt from *Betty Shabazz: A Life Before and After Malcolm X,* by Russell Rickford, published by Sourcebooks, Inc., used by permission.

Excerpt from *The Best of the Kenyon Review,* edited by David Lynn, from essay "Some Food We Could Not Eat" by Lewis Hyde, published by Sourcebooks, Inc., used by permission.

Published by Sourcebooks, Inc.
P.O. Box 4410, Naperville, Illinois 60567-4410
(630) 961-3900
FAX: (630) 961-2168
www.sourcebooks.com

Library of Congress Cataloging-in-Publication Data
Fiske, Edward B.
Fiske New SAT Insider's Guide/ Edward B. Fiske, Bruce G. Hammond.
    p. cm.
ISBN 1-4022-0163-X (alk. paper)
1. Scholastic Assessment Test—Study guides. I. Hammond, Bruce G. II. Title.
LB2353.57.F59 2004
378.1'662—dc22

                                                          2004003978

Printed and bound in the United States of America
          DR 10 9 8 7 6 5 4 3 2 1

*To Brent Colley,
the world's greatest Hokie fan*

CONTENTS

INTRODUCTION

Cutting through SAT Hysteria

There are many stressful moments in the life of a teenager—like hearing your name on the school intercom followed by the words, "Please report to the main office." Or the awkward silence on a phone line just before you summon the courage to ask, "Are you busy Saturday night?" For pure humiliation, nothing beats the sight of your mom striding close on the heels of the tour guide at First Choice U., notebook in hand, asking yet again about campus safety and whether it is really true that boys and girls share the same bathrooms.

But these moments are kid stuff compared to the phrase that strikes like a thunderbolt through the heart of every high school student:

"Open your test booklet, read the directions, and begin."

Welcome to your worst nightmare: the SAT.

The SAT wasn't always this scary. Though it has existed in its modern form for nearly sixty years, only in the last two decades has the hype become hysteria. Before 1957, students weren't even informed of how well they did on the test. (The College Board communicated directly with the colleges and the student was left out of the loop.) But those were the days when getting in had more to do with where you went to school and who your parents were than your SAT scores. Since the mid-1970s, there has been a steady ratcheting up of the pressure on test-takers as competition to get into the nation's elite colleges has intensified. In the past fifteen years alone, applications to the Ivy League have spiked about 50 percent. At the most desirable colleges in hot locations—like Columbia and NYU in New York City or George Washington in D.C.—applications have more than doubled.

Competition has also heated up among the colleges, which are almost as obsessed with looking good in the rankings as the students are with getting in. Average SAT scores are an important yardstick for the colleges; though they never admit it publicly, the colleges are somewhere between eager and desperate to enroll students with high scores. At colleges that offer merit scholarships, such awards are often available only to students who meet minimum score cutoffs. Despite a growing backlash against standardized testing, and the decision of a few dozen selective colleges to make the test optional, the importance of the SAT for college admission is greater than ever before.

Does all this make you a little nervous? Join the club. Colleges say that a high SAT score is only a small part of the formula for getting in—and certainly less important than your high school transcript. It is true that you can't get in at a selective college without top grades. But thousands of students nationwide rank at or near the top of their high school classes, and you can bet that these students also write good essays

and get great recommendations. When the colleges evaluate their hordes of eager applicants, only one part of the application ranks each student neatly on a universal scale: the SAT.

It is no coincidence that the nation's most prestigious colleges have the highest average SAT scores. In 2003, the average scores of students admitted to the likes of Harvard or Stanford hovered around 750 on both the Verbal and Math sections—scores achieved by less than 1 percent of the test-takers. At Brown, a slightly less selective institution, the averages were closer to 700 Verbal and 700 Math. (All SAT sections are graded on a scale of 200–800, with the national average on each hovering just over 500.) Indeed, the average SAT scores at virtually all selective colleges can be predicted almost exactly by their place in the admission pecking order. To put it another way, students with high test scores are much more likely to be admitted at selective schools than those with lower scores.

The link between SAT scores and admission chances is strong—and would be good reason by itself to make students nervous about taking it. But the scariest part of the SAT is not the fact that it is important, but rather that the results are so unpredictable. From the time they are fresh-faced babes in elementary school, students get grades from a teacher to tell them how they are doing. There is no mystery about grades in

THE POWER OF LEARNING BY DOING

Imagine two people learning how to play a new game. Like basketball. Suppose one of them listens to weeks of lectures on the finer points of the game—how to dribble, how to shoot, how to run a back-door play, how to execute a baseline spin move from the low post. Suppose another person spends all that time actually playing the game. Who do you think will be the better player? Like basketball, taking the SAT is a game that is best learned by actually doing it, not by listening to experts talk about it.

Let's Get Started

We hope that you will find the layout of this book logical and easy to follow.

"Inside the New SAT" gives you the essential facts about the SAT: the nuts and bolts of the new (and old) versions, what the changes will mean for students like you, the role of the SAT in the college admission process, a rundown of exactly what the SAT measures, and an inside look at whether you can psych out the test.

> **"Making the test into a mental game is distracting and can be demoralizing."**
>
> **—640 V, 760 M**

We'll also cover the Preliminary SAT (PSAT) and give you tips on the other major standardized test, the ACT.

"SAT Prep Courses: Straight Talk from Students" lays out the findings of our survey and is chock full of quotes from students who did well on the test about their strategies for beating the SAT, and whether they thought their SAT prep courses improved their scores. If you still want to take a prep course after reading this chapter, be our guest.

"Taking Charge of Your SAT Prep" offers advice on how to prepare for the SAT, including when to take the SAT, how many times to take it, and how to design your own prep course. Based on our surveys, we'll reveal how focused practice can help you devise all-important strategies for skipping problems, making educated guesses, and honing your speed and stamina.

Chapters 4–6 provide a closer look at the Writing, Critical Reading, and Math sections that will comprise the New SAT. Anyone taking the test before March 2005 can skip the Writing chapter and head to Critical Reading, which includes the material in the existing Verbal section. Overviews of the two kinds of questions that will be dropped, analogies in the Verbal and quantitative comparisons in the Math, are also included. Instead of offering long-winded explanations of topics you already understand, we'll give you an inside view of the nastiest tricks the test-makers will throw your way—and how you can beat them at their own game.

"Word for Word: Quotes from the Students about Prep Courses" consists of extensive quotes about test prep from students who took Princeton Review and Kaplan courses, as well as from students who took one-on-one tutoring. Treat this chapter like an appendix. If you doubt our conclusions or want to hear more student voices, this chapter has what you are looking for.

To help you navigate, the first three chapters begin with an "Answers to Your Questions" box that outlines the topics, in order, that will be covered. The chapters on the three sections of the SAT likewise begin with a box that summarizes the types of questions that will be discussed in each.

So what are you waiting for? Don't let procrastination slow you down. You can do it, and the time is now.

school—if you master the material, you get an A. Study hard and you will be rewarded. Though a few slacker-geniuses can get As without doing much, and though some teachers give grades that seem arbitrary, in most classes grades make sense and students know what to do in order to improve them.

The SAT replaces the predictability of school grades with a new standard. SAT scores are reported on a precise numerical scale, yet exactly why particular students get particular scores is often a mystery. The scores usually reflect school grades, more or less, but they also invariably rewrite the pecking order of who is "smarter" than whom. Consider two students who take the same classes in the same school and get the same grades. Call them 1440 Fred and 1220 Teresa. Both have 3.83 grade point averages in the toughest courses, and both took the same prep course for the SAT and studied the same amount. Yet Fred scored 220 points higher. Was it luck? Test-taking skills? Is Fred really a better student than Teresa, even though they have been running neck and neck since middle school? Is Fred better prepared for college? In the big picture, both students scored far above the national average, but that is small consolation to Teresa, who will be less likely to qualify for admission and scholarships because of her lower score. Nobody will ever be able to say for sure why Fred scored 220 points higher, or what, if anything, Teresa could have done to close the gap.

There are several reasons for the confusion surrounding the SAT. Most importantly, nobody can agree on what the SAT measures. Even the test-makers don't have a ready answer. Academic skills are obviously important, but so too are test-taking techniques. The imprecision of standardized testing is another source of uncertainty. Like public opinion polls quoted in the media, the SAT is not a perfect measure

COLLEGE BOARD AND ETS: WHO ARE THEY?

Even many educators don't understand the difference between the College Board, which owns the SAT, and Education Testing Service (ETS), a test-development organization that has a contract to design and administer it for the Board. Often, we'll refer to these two collectively as "the test-makers." The Board will be our primary subject when we're talking about policies and public statements related to the SAT, including the types of test questions. ETS will be our focus when we take a closer look at how particular questions are designed.

of what you know because it doesn't test all your knowledge, but only a sample of it. On the SAT, everybody has a "real" score—the average of what they would get if they took the test an infinite number of times. The odds are about one in three that your score on any particular section will vary from your real score by at least 30 points, and there is about a 10 percent chance that your score will be off by at least 60 points. And that doesn't factor in what will happen if you simply have a bad day.

With such an air of mystery surrounding the SAT, it is no wonder that the test causes such fear and loathing among high school students and their parents. Admission officers try to downplay its importance, but their assurances ring hollow. The test-makers say that the SAT is a test of reasoning, but who really believes that?

The combination of the pressure surrounding the SAT, and all the double-talk about the test from the higher education establishment, paved the way for another player on the college-prep scene: the multi-million-dollar SAT coaching industry. Skillfully playing on the anxieties that so many students logically feel, many prep outfits promise top-secret techniques that will help students outwit the test. Others administer hour upon hour of drills and homework. Many do both. The tab for all this extra cramming frequently tops $1,000.

There has always been a large fly doing the backstroke in the ointment of test-prep.

No one has been able to prove whether it really works. Ask the College Board and you'll learn that the SAT "measures skills developed over a long period of time." Translation: forget studying because there's nothing you can do.

> **"Thinking like the test-maker was good and bad because sometimes I forgot to just think about what I thought."**
> **—590 V, 720 M**

According to the Board, taking a coaching course to prepare for the SAT is unlikely to increase your combined score by a total of more than 30 points. Various studies, most done at the request of College Board and ETS, show this to be true. No surprise here—if test prep were found to be effective, the validity of the test would be undermined. For their part, the test-prep companies claim eye-popping average score gains of as much as 140 points and more on a student's combined Verbal + Math score. They have studies of their own which (surprise!) back up their side of the story chapter and verse.

Suspicious of the test-makers, and not quite trusting the coaching outfits, families can be forgiven if their thinking about the SAT is all over the place. The boy next door says his combined SAT score went up 150 points with Princeton Review? Take a prep course. Cousin Amanda says her score went down 20 points after a Kaplan course? Don't take a prep course. But isn't there a guarantee that my score will go up? Take a prep course. My college counselor says I can probably prepare just as well on my own? Don't take a prep course.

Under the stress of the college search, the allure of the test-prep companies is often irresistible. Facing tens of thousands of dollars in tuition payments, many families are willing to cough up an extra grand on the chance that it might help.

The Truth about the SAT

The purpose of this book is to clear up the confusion once and for all. Hype and hysteria have been swirling around the SAT for years, but now is a particularly crucial time because the test is about to undergo its most significant revision in decades. The new SAT, to be debuted in March 2005, has raised anxiety to a fever pitch. We begin the book with straightforward answers to questions such as:

- How will the SAT change? And what will the changes mean for me?
- What does the SAT really measure?
- How important is the SAT?
- Is it possible to psych out the SAT?

After a balanced look at each these issues, we found that the truth differs in important ways from the party line offered by the colleges, the College Board, and the giants of test prep. But the majority of the book is devoted to answering the two central questions:

- What is the best way to prepare for the SAT?
- Are coaching courses really worth the money?

In over twenty years of writing and counseling about college admission, we have heard variations of these two questions over and over again. Prior to doing the research for this book, even we did not have a ready answer. Unbiased information about prepping for the SAT is hard to get. Even among education professionals, attitudes toward SAT preparation and coaching courses have always been shaped by biases and hunches rather than hard information. Many educators resent the College Board and its stranglehold on the college admissions process. Believing that the SAT is arbitrary and discriminatory, they are inclined to believe the claims of the test-prep companies that the SAT is a rigged game that can be outsmarted if you know the rules. On the other side are educators—including most admissions officers—who believe the SAT has a useful role in college admissions even if it does have flaws. These people are generally suspicious of the slick marketing and dubious claims of the test-prep companies.

For many years, we quoted an admissions officer who said "you pay your money and you take your chances." A pithy turn of phrase but not particularly enlightening. To get beyond the propaganda of the test-makers, the admission officers, and the test-prep giants, we needed an independent voice. It occurred to us that with all the purportedly "inside" information circulating about the SAT, there was one source conspicuously lacking: the students who have actually taken the test.

Since 1981, the *Fiske Guide to Colleges* has offered the inside story on the nation's best and most interesting colleges by reporting straight talk from students coast to coast. This book brings the same kind of insight to the SAT. In what turned out to be one of the largest independent studies ever conducted about preparing for the SAT, we distributed nearly 1,400 surveys to students and received responses from 815 students at 67 high schools. We sought a broad sample of students that included both those who paid for test prep and those who prepared on their own. Our main priority was simple: find out what works. How did students who did well prepare for the SAT? Which prep techniques did they find useful? We also wanted to take a hard look at coaching courses. Would those who got

tutoring or coaching score higher than those who did not? Would those who paid big money see results?

After reading and tabulating 815 surveys, the answer came back loud and clear. The 425 students who did not take a prep course or get a tutor scored a combined 1291, while the 390 students who did take a prep course averaged 1257. The average score for the 119 students who took a course or got tutoring from Princeton Review or Kaplan was 1278.

Surprised? We were. But the more we analyzed our results, the more they made sense. Here are a few of the many insights that you will learn in this book:

- why the highest-scoring SAT-takers seldom benefit from prep courses
- how high-scoring students use their wits to beat the SAT
- why taking full-length practice tests— and analyzing the results—is the single most effective way to prepare

Most importantly, you'll get the collective wisdom (and occasional wit) of 815 students who averaged a combined score of over 1270. If your goal is to score high, there is no better source than students who have recently done so. You'll learn how they prepared for the test—what worked for them, what didn't work, and what they wish they had done differently.

Doing It on Your Own

This book is differs from most SAT prep guides because it does not offer a surefire formula for acing the test. Our bottom line, reinforced by the hundreds of surveys we received from students with firsthand experience, is that most students will be best served by devising their own strategy rather than using a prepackaged approach designed by others. Our job is to report the findings of our surveys—including countless techniques used by real students—and let you choose the methods that make the most sense. We'll offer plenty of guidance on how to shape your approach to the SAT, but you're the one in control.

The most important impact of this book, we hope, will be to unleash the initiative of America's brightest students. (By virtue of buying the book, we count you among that group.)

> **"It seemed that the instructors became talking books. Everything they told us I had already read."**
>
> **—610 V, 690 M**

As our survey makes clear, the savviest students have known all along that they could beat the test on their own. But hype and peer pressure can be powerful forces, and untold thousands of parents and students have been buffaloed into wasting their money on tutors and prep courses. We'll tell more than a few sad stories of such experiences.

There is a strong basis in learning theory for the effectiveness of preparing on your own. Modern research on the brain has proven that initiative and learning go hand in hand, and that active learners retain far more than those who passively listen to others. Memory, it turns out, is constructed rather than absorbed. Students are far more likely to retain knowledge that they themselves have shaped into a meaningful whole. Test prep is not brain surgery or theoretical physics. Every student who takes the SAT has already studied the subject matter on the test. Some students may not want to put out the effort to design their own approach, but all *can* do it if they put their minds to it.

There is an old saying that the best way to learn a subject is to teach it to someone else. Ever wonder why that is so? In the process of explaining something to another person, we are forced to design our own way of ordering the information. We may have already "learned" the material, but we will know it much better after creating a mental blueprint for how to teach it. This blueprint stays in our head and is the context for remembering. When the chips are down, we are far better able to recall information from a blueprint we have made ourselves than one that was handed to us on a silver platter. In studying for the SAT, the most successful students are the ones who teach themselves.

Another insight from our survey that is backed up by learning theory is this: the best way to master the SAT is through focused practice. Instead of cramming their heads full of tricks, top-scoring students experiment with problem-solving methods under conditions that simulate the real test. They learn to handle SAT questions through repetition, and they try various techniques until they find what works for them. They learn how to deal with time pressure by repeatedly facing that pressure in practice, and then developing strategies for dealing with it. And what about all those secret ways to psych out the test advertised by the test-prep companies? Suffice it to say that such gimmicks are more effective at selling prep courses than helping real students score high on the SAT.

We could probably sell more books with a foolproof, patented, guaranteed-or-your-money-back system to beat the SAT, but that would be dishonest. Students learn differently. A great technique for one student may befuddle and unnerve another. Take reading comprehension. Some students swear by reading the questions first, then reading the passage. Others get distracted by reading the questions first. Still others skim the passage and then focus on the questions. The strat-egy you choose is less important than making a choice—your choice.

This book offers a menu of all the best techniques from hundreds of high-scoring students, including:

- how to get your brain in shape and the importance of pacing yourself
- how to get inside the minds of the test-makers and understand what they are looking for
- how to zero in on the correct answer even if you are not sure what it is
- how to overcome your anxiety and approach the test with confidence

Along the way, you'll learn strategies that cover every type of question you'll encounter on the SAT. We'll lay them all out, then guide you toward your own unique strategy for conquering the test.

According to our survey, the number-one reason why students take an SAT prep course is to pay an adult to force them to focus on the SAT. With that kind of attitude, no wonder students do better when they have the initiative to prepare on their own. With the publication of this book, there are no more excuses. Think of us as a $15 alternative to a $1,000 prep course.

1 INSIDE THE NEW SAT

ANSWERS TO YOUR QUESTIONS

- ▶ Why is the SAT changing?
- ▶ How will it change?
- ▶ What about the PSAT?
- ▶ How important is the SAT in admission?

- ▶ What about the ACT?
- ▶ Can you psych out the SAT?
- ▶ What does it take to beat the SAT?

Most readers already know what the letters SAT stand for—or think they know. Scholastic Aptitude Test? Think again. That name bit the dust in 1990. Scholastic Assessment Test? The College Board ran that one up the flag pole in the early '90s, but no, SAT does not stand for that either. The truth is that SAT no longer stands for anything. It is a brand name—like Kmart or Exxon.

The story of the SAT's incredible changing name is convoluted but crucial to understanding the test. The roll-out of the New SAT I in March 2005 will represent a major change in the way the test is put together. Understanding how and why is important to any student who wants to master the test.

The Scholastic Aptitude Test was first administered back in 1926, when everybody thought they knew what aptitude meant. The SAT was an intelligence test, designed to distinguish students who had the potential for higher education from those who did not. In the days when people believed in the validity of IQ—intelligence quotient—it was a perfectly logical exercise. By the 1960s, the SAT had gained wide usage by selective colleges and universities. Previously, the most important questions in college admissions had been "Where'd you go to school?" and "Who's your daddy?" The SAT played a crucial role in opening the doors to gifted students who were not born with a silver spoon.

> **"The most important thing about the SAT is not to be surprised."**
>
> **—730 V, 720 M**

The College Board's fondest hope was that the SAT would become a universal measure of scholastic aptitude—not to be confused with scholastic achievement. The latter was the domain of the ACT (discussed below), the Achievement Tests (now called "SAT II: Subject Tests"), and the Advanced Placement tests. Unlike all of these, the SAT I was not intended to measure what students learned in school. It aimed higher.

But the old SAT was like a spiffy new shirt with a teensy-weensy thread hanging from the sleeve. Give that thread a yank and the whole thing might come unraveled. The root of the problem with the SAT lies in the complexity of the human brain and in the fact that modern research has figured out that intelligence is a complicated, multifaceted thing. Some people have excellent spatial understanding but are lousy in interpersonal awareness. Some people can speak brilliantly but are unable to translate their insight into writing. Some people are speedy in processing information; others process more slowly but produce thoughtful, nuanced answers to complex questions. Three hours of oval blackening will reward students who excel in the particular set of skills and abilities measured by the test, but this exercise may also punish students who have other skills that are just as important—or even more important—for success in college and in life.

The realization that intelligence cannot be measured by two numbers was a major problem for the College Board and its SAT. The SAT was not supposed to be an achievement test, and it clearly was not an adequate measure of intelligence. So what did it measure?

Answering this question is complicated by the fact that students with higher incomes consistently score better on the SAT than they should in relation to lower income students with similar grades. At the same time, members of some minority groups score more poorly than their school performance suggests they should, and girls, who on average get better grades than boys, score less well on both sections than do boys. The College Board says that the test merely reflects the inequities in society.

By 1990, the word "aptitude" had become an embarrassment. It suggested that the ingredients of success were inborn rather than learned. But "scholastic assessment" was no better. By design, the SAT did not measure classroom-acquired knowledge. The College Board already had a complete line of scholastic assessment tests in the form of what is now known as the SAT II: Subject Tests.

Faced with the problem of defending a test that measured neither intelligence nor achievement, the College Board gamely soldiered on. Its brain trust hit upon a new unifying concept for the test—"developed reasoning ability." In effect, the Board was claiming that the SAT measured ability that was linked to schoolwork yet was broader than school learning and, at the same time, was neither a measure of innate ability nor a proxy for socioeconomic status. Is that confusing enough for you? It was a tangled web to weave. Interviewed in 1999 by the PBS television program *Frontline*, Wayne Camara, head of the College Board's Office of Research, summed up the argument this way:

[The SAT] is not an IQ test. It's far from it. Developed reasoning skills measured on a test like the SAT will link directly to the breadth and the depth of the curriculum students have been exposed to in school, but also out-of-school learning. Students who have read an incredible amount, whether it's in-school assignments or out-of-school assignments, are more likely to do better on tests like the SAT but also in college.

So it's not an achievement measure, which would be redundant with what grades are. But it's certainly not an IQ test, which would be an innate measure of ability. It's much more developed reasoning— the type of skills students develop over an extended period of time.

The idea that SAT measured reasoning ability—but not necessarily reasoning ability developed in school—would prove to be untenable. If life outside of school was part of the equation, there was too much probability that SAT scores would be shaped by factors such as family income, ethnicity, and other socioeconomic factors. The notion of developed ability was like blood in the water for the critics.

The mortal blow for the old SAT was a thunderbolt unleashed in February 2001, by the then president of the University of California, Richard Atkinson. Out of the blue, he announced that he would recommend that UC drop the SAT I as an admissions requirement. Atkinson, a psychologist, lashed out at the SAT I as "aligned neither to standards nor school curriculums" and went on to say:

> Simple fairness tells me this is wrong. We are, after all, a society built on twin notions: first, that actual achievement should be what matters most; and second, that people should be judged on the basis of what they have made of the opportunities available to them. Therefore, it seems only right that college-bound students should be judged on what they have accomplished during four years of high school, not on the basis of a single standardized exam designed to test undefined notions of "aptitude." For those reasons, I am recommending to the faculty that the SAT I no longer be required for students applying to UC.

Atkinson stressed that he is not against standardized testing per se—just tests that are not connected to high school curriculum. He reaffirmed UC's use of the SAT IIs, describing them as a better predictor of college performance than SAT I, and called for the design of new standardized tests geared toward what students learn in school.

It would have been interesting to be a fly on the wall at College Board headquarters when Atkinson's announcement came over the wire. "To drop the SAT would be like deciding you're going to drop grades," pouted Gaston Caperton, president of the Board. With 175,000 students on eight campuses, UC was the SAT's largest institutional user and a client that College Board could not afford to lose. Almost before the ink had dried on Atkinson's statement, the Board was busily cobbling together a New SAT that would appease Atkinson and the critics. Barely four months later, the Board announced plans for the changes scheduled to be implemented in March 2005.

How the Test Will Change

Goodbye 1600, hello 2400. The most obvious change in the SAT will be a new way of computing combined scores. The old SAT consists of the familiar Verbal and Math sections graded on the 200–800 scale. The new version will have three sections: Writing, Critical Reading, and Math. Total testing time will increase from 3 hours to 3 hours and 45 minutes. With three sections instead of two, the holy grail of standardized test-taking will henceforth be 2400—a combined perfect score on all three.

It should surprise no one that the New SAT will have a split personality. Its roots as an aptitude test are still apparent, yet it has been dressed up with new material to make it a more credible indicator of what students learn in school. The Verbal section, renamed Critical Reading, will have one major change: the much-dreaded analogies will be deleted. (See box.) In their place, students will get a bigger dose of reading comprehension. Existing passages of up to

800 words will stay, and additional short passages, called Paragraph-Length Critical Reading, will be added.

The Math section will have two significant changes: higher-level math will be added, and quantitative comparison questions will be dropped. Most of the new topics are normally learned in Algebra II. They range from radical equations and negative exponents to quadratic equations. Geometric notation will now be used, and basic trigonometry will appear as an alternative method to solve

OLD SAT
Total Time: 3 hours

Sections
3 Verbal (2 of 30 minutes, 1 of 15 minutes)
3 Math (2 of 30 minutes, 1 of 15 minutes)

1 unscored section

Types of Questions
Verbal
Sentence completions
Analogies
Critical reading

Math
Conventional multiple-choice
Quantitative comparisons
Grid-ins (student-produced responses)

NEW SAT
Total Time: 3 hours and 45 minutes

Sections
3 Critical Reading (2 of 25 minutes, 1 of 20 minutes)
3 Math (2 of 25 minutes, 1 of 20 minutes)
2 Writing (1 of 35 minutes, 1 of 25 minutes)

1 unscored section

Types of Questions
Critical Reading
Sentence completions
Paragraph-length critical reading (100 words)
Reading comprehension (500–800 words)

Math
Conventional multiple-choice
Grid-ins (student-produced responses)

Writing
Student-produced essay
Identifying sentence errors
Improving sentences
Improving paragraphs

some problems. New statistics concepts will include scatterplots, matrices, and geometric probability. The role of a calculator, scientific or graphing, will expand.

Few students will shed any tears over the axing of the analogies. A fixture on the SAT since 1936, analogies have long been synonymous with the test. But in recent years, they have also been a poster-child for the disconnect between SAT and the typical high school curriculum. An example:

ANALOGIES : COLLEGE BOARD ::
  (A) achievement : ACT
  (B) aptitude : test
  (C) essay : writing
  (D) calculator : math
  (E) albatross : Ancient Mariner

British literature buffs will immediately recognize that the correct answer is (E) albatross: Ancient Mariner. Just as the albatross symbolized the Mariner's guilt in Samuel Taylor Coleridge's epic poem, so the analogies are an embarrassing symbol of the SAT's failure to keep up with the times. Simply put, the analogies are irrelevant to anything in school curriculum or in real life. UC's Atkinson said he was moved to consider dropping the SAT when he visited an elite private school where the curriculum in the middle grades included cram sessions on SAT-style analogy questions. The College Board itself now admits that the analogy questions encourage rote memorization of

vocabulary. If only the Board had said that a couple of years ago.

Quantitative comparison questions are also being dropped because students never see questions like these anywhere except on the SAT. Quantitative comparisons ask the student to evaluate two mathematical expressions with four possible answers. Here is an example:

SUMMARY DIRECTIONS FOR COMPARISON QUESTIONS
Answer:
A if the quantity in Column A is greater;
B if the quantity in Column B is greater;
C if the two quantities are equal
D if the relationship cannot be determined from the information given.

$$6x - 12 = 42$$

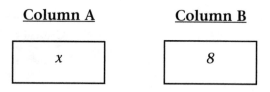

Column A	Column B
x	8

Answer: A. (Since x must equal 9, Column A is greater than Column B.)

Like the analogies, this type of problem never sees the light of day in a classroom and therefore will be axed. As with the old SAT, a few math questions will require students to produce their own answer. The bulk of the questions will remain in the conventional five-question multiple-choice format.

The biggest news comes in the addition of a new section, Writing, created with material lifted from the former SAT II: Writing Test. Multiple-choice questions, also in the format of those on the SAT II: Writing Test, will come in three types: identifying sentence errors, improving sentences, and improving paragraphs. All three kinds are in multiple-choice format and require students to choose the most appropriate word or phrase to be inserted to correct an error or make an improvement.

The most anticipated addition will be a 25-minute essay that the College Board hopes will give the SAT new credibility. A writing test had been high on the University of California's list of priorities. The format will be similar to that of the current SAT II: Writing Test and will feature open-ended prompts that allow students to express a personal opinion. An example: *"Necessity is the mother of invention." Plan and write an essay in which you develop your point of view on this issue. Support your position with reasoning and examples taken from your reading, studies, experiences, or observations.*

As with the old SAT, the new version will include one unscored "experimental" section that will be used to test new questions and may be Critical Reading, Writing, or Math. This section does not count toward a student's score.

The addition of the Writing section will be accompanied by a slight decrease in the time devoted to Critical Reading and Math. Taken as a whole, the changes will add 45 minutes of testing time and increase the registration fee to about $40.00. As a footnote, UC's Atkinson hailed the changes as soon as they were announced. "I give enormous credit to the College Board and to its president, Gaston Caperton, for the vision they have demonstrated in bringing forward these changes and for their genuine commitment to improved educational attainment in our nation," he said in a statement.

And the part about UC dropping the SAT I? It won't happen. Having successfully prodded the College Board into action, Atkinson and UC reversed their decision soon after Caperton announced his plan to change the test.

The New PSAT and the National Merit Program

Although most of the hype is about the New SAT, there will also be a new Preliminary SAT beginning in October 2004. The Preliminary SAT is a modified version of the real thing, administered once a year in October to eleventh graders and many tenth graders depending on high school policy. The PSAT is also the qualifying test for the National Merit Scholarship Program, the largest and best-known scholarship/recognition program in the country.

The changes to the PSAT are less significant than those to the SAT. The PSAT has consisted of Verbal, Writing, and Math sections since 1997, when a Writing section like the one on the New SAT was added. A major difference: the PSAT consists only of multiple choice questions (no essay). It will stay largely the same, and the Verbal portion, renamed Critical Reading, will include the same kinds of questions as the New SAT while also dropping the analogies. As with the SAT, the PSAT math sec-

OLD PSAT	NEW PSAT
Total Time: 2 hours and 10 minutes	**Total Time: 2 hours and 10 minutes**
Sections	**Sections**
2 Verbal (25 minutes each)	2 Critical Reading (25 minutes each)
1 Writing (30 minutes)	1 Writing (30 minutes)
2 Math (25 minutes each)	2 Math (25 minutes each)
Types of Questions	**Types of Questions**
Verbal	**Critical Reading**
Sentence completions	Sentence completions
Reading comprehension (500–800 words)	Reading comprehension (500–800 words)
Analogies	Paragraph-length critical reading (100 words)
Writing	**Writing**
Identifying sentence errors	Identifying sentence errors
Improving sentences	Improving sentences
Improving paragraphs	Improving paragraphs
Math	**Math**
Conventional multiple-choice	Conventional multiple-choice
Grid-ins (student-produced responses)	Grid-ins (student-produced responses)
Quantitative comparisons	

tion will lose the Quantitative Comparisons and feature some higher-level math, but it will not include anything from Algebra II. Though there will NOT be an essay on the new PSAT, schools will be given the option of administering one for practice. Total testing time will be two hours and ten minutes—an hour and thirty-five minutes shorter than the New SAT. The new PSAT will have one less of each kind of section and will not have the 25-minute unscored section. If you are reviewing for the PSAT, all the advice in this book applies.

Unlike the SAT, students register for and take the PSAT through their high schools, which have the option of administering the test on a Wednesday or a Saturday. Students who are homeschooled should contact a local high school and arrange to take the test there. Students occasionally run into problems if their school arranges a Saturday administration that conflicts with an athletic contest or other event. In such cases, they are allowed to take the test at a school other than their own, and those with conflicts should investigate local schools that may be giving it on Wednesday. If all else fails, missing the PSAT is not a disaster. The scores are not generally reported to the colleges and carry little significance once a student completes an SAT. The main value of the PSAT is practice. Most schools keep each student's test booklet on file, and when the score reports come back in December, students can see exactly which questions they missed. The PSAT is scored in a similar way to the SAT, but instead of 200–800, the scale is 20–80.

The long form of the Preliminary SAT's acronym is PSAT/NMSQT, the latter part standing for National Merit Scholarship Qualifying Test. Eleventh graders who take the PSAT are automatically entered in the competition. Each student's scores in the Critical Reading, Writing, and Math sections are added together to create a Selection Index. The top 1.25 percent of eleventh grade scorers, more or less, earn the status of National Merit Semifinalists. The next-highest 3 percent are designated as Commended Students and receive a certificate for their efforts. One footnote: the 1997 decision to add a Writing section to the PSAT was made under the threat of legal action. At that time, many more boys than girls were earning Merit Scholarships, and since girls tend to do relatively better than boys in Writing, the new section was intended to boost the number of female winners. It did, though the goal of a fifty/fifty gender split remains elusive.

Since National Merit mandates a fixed proportion of winners from each state tied to its population, your odds of qualifying can vary depending on where you live. That spells trouble for students from highly educated states like Massachusetts, where the Selection Index necessary for Semifinalist status has traditionally been about 221. In less high-falutin' places like Wyoming or Mississippi, the qualifying score has been closer to 200. (The exact score in each state may vary from year to year depending on the number of high scorers.)

Once the Semifinalists are announced—in September of twelfth grade—they have about a month to write an essay and complete a short application that is coupled with a counselor recommendation. Advancing to Finalist is a snap as long as the student's grades are in the A range. About 90 percent of Semifinalists become Finalists when the new crop is announced in early February. From here, about 2,400 of the highest scorers are awarded one-time scholarships from National Merit of up to $2,500. Major corporations also make awards, usually to Finalists who are dependents of their employees or residents of areas where the corporations do business. About two hundred four-year colleges offer scholarships to Finalists, including some that make a cottage industry of enrolling Finalists with full-ride scholarships. But don't count on anything but a yawn from Ivy-caliber schools, which are overrun with applications from National Merit honorees.

In all, just over half of the Finalists receive a scholarship. Whether or not Finalists get money may have less to do with merit than where they choose to go to college, where they live, and where their parents work.

National Merit also sponsors the separate National Achievement Scholarship Program for outstanding Black American high school students. The mechanics of the program are similar to those of the main program, and just over 775 students are ultimately named as Finalists and are thereby eligible for scholarships. African American students can enter both the National Achievement and National Merit programs.

How Important Is the SAT?

To hear students talk, you'd think that college admission was all about SAT scores—with maybe a quick glance at a student's transcript and letters of recommendation. Keenly aware of the hype, colleges are quick to downplay the importance of scores. High school counselors fall somewhere in the middle; they seek to ease student overemphasis on the SAT while believing in their heart of hearts that the SAT is more important than the colleges are willing to admit.

We spoke to several college admission officers to get their views. "The SAT is one factor in our evaluation of academic achievement and potential," says Jerome Lucido, vice provost for enrollment at the highly selective University of North Carolina at Chapel Hill. "This evaluation includes coursework, grades, rank in class (or its many proxies), awards, achievements, and teacher recommendations. We also consider many personal factors. It is clear, then, that SAT plays a much smaller role in the overall decision than students would believe from the rumors they hear, from the rhetoric of the coaching companies, or from the popular press."

If you polled the admissions directors of fifty highly selective colleges, every one of them would probably agree with this statement. While downplaying the importance of the SAT, admission officers defend its usefulness as one part of the application. In doing so, they walk a fine line. Even the College Board admits that grades in school are the best indicator of college readiness. But the colleges (and the College Board) maintain that the combination of high school grades and SATs is a better predictor than either measure by itself. "The tests are a national measure for all applicants so it helps to equalize consideration of candidates across a wide national and international spectrum," says Karl Furstenberg, dean of admissions and financial aid at Dartmouth College.

David Erdmann, dean of admissions and enrollment at somewhat selective Rollins College, expands on this reasoning: "Our experience is that grading systems, rigor, curriculum, standards, and expectations vary from school to school. Recommendations have the same flaw. The best recommendation for the top student at one high school may have the same praise that might have been heaped on the middle student at another high school. We believe that recommendations typically favor independent school students where the teaching load is lighter, where putting the best foot forward is an expectation, and where the recommendation is generally in greater depth. Essays suffer the same inherent flaw, or can, where the opportunity for assistance is greater. SAT or ACT scores help to level the playing field."

> **"DON'T FREAK OUT! That's the best advice. The SAT is serious but if you are too tense it won't help and it will cause physical and emotional distress."**
>
> **—710 V, 800 M**

We suspect that many admissions officers would also agree with this statement. Yet if it is true that the SAT is the only universal yardstick—or at least true that admission officers perceive it to be—that fact strengthens the hand of those who say that the SAT may be more important than the colleges say it is. Public perception of the SAT as a universal yardstick also plays a role. To a greater or lesser degree, all admissions offices feel pressure to maintain high average SAT scores among their entering classes—high scores look good, and scores are a factor in the rankings produced by *U.S.News & World Report.*

The correlation between high scores and admission to top colleges is exceptionally strong. Dartmouth and UNC at Chapel Hill provide the following figures based on combined scores from the old SAT:

SAT SCORE	PERCENT ACCEPTED	
	Dartmouth	UNC
1600	80	95
1400–1590	36	68
1200–1390	14	39
1000–1190	11	22
800–990	0	11
600–790	0	2

Of course, the colleges would be quick to point out that students who have high scores tend to bring other qualities that make them stand out. Then again, many of the low scorers who get in are athletes or others with special talents.

The gulf in perception that separates those on the high school side and those in college admission offices may lie in how each one sizes up the competition. Top students see themselves as competing against other top students. The student with a 2.5 GPA in a particular high school is not likely to be applying to the same colleges as classmates with a 3.7 or 3.8. Given that students with similar academic records apply to the same schools, what makes the difference? These students all get good recommendations and can generally write a good essay. Today's trend toward grade inflation accentuates the issue. Capable, hard-working students inhabit an increasingly narrow band of grades in the A/A-/B+ range. The SAT is often the only factor that puts meaningful distance between them. A strong student who does not test well may score in the 500s or 600s on each section for a combined score in the 1200s; a student with the same A average who is an SAT whiz may get 700s for a combined score in the 1400s or 1500s.

All this begs an important question: does the SAT measure real abilities? Or merely test-taking skills? We'll weigh in on this raging debate a bit later. For now, suffice it to say that if you're an able student with a strong transcript, your SAT score will determine your fate at selective institutions as much as or more than any other part of your application.

Before we leave the topic of the SAT's importance in admission, it is worth noting that most public universities that are less selective than UNC at Chapel Hill use a different model. With lots of applicants and relatively few admission officers, these institutions tend to rely on test-score cutoffs for admission, though there is often an alternate route to getting in for students who do not achieve the requisite score. The University of Arizona is a typical example. For in-staters, U of A requires that students meet one of the following four criteria for automatic admission: 1) rank in the top 25 percent of the high school class, or 2) have a 3.0 GPA, or 3) a 1040 SAT, or 4) a 22 ACT. Students who do not meet any of these requirements may be admitted if they fulfill other criteria.

Still other schools create a formula for admission that encompasses minimum GPA and test-score requirements. Depending on the formula, it is sometimes possible to compensate for a low test score with a high GPA. Most colleges that use a specific score formula are up-front about it on their websites. Standardized test scores are not necessarily more important at these institutions than at the highly selective places, but at least you know where you stand.

What about the ACT?

Ask someone from Connecticut about the ACT and you may get a blank stare. The same goes if you ask about the SAT in Iowa. The world of college admissions is divided into two fiefdoms of roughly equal size. The SAT was created by a group of Ivy Leaguers as a sorting mechanism for elite East Coast institutions. It is also the dominant test on the West Coast, thanks in part to the influence of the University of California. The SAT is designed to make subtle distinctions between the abilities of above-average students. The ACT was conceived by professors at the University of Iowa in the late 1950s and has historically served the Midwest and Mountain West. It is designed to assess the academic preparation of students of a wider cross-section of students. The SAT is more than thirty years older, and with 1.4 million test-takers a year, it is still the most widely used college entrance exam. But the ACT has been gaining ground in recent years as more students on the coasts seek an alternative to the SAT.

The ACT includes sections in English, math, reading, and science reasoning that are scored on a 36-point scale. The average composite ACT score is between 20 and 21. The vast majority of colleges will accept either the SAT I or ACT to satisfy their core testing requirement. A few highly selective institutions, especially those that are technically oriented, prefer the SAT I because it makes finer distinctions on the high end of the score scale.

For students who are disappointed with their SAT scores, the ACT offers another chance to do well on a standardized test. Though the two tests are used interchangeably, their personalities are far different. While the SAT has always been a sorting mechanism for selective institutions, the ACT was originally created less to help with admission decisions than to determine course placement. While the SAT purports to measure "reasoning," the ACT is an achievement-based test. In practical terms, that means the ACT has more straightforward questions about material you have learned in school while the SAT offers riddles that test big-picture thinking ability. The SAT has always emphasized vocabulary to a much greater degree than has the ACT, which focuses mainly on grammar and usage in its English section. In math, the ACT has stressed knowing the right formulas to solve problems while the SAT gives students the formulas and asks them to solve problems that require more creativity. Time pressure is often a factor on both tests.

The introduction of the New SAT will blur these distinctions somewhat. The College Board is pledging to make the SAT more achievement-oriented—and more like the ACT. For its part, the ACT will offer an optional 30-minute essay similar to the one on the New SAT beginning in February 2005. Up to now, most colleges have said that either the SAT or the ACT will satisfy their testing requirement. But beginning with the Class of 2006, colleges will also specify whether they require a test with a writing component (i.e., the New SAT or the ACT with Writing Test). If your colleges do not require a test with an essay and you don't want to deal with writing one, you can still take the ACT without the essay.

The accompanying chart compares scores on the old SAT with those on the ACT. Students who score significantly better on the ACT may want to consider submitting only these scores to the colleges. If the scores are about even, submission of both sets of scores is probably the best strategy.

ACT–SAT I Conversion Chart

Here is how scores on one correlate with the other, more or less. If a student gets a 23 on the ACT, for example, that's roughly the same as getting a 1070 on the SAT. Look for a revision of these numbers when data on the New SAT become available.

ACT–SAT I CONVERSION CHART

ACT	SAT I
36	1600
35	1580
34	1520
33	1470
32	1420
31	1380
30	1340
29	1300
28	1260
27	1220
26	1180
25	1140
24	1110
23	1070
22	1030
21	990
20	950
19	910
18	870
17	830
16	780
15	740

Is It Possible to Psych Out the SAT?

The biggest brouhaha over the SAT concerns the extent to which it measures real abilities as opposed to mere test-taking savvy. Critics say that knowledge of test-taking techniques plays an outsized role in doing well. The most extreme version of this argument holds that an SAT score is simply a measure of how well a student takes the SAT. By getting inside the mind of the test-maker, the theory goes, students can find the answers to many questions without regard to the subject matter that the question addresses. The most prominent advocate of this view is Princeton Review, which grosses millions each year selling this approach. Independent testing watchdog groups, which generally oppose high-stakes exams such as the SAT, have also bought into this theory because it helps bolster their arguments against the test.

The kernel of truth to this view relates to how ETS designs the SAT. As with many tests that attempt to measure broad abilities, on the SAT most of the questions are chosen based not on whether the answer is an important piece of knowledge, but on how many students get the question right or wrong. For each SAT, there must be a constant proportion of easy and hard questions so that the scores come out right. A 600 on one administration of the SAT must mean the same thing as a 600 on the next administration. Since the easy questions come at the beginning and the hard questions at the end in all sections except Reading Comprehension, students must be wary of obvious answers near the end of each section because they are often tricks designed to fool average test-takers. Princeton Review illustrates this principle with a fictitious character, Joe Bloggs, who represents the average student. Joe Bloggs gets the easy questions right and the hard questions wrong. Here is an example:

If $4^r = s$, which of the following equals $16s$?

(A) 64^r
(B) 4^{16r}
(C) 16^r
(D) 4^{2+r}
(E) 4^{r^2}

This problem is a relatively hard one that Joe Bloggs is likely to miss. In order to get it right, students must understand how to manipulate exponents. For those who don't know the math, response (A) may seem like a logical answer. If we multiply s by 16, shouldn't we also multiply 4^r by 16, thereby giving us 64^r? Of course not. 64^r is a wildly different expression than 4^r, depending on the value of r. The answer is (D) because by changing the exponent from r to $2 + r$, we are multiplying 4^2, which is 16, by the original expression 4^r.

The technical term that test designers use for a Joe Bloggs answer is a "distracter"—an answer made to appear right that is actually wrong. The SAT is full of distracters because

ETS and the College Board want only a few students to score high. At this point, a tip of the cap is due Princeton Review for highlighting an insight that can be summarized as follows: **watch out for easy-looking questions at the end of sections.** Much of the hoopla related to getting inside the mind of the test-makers has its origin in this technique.

> **❝I always skip hard questions so that I won't be rushed and mess up the easy questions.❞**
>
> **—710 V, 740 M**

As far as we can tell, there is not much more than this to "psyching out the test-maker." Everybody knows the test is tricky—but which tricks do *you* usually fall for? The way to find out is by taking the test over and over and learning from your mistakes. We recommend that students be wary of venturing too far into the realm of reading the test-makers' minds, a tangent that can take you away from focusing on your own strengths and weaknesses. The material on the test, based as it is on subjects that all students have studied, is almost always a more reliable guide to finding the answer than shadowy theories about the test-makers' tendencies. If you have the brain power to outsmart the test-maker, the chances are excellent that you can solve most problems based on the content of the questions.

In our survey of 815 students nationwide, we found few students who referenced test-taking techniques of this nature as the most important part of their test prep—or even as a useful part. The allure of learning inside secrets is powerful, but most students find the reality of it less than they imagined. "Making the test into a mental game is distracting and can be demoralizing," says one student who scored 640 V, 760 M. Says another student, who got 590 V, 720 M, "Thinking like the test-maker was good and bad because sometimes I forgot to just think about what I thought." A Princeton Review prepper who scored 620 V, 620 M was simply confused: "I didn't know when to apply their methods. With dozens of kinds of math tricks, it's difficult to know when to use what." Adds another student who took a Princeton Review course and scored 620 V, 620 M, "Joe Bloggs answers and educated guesses don't always work and I found it more difficult to figure out when to use them than to just do the problem." A third student with 600 V, 600 M maintains that "trying to think like the test-maker wastes too much time."

The biggest problem with the psych-out-the-test approach is that it adds to the mental burden that students carry into the test. Students responding to our surveys told us that the most important key to

POLITICAL CORRECTNESS AND THE SAT

Pity the poor white male. Once the top dog in American society, he is fast becoming a pariah—at least if you judge by portrayals in the SAT. We analyzed the Sentence Completion questions in ten SATs administered from 1995–2002 that form the contents of the third edition of *10 Real SATs*, a book published by the College Board. In these questions, the test-makers invent sentences and leave blanks for students to fill in. The subject matter of the sentences does not directly relate to the questions, but it does reveal the extent to which the test-makers are trying to combat the perception that the test is biased against females and minorities. There were a total of 181 Sentence Completion questions in 20 sections, and most of them dealt with fictitious characters. But 32 real people were mentioned. The list included 22 women, 8 African Americans, 5 Hispanics, and 3 Asian Americans. The 10 males included 7 minorities and 2 from overseas. The lone American white male was Thomas Jefferson, referenced in a question about his decision not to condemn lotteries.

The questions mentioned a total of 13 fiction writers by name. Nine were from minority groups and the other 4 were white women. Included were distinguished authors such as Maya Angelou, Toni Morrison, and Virginia Woolf, and somewhat lesser-known figures such as Toni Cade Bambara, Maxine Hong Kingston, Clara Rodriguez, and Li-Young Lee. The diversity was admirable in all respects but one: no white males.

Males took it on the chin in the questions that referenced fictitious individuals. The females included Veronica, the gifted physicist; Gwen, who decided to become a medical ethicist; and Carmen Sanchez, the company president who set a good example for her employees. The males included some shadier characters; every negative reference was to a male. One lad committed an act so "heinous" that it was "appalling" even to him. A certain Mr. Edwards "shocked his associates by reacting violently" without provocation. Another poor bloke "is no scholar" even though he "can regurgitate isolated facts."

A young man named Steven, presumably watching his weight, "found it particularly difficult to forgo chocolate." The behavior of other males was "bizarre," "inexplicable," and "dilatory," while another stirred "violent enmity." A boy named Andrew apparently avoided these pitfalls, though he turned out to be "excessively cerebral."

The closest thing we found to a negative reference to a woman was to a female doctor who "vacillated so frequently on disease prevention" and a female prime minister who "was notoriously intransigent regarding issues of national security."

Our purpose is not to question the value of diversity. We're simply saying that on a test where speed is crucial, it is an advantage to be able to size up female- and minority-centered questions at a glance. For instance, you may find yourself puzzling through pairs of words in which you know the definition of one word in the pair but not the other. If so and the question deals with women or minorities, pick the pair with the most positive word.

The test-makers emphasize female- and minority-friendly content because white males do better on the test. Students of all backgrounds can use this tendency to boost their scores.

doing well on the SAT is a relaxed mind-set. Yet prep courses often make the SAT more complicated and stressful than it needs to be. "I feel the program's pressure truly made me nervous and resulted in my lower scores," says one student who took a prep course and was "greatly disappointed" with his 610 V, 590 M. Another student took a prep course and scored 550 V, 590 M on his first SAT. For the second and third, he "slept more and told myself it isn't that big of a deal." His final scores: 620 V and 650 M.

Students told us that course instructors are often less concerned about the needs of their students than in bragging about how they can outsmart the test-makers. "The prep course concentrated too much on stressing ETS is trying to trick you instead of spending time doing practice tests," says a student who scored 570 V and 610 M. We are inclined to agree with the 680 V, 670 M scorer who says, "I feel that the people who pay hundreds of dollars for tutors, study and practice for the test for hours, and take the test like eight times, do less well than those who just relax."

The people who emphasize getting inside the mind of the test-makers are cashing in to the tune of millions of dollars. But they've got it all wrong: the real key isn't to psych out the test but to psych up yourself. Instead of trying to cram your head full of someone else's tricks, focus on your own preparation:

- your way to beat test anxiety
- your way to increase your test-taking speed
- your way to approach the Reading Comprehension
- your way to figure out the tough math problems

Just as an athletic team should focus mainly on its own play rather than worry about what the other team will do, so must SAT-takers be primarily concerned with conditioning their minds to score high.

What It Takes to Beat the SAT

Everyone wants to know what the SAT really measures. Intelligence? Reasoning ability? Factual knowledge? Mere test-taking wizardry? Good guesses all—but all wrong.

Nominally, the New SAT includes sections on reading, writing, and math skills. Strong ability in each of these is essential to scoring well. Some students may need to brush up on math, others may need to work on their vocabulary or their mastery of written English. Subject matter matters.

But just as important are qualities that you'll never read about in a College Board brochure. Here is our assessment of what really matters on the SAT:

A Clear Head Under Pressure

Nothing is more important to success than the ability not to stress out. A tense brain processes information more slowly and makes more mistakes than a relaxed one. In the primeval forest of 10,000 years ago, anxiety meant fight or flight. Anybody who takes a 3-hour-and-45-minute test while fighting that impulse is bound to score lower than someone who is less anxious. The students who do best on the SAT are generally calm and confident. The heightened alert of a testing situation may actually help them think more clearly.

Speedy Thinking

Students who think faster do better on the SAT. Students who think more slowly do not have time to finish the test, or they miss questions because they are worried about not having enough time. Speed takes the pressure off and gives students time to go back and check their work. Speed is especially crucial on the critical reading, where many students get bogged down and stressed out. And what about trying to write a decent essay in 25 minutes? Quick thinkers are not always the deepest thinkers or the most nuanced. But as long as the College Board and ETS use time pressure as a sorter, fast workers will come out on top. The College Board has never provided an adequate educational reason why the test should be timed. (The Board does argue that the SAT reflects the fact that many tests in college are timed.)

Ability to Stay Focused

Chess players make good SAT takers. Why? Because they know how to put their minds inside a game that has many angles. A good test-taker never loses focus on what the game is—to get the questions right. Some students make the mistake, for instance, of getting really interested in the reading comprehension passages. Bad idea. They waste valuable time learning about a fascinating subject when they should focus on the questions and then move on. Some bright students get confused because they let outside knowledge intrude into the logic of a question and its answer. Many SAT questions have more than one answer when removed from their context. A good test-taker edits out this noise without thinking about it. She is focused, surgical, and sequential. Gets the right answer— moves on to the next.

> **“Because the multiple-choice answers are supposed to mess you up, if you dwell on any one too long you'll probably get tricked and miss it.”**
>
> **—790 V, 800 M**

A Feel for Proper English

Don't count on your literature class to give you the skills necessary to do well on Critical Reading and Writing. Exposure to good grammar from the time you were knee-high is much more important. Many students, for instance, cannot define the subjunctive mood but know that "if I was going to the store" is incorrect. (It should be "if I *were* going to the store.") Many students can get sentence completion problems without even looking at the answers by being familiar with words commonly paired together. For example, you might encounter a problem such as, "Because there were _____ circumstances, he was not punished for his misdeed." The answer to this portion of the question is

NEW SKILLS FOR A NEW SAT

The main keys to success on the New SAT are the same as those on the old one. But the relative emphasis will change. Here are the most important new developments:

▶ **Verbal skills will be twice as important as math.** With the addition of the Writing section, verbal skills outweigh math by 2:1. Cynics see this as partly an effort to boost the scores of girls, much as the College Board did in adding a Writing section to the PSAT.

▶ **Vocabulary will be less important.** The analogies hinged largely on word definitions. Though some sentence completion and reading comprehension questions will still emphasize vocabulary, word meanings in these questions can be figured out in the context of a sentence or paragraph.

▶ **Advanced math knowledge will matter more.** The old SAT included math rooted in simple formulas that everyone had learned by first-year algebra and geometry. The trick has always been knowing how to set up the problem. This emphasis will remain strong, but the new math will require more formula know-how.

▶ **Students must write an essay.** Bet you're glad to get this breaking news. The emphasis is on composing thoughts quickly and getting them down in an organized way with concrete examples to back up your point of view. Preparation will potentially make a bigger difference here than anywhere else on the test.

"extenuating"—easy for someone who knows that "extenuating" and "circumstances" often go together.

Reading and Word Power

Though the decision to drop the analogies will mean that the New SAT has less emphasis on knowing definitions, vocabulary will still be very important. The Sentence Completion questions in Critical Reading are really vocabulary questions, and the Reading Comprehension section also tests vocabulary. The number-one, all-time best way to prepare for the SAT—even better than having dinner every night with your college-educated parents—is to read, read, read (with a dictionary). Reading helps you recognize words and know their meaning, but that is only the beginning. Most students don't realize that the SAT math is also in large measure a reading test. The math questions spin scenarios that must be kept straight in the student's mind—a skill that is developed by reading. Readers develop the focus necessary to stay tuned to the test and the ability to move through it quickly.

Problem-solving Ability and Short-term Memory

Notice we didn't say "mathematical" ability? The SAT Math section uses math to test students, but it isn't about math. The Math section takes problems that everyone knows how to solve and disguises them. Or it adds a tricky twist, like asking for the greatest integer that is less than the solution to a particular computation. We offer an overview of such shenanigans in our chapter on the Math section. For now, suffice it to say that knowing how to solve math problems is less important than understanding how to stay on top of complicated scenarios. A lot of it boils down to simple short-term memory. Many questions are difficult not because they require challenging computations, but because they stack up elementary ones in confusing ways. Keeping it straight is the name of the game.

> **"Approach the SAT as a series of problems to solve, not a test that will determine the rest of your life."**
>
> **—700 V, 760 M**

Stamina

Though less important than speed, stamina will get more important with the 3-hour-and-45-minute format of the New SAT. In your daily school life, when do you ever focus for 3 hours and 45 minutes non-stop? Maybe at exam time but probably not even then. Taking the SAT is like running a marathon—it takes training to discipline your mind and body to focus for that period of time. Students who do poorly on the SAT generally lose focus halfway through the test.

Developing Your Own Approach

As usual, the truth about the SAT is somewhere between the College Board's public pronouncements and the overheated rantings of the critics. The SAT does measure real abilities that are important to academic success. If your academic skills are limited, no amount of hocus-pocus will get you a high score. On the other hand, there is no good reason why these particular characteristics should be valued more than many other skills and characteristics that lead to success in college and in life, skills that the SAT does not measure. Is the SAT tilted in favor of certain types of people and against others? Definitely.

The good news is that preparation can make a difference. If you're a white-knuckle test-taker, practicing the test can help you increase your comfort level. If speed is your problem, techniques can be learned to buy you some extra time. By fine-tuning the pace at which you move through the test, you can further ease your anxiety. If you are uncertain in your writing skills—or even if you're not—some concentrated planning for the new essay is likely to improve your score. If math gives you trouble, focused preparation will increase your comfort level and make you a little more intuitive when the chips are down. By trying out various problem-solving strategies, you can find the ones that will help you most.

A miracle is probably not in the cards, but there is plenty you can do to raise your score. We'll tell you how—based on the insight of hundreds of high-scoring students.

2 SAT PREP COURSES
STRAIGHT TALK FROM STUDENTS

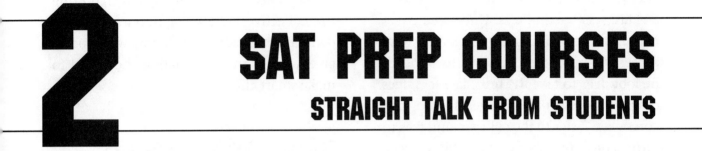

ANSWERS TO YOUR QUESTIONS

▶ **Do coaching courses really work?**

▶ **If not, why are they so popular?**

▶ **What do students say about prep courses?**

▶ **What advice do students have about preparing?**

Anyone who managed to remain semi-conscious in AP English may have a vague recollection of Odysseus and his encounter with Scylla and Charybdis. Don't remember that one? It was when Odysseus had to steer his ship between Scylla, a six-headed monster, and Charybdis, who swallowed boats in a whirlpool and then spit them back out. Still doesn't ring a bell?

When it comes to taking the SAT, the seas are ruled by two giants that are just as powerful, if slightly less menacing.

One of them is a two-headed monster, the College Board and ETS, which uses the

SAT to create a mixture of fear, confusion, and exhaustion in its prey. After the reasoning test has neutralized the reasoning powers of each hapless student, College Board and ETS proceed to one of their most important tasks: extracting fees. Under the cover of an acorn logo and nonprofit status, they devise ever-more creative ways to bring in the loot: fees to take the tests, late fees, fees to report scores to the colleges, fees to rush scores even faster to the colleges, and fees to learn scores by phone. For the College Board and ETS, the SAT is a cash cow. They roar with rage when anyone suggests that the test can be beaten with coaching.

The other giant of standardized testing seduces its victims with a soothing melody about acing the SAT. It whispers things like, "The SAT is a scam" and "We guarantee your SAT score will improve by at least 200 points." Ah, the siren song of Princeton Review—the biggest name among the legions of tutors and test-prep gurus nationwide that offer a magic bullet to slay the standardized test monster. While College Board and ETS create fear and loathing, the test-prep giants play on it. Though not a whirlpool exactly, the test-prep industry can suck you under and spit you out—minus $1,000 and a few dozen hours of your time.

Are the College Board and ETS correct in their claims that coaching for the SAT won't help (much)? Can the right coaching guarantee that your score will rise? It occurred to

us that one way of answering this question might be to ask people with firsthand experience. We went to the ultimate source for straight talk about the SAT—the students who had just finished taking it. By reporting the collective wisdom of hundreds of students from dozens of schools, we hope to give families the information they need to make smart choices.

The Story Behind the Survey

In February–April of 2003, we conducted what turned out to be one of the largest independent surveys of SAT preparation practices ever done. We began by enlisting the help of high school guidance counselors who had been generous as expert consultants to the *Fiske Guide to Colleges* and the *Fiske Guide to Getting Into the Right College*. Several years before, we had begun seeking the input of college counselors across the nation about the Fiske Guide series. Of this group, 70 agreed to distribute and collect the survey from up to 20 students. A high proportion of these counselors work at private and suburban public schools, and a few are independent counselors. We chose this population because we knew that it would include a high proportion of top scorers—useful for their insight into scoring high on the test—and a high proportion of students who paid for test-prep services.

Most previous studies—whether sponsored by the test-prep companies, the test-makers or someone else—consisted of a before-and-after analysis of a particular group. Their method: give the SAT to a group of students who know nothing about it, give them a prep course, and test them at the end. But studies such as these, typically done at the behest of the test-prep giants, are open to the possibility of manipulation. The first SAT taken by the students—the one used as a benchmark to measure improvement—is often not a real SAT but an imitation designed by the company doing the study. Assuming that these imitations approximate a real SAT, they carry none of the pressure of a real one. Furthermore, there is no guarantee that the students chosen to be part of the studies are typical of all test-takers—indeed, some studies are conducted on a sample of students whose scores are known beforehand.

> **"Don't buy into the frenzy out there. Some of these prep companies try and 'sell' you packages you don't need."**
>
> **—680 V, 640 M**

Most importantly, these before-and-after studies were asking the wrong question. The issue is not whether preparing for the test can make a significant improvement in your score. Just about everyone would agree that it can. The real issue is: *can a coaching course or tutoring improve your score more than preparing on your own with books and software?*

Our first order of business was to divide the surveys into two piles: those who had received face-to-face instruction, and those who had not. Among the first group were students who had paid for one-on-one tutoring and those who had participated in a coaching course offered by a private firm or at their school, including a few students who had received a prep course for the PSAT. Many in this group had paid hundreds of dollars for their course, though those who took a school-based course typically paid less, and a few got the course for free. This group also included a handful of those who had taken an online prep course.

Eye-Opening Results

From the total of 815 students, 390, or 48 percent, had received coaching while 425, or 52 percent, had prepared on their own. Our most important question was whether those who had face-to-face instruction earned higher scores than those who had not. Based on the highest verbal and highest math score of each student, we found that students who did not take a prep course scored higher than those who did.

> Average score for **coached** students:
> 636 Verbal, 621 Math
> Average score for **uncoached** students:
> 645 Verbal, 646 Math

The distribution of combined scores for coached and uncoached students, based on highest verbal and highest math, is below. Included are the total number of students, coached and uncoached, who earned a combined score in each range. Percentage figures represent the proportion of the total within that range:

Score	Coached	Uncoached
Below 1000	31 (53 %)	28 (47 %)
1000–1090	32 (50%)	32 (50%)
1100–1190	64 (56%)	50 (44%)
1200–1290	87 (48%)	93 (52%)
1300–1390	87 (49%)	90 (51%)
1400–1490	74 (48%)	79 (52%)
1500–1600	15 (22%)	53 (78%)

Two surprising findings emerge from these data. First, students who got face-to-face coaching for the SAT actually scored lower, on average, than those who did not. Those who took a prep course received an average combined score of 1257, while those who did not averaged 1291. In each score interval below 1500, there are approximately equal numbers of those who received coaching and those who did not.

Second, among students who scored above 1500, a much smaller fraction received coaching than among students who scored lower. High scorers typically prepared for the test on their own. And as we will see below, students in this group who did take a coaching course or tutoring generally found it to be a waste of time. The difference of 34 points between the combined scores of the two groups is due primarily to the fact that those who scored above 1500 were less likely to have taken a prep course.

Princeton Review and Kaplan

An important emphasis of our study was to examine the results achieved by students who took coaching courses from the two major national test prep companies, Princeton Review and Kaplan. Of the 815 students in our survey, 72 reported that they took a Princeton Review classroom course, 46 took a classroom course from Kaplan, 5 went to Princeton Review for one-on-one tutoring, and 1 took an online course from Princeton Review. These totals include students who took a standard classroom course from the two firms—typically lasting about 40 hours—and students who took a school-based course of variable length offered by one of the two firms. Five ambitious souls took a class or tutoring from both Kaplan and Princeton Review.

The combined group of Kaplan and Princeton Review preppers included 119 students from 44 schools in 21 states. The results? The Kaplan preppers had an average score of 637 Verbal and 665 Math for a combined score 12 points higher than those who did not take a prep course. Princeton Review's averages were 624 Verbal and 640 Math, 26 points below the non-prep average.

These differences are probably meaningless. It may be that students with high verbal scores are less likely to take a prep course, or that prep courses have slightly better success in raising math scores. But the bottom line is that prepping with Kaplan or Princeton Review did not correlate with higher scores among our survey participants.

Below is the combined distribution of scores, based on each individual's highest verbal and math score, of the 119 students who prepped with Kaplan or Princeton Review. The first percentage figure refers to the percentage of Kaplan/Princeton Review preppers who were in that interval. The second is the percentage of all students in the survey who scored in that interval.

Score	# Kaplan/ Princeton Review Prep	% Kaplan/ Princeton Review Prep	% of entire survey
Below 1000	6	5	7
1000–1090	7	6	8
1100–1190	24	20	14
1200–1290	27	23	22
1300–1390	22	18	22
1400–1490	27	23	19
1500–1600	6	5	8

These numbers show that the distribution of scores of those who took a Princeton Review or Kaplan course differs little from the distribution of those who did not. Some students who took Princeton Review or Kaplan scored high, others scored low, still others scored in the middle.

It should be noted that while many of these students took the standard Princeton Review or Kaplan course, others took school-based courses offered by personnel from these companies. Such school-based courses can be shorter in duration than a full-blown Princeton Review or Kaplan course.

Nevertheless, our survey offers strong evidence that a prep course with Princeton Review or Kaplan is not likely to be more effective than preparing for the SAT on your own. Because many of the students who do prepare on their own use Princeton Review or Kaplan materials, one obvious piece of advice is to save your $1,000 and buy the book for about $15. But we also have our doubts about the techniques of the test-prep giants, which we will address below.

Score Increase Claims: A Closer Look

It should come as no surprise that our results are at odds with what the big test-prep companies say. In recent years, Princeton Review has advertised an average score increase of 140 points for students who take its classroom prep course. The company

WHEN MOM AND DAD PUSH THE PREP COURSE

A majority of the students in our survey who paid for SAT coaching said that the idea came from mom and dad. That's understandable—parents are the ones who pay the bill. But our questionnaires found numerous instances when over-stressed parents crammed a cram course down the throat of an unwilling student. One my-mom-made-me-do-it prepper describes his course as "a waste of time and money," adding that "what helped was sitting down by myself and becoming comfortable with the format." He scored 700 V and 730 M. Another student says his math tutoring was "worthless" and that he reacted negatively "because it was not my choice." His scores were 760 V, 690 M and he advises students to take practice tests and prepare on their own. Yet another student was prodded by his parents to get tutoring in math after he scored "only" 640 the first time. "It was boring and I wasn't told anything I didn't already know. I'm just glad my parents paid for it, not me," he tells us. And his math score the second time? 640 again. Asked about the benefits of her prep course, another student who scored 520 V and 630 M replied: "It pleased my parents." Were the benefits worth the cost? "NO!"

cites a study conducted at its behest in 2002 by a corporate communications firm. The sample included 693 students, out of which 138 provided usable responses. The average combined score increase for the latter group was 136 points. We have three observations about the study:

- Princeton Review selected the students who would be included in the survey pool
- An unknown number of the score increases were computed based on a Princeton Review diagnostic test rather than a real SAT
- Only 20 percent of the students in the initial sample were included in the results

Kaplan does not claim an average score increase for its students. According to a statement from Justin Serrano, the Executive Director of Kaplan Test Prep, "Score improvement statistics can be manipulated to create the appearance of a particular test score improvement, when, in fact, those results were based on small samples of students with nonrepresentative score distributions."

There are no guarantees in college admission—unless you sign up for an SAT coaching course from the leading test prep companies. "We guarantee your SAT score will improve by at least 100 points, or we'll work with you again for up to a year FREE," says Princeton Review. In other words, there is good news and bad news: you don't get your money back, but you can enjoy another free year of the same preparation that didn't work the first time. Kaplan does offer a money-back guarantee. The hitch: Kaplan guarantees only a score increase. If you go up 10 points, no dice. Given that the College Board says that the typical student goes up nearly 30 points between tests anyway (from eleventh to twelfth grade), this guarantee is less than scintillating. In order for the guarantees to apply, students must attend all the sessions and do all the homework. (At press time, Princeton Review had upped its score-increase guarantee to 200 points for the New SAT.)

Princeton Review says that the average composite score increase of students who take its classroom course is 140 points. Of the 78 students who took our survey and reported taking a class from Princeton Review, 72 responded to the question: **"How much do you think your prep course increased your composite SAT score?"** The results:

None	8
50 points or less	19
60–100 points	30
110–150 points	11
160+ points	4

The totals include students who took a Princeton Review classroom or school-based course, one-on-one tutoring, or an online course. School-based courses are sometimes shorter than the Princeton Review's regular classroom course and the 100 point score-increase guarantee may not have applied in all cases.

Why the Myth Won't Go Away

If the case for an SAT prep course is so weak, why do families continue to spend millions on them every year? The reasons are complex. With the cost of a year at Prestige U. now pushing $40,000, some families don't seem to mind ponying up another $1,000 with an "it-can't-hurt" philosophy. Common sense says that preparing for the SAT—whether on your own or through a course—can indeed improve your score. The fallacy, skillfully perpetuated by the test-prep giants, is the notion that families face a choice between spending big dollars for a prep course or doing nothing. But that's not the way it is.

Part of the reason for the test-prep mania lies with the College Board's lack of credibility on this issue. For decades, the Board insisted that preparation could have no meaningful impact on a student's score. While still pooh-poohing the impact of test prep, the Board now sells its own line of test-prep books and software. Hmm. Also crucial was the Board's inability to develop a convincing explanation of what the SAT really measures. Is the test really about "reasoning?" Or does it merely use simple subject matter to create tricky questions?

THE VOICE OF EXPERIENCE

We found a true expert on test-prep in the person of a 540 V, 670 M scorer who took three coaching courses—one from Princeton Review, one from Kaplan, and a third with another commercial firm. What did he learn?

"Hey, it's a business. You're just fooling yourself when you think that money will buy you knowledge."

He says his family spent "a lot" on prep courses that "became tedious and a burden." The bottom line? "I advise preparing on your own with books or software. Keep in mind that the prep courses work with the same books. Buying them and not attending classes can save a lot of money."

The disconnect between how College Board talked about the test and how students experienced it created an opening for anybody who could sell straight talk. Prior to 1980, test prep was a relatively sleepy industry dominated by Stanley H. Kaplan, the forerunner of today's Kaplan that was founded in the 1940s by its avuncular proprietor. But the industry took off in the 1980s with the rise of Princeton Review and its hipper-than-thou image and aggressive guarantees of score improvement. Countless other regional, local, and online companies have gotten into the game.

In the world of SAT coaching, perception is reality. Many students will never know for sure whether or how much their scores have increased because they take a prep course before their first SAT (or PSAT). But if you've been told again and again that your scores will increase, the common tendency is to believe it. Naturally, there are some instances when test scores do increase dramatically: from coaching, a good night's sleep, lack of a headache, the imponderables of fate, or the statistical margin of error in the SAT. When this happens after a prep course, students are sure to attribute the rise to their course and spread the word far and wide, leading to the "so-and-so increased by 200 points" buzz. Students whose scores do not go up after a prep course are disappointed and embarrassed. They're also a lot less likely to brag about it in school. It's a bit like people who talk about their experience in the stock market. They're not likely to bend your ear about the clinkers.

Students Talk About Their Prep Courses

Many people assume that an adult standing in the front of the room, with students listening attentively, will automatically raise scores. But studies among college students have shown that those who listen to a lecture learn no more than those who get a transcript of what was said. That bodes ill for national test prep companies because many instructors are recent college graduates who rely heavily on company books. "What was taught in the classroom was the exact same thing printed in the Kaplan book I bought from the bookstore," complains a 740 V, 690 M scorer. Another student who prepped at a local firm and scored 610 V, 690 M writes, "It seemed that the instructors became talking books. Everything they told us I had already read.... The instructors often didn't know the answers to questions outside our homework."

Despite the subjectivity involved, we wanted to know about students' perceptions of whether coaching increased their scores. The survey gave students a choice of five responses to how much they thought their composite score increased: None; 50 points or less; 60–100 points; 110–150 points; or 160+ points. The most common response was 60–100 points, followed by 50 points or less. Together, these two responses formed a solid majority across all score intervals and all test prep companies. Lesser and approximately equal numbers of students believed that their score went up not at all, or 110–150 points, and a smaller fraction believed that its scores had gone up 160 points or more. There was only one systematic difference in the responses. Those who scored lower than 1100 were less likely to believe that their score had jumped more than 100 points.

> **"They just gave us practice tests and went over the given answer explanations, something I could have done in my own time. They said they would promise to raise your score, or you may take the course again for free. But since I am a senior and I am not going to take the SAT again then that does not help me."**
>
> **—580 V, 560 M**

Of the students who thought that their prep course was worthwhile, few cited test-taking strategies or the insight of the instructor as the reason why it was useful. The most commonly cited benefit was access to practice tests; a close second was having someone on the scene to make sure they got done. "The course itself did not provide many helpful hints but did force me to take practice tests," says a 600

V, 600 M scorer. "My tutor made me do the work on the tests," admits another student who scored 690 V, 710 M. "If he hadn't forced me to do it, I probably wouldn't have done it."

Many students tended to be forgiving when coaching courses failed to deliver the promised score increases. "I learned a lot of great strategies but did not improve my score by the 100 points that were guaranteed," said a 650 V, 550 M Princeton Review student of her prep course. "I would still recommend it to other students because I know that it can be very helpful for many students."

> **"If you are one to cheat yourself, to take short cuts and to lose motivation, take an SAT course with outlined rules and requirements."**
>
> **—560 V, 650 M**

"I only increased 10 points," wrote a 540 V, 560 M Princeton Review prepper who elsewhere noted, "I would recommend this course. It was very helpful learning the tips on how to take the SATs." Another Princeton Review student with a combined score of 550 V, 630 M had an interesting hypothesis about score increases: "Each time I took a practice test my score improved. I think the tests they gave got easier, because my real SAT score was a lot lower than my final practice score." One 640 V, 590 M scorer was perturbed by what she perceived as Princeton Review's lack of follow-through. "Princeton Review did not keep its word about private tutoring if I didn't go up 100 points from my first practice test. I had to find a tutor on my own." (Princeton Review's guarantee for private tutoring is the same as for its classroom courses.)

The Test-Prep Syndrome

A final reason why families don't balk at ineffective prep courses might be styled "The Test-Prep Syndrome." This is the tendency to identify with one's tutor after long hours in captivity cramming for the SAT. It is human nature, especially among adolescents, to bond with adults who give them time and attention. "I had an amazing and inspiring tutor who motivated me to do well on the SATs," wrote one student who scored a combined 1090, "My tutor opened my mind to so many wonderful things. Her and I established a close relationship and I enjoyed working with her so much." Unfortunately, this student's scores went down 10 points after working with the tutor to the tune of $110 per hour. Were the benefits of this tutoring worth the cost? Perhaps. The tutor is probably a fine person who will get a solid endorsement when another family is seeking an SAT coach.

From a mixture of hype, anxiety, and the very real student/tutor relationship, SAT coaching has become a fixture on the landscape of the college admission process. Faced with the anxiety of a high-stakes test, families find comfort in the belief that buying a service will help cope with the problem. Just be forewarned that extra hand-holding might not mean a higher score.

A Closer Look at the Questionnaires

Below, we summarize the responses to our survey with reference to the highest combined score achieved by the students: those who scored 1500 or better in the first cohort, those who scored 1300–1490 in the second cohort, etc. Each group seemed to have its own personality, which hinted at why the students got the scores they did.

The surveys offer a revealing glimpse of attitudes and experiences of today's students related to the SAT and preparing for it. They also provide strong evidence of the

ANATOMY OF A 1600

Julie Zhou is anything but a test-prep geek. From rock climbing to the math club, she did it all. But when the time came to take the SAT, she was focused. On her first try, she notched a spiffy 1550 with 750 Verbal and 800 Math. Good enough for most people, but not for Julie. "I realized from the results of my first SAT that my vocabulary skills needed the most improvement," she recalls. "I really focused on that aspect of the test and scraped together a long list of words provided by my school, prep books, and books I read for enjoyment and studied until I knew them all." Her regimen also included plenty of practice tests. "They were effective in letting me get the feel for the test. I usually didn't work an entire test all the way through, instead concentrating on my most difficult sections." Julie describes her preparation for the math section as "finding new ways to check my answers." By knowing the angles backwards and forwards, she could leave herself more ways of solving a problem and more methods to ferret out mistakes. Another piece of advice from Julie: "Towards the end of each section, the most tempting answers are always wrong." Her hard work paid off when she took the SAT a second time and nailed a 1600. "Be cautious but confident," she advises, "You are all capable of owning this test with adequate preparation."

Julie Zhou graduated from The Westminster Schools in Atlanta, Georgia. She now attends Harvard University.

overwhelming importance of the SAT in the lives of ambitious, high-achieving young people. By grouping the responses according to test score, we are consciously accentuating that emphasis for the purpose of this study. The reader can draw his or her own conclusions as to whether emphasis on the SAT has gone too far.

Readers should also be reminded that students in the survey are part of a selective group. In many cases, they attend schools where the average SAT score is 1200 or higher. Their perceptions of a "good" or "bad" SAT score are shaped accordingly.

Students Who Scored 1500–1600

You know who they are. You've seen them in your honors classes. They're the geniuses, the uber-testers, the disgustingly smart people who are always busting the curve in AP Calculus BC. On the SAT, they scored in the top one-half percent of test-takers and most of them will attend places like Harvard and Brown. They make you want to blow chunks.

But who are these people and how did they get such high scores? By studying day and night? Prep courses up the wazoo? Not exactly. It turns out that students who scored above 1500 were mostly nonchalant about their achievement. A total of 68 students in our survey scored 1500 or better—including four that registered a perfect 1600—but only 15 had coaching of any kind. "Test prep is stupid. The less I prepped the better I did," chirped a 790 V, 720 M scorer. This lad says he prepared less than five hours for his first SAT and got a combined 1380, then did nothing before the second test and went up 130 points. In response to a question about how he prepared for his second SAT, a 770 V, 800 M scorer replied, "I ate breakfast." As a group, the 1500s were more confident and less likely to take the test multiple times. Forty-three percent didn't bother to take it twice, including two who scored 1590 on the first try and apparently felt no desire to go for a 1600.

It may be that the 1500+ scorers had good reason to be confident, and perhaps

AN UNSOLVED MYSTERY

One survey participant scored 1400 on her first attempt, then plummeted to a 1260 on her second. "I have no idea how my score dropped, although I didn't go to bed until 2:00 a.m. the night before but I thought I did really well. Mom made me take it the second time."

they only took the test once because they got the score they needed, but we think their relaxed air may have something to do with why they aced the test. "Don't freak out," declares a 710 V, 800 M scorer bound for University of Illinois at Urbana-Champaign, "The SAT is serious but if you are too tense it won't help and it will cause physical and emotional distress."

Despite the laid-back tenor of the high scorers, plenty of them worked hard to improve their scores. One student prepared on her own for more than 30 hours per week for her first SAT and got a combined 1290. For two subsequent tests, she accelerated her efforts, working more than 40 hours per week with a study book she created herself. The result was a 1510. Another student finally pulled a 1600 on her fourth try with more focus on prep books.

As a group, the 1500 scorers undermined the idea that coaching courses are the route to a stratospheric score. Of the 15 students who got tutoring or coaching, most said it was not worth the cost. "I didn't learn anything!" writes a frustrated 760 V, 790 M scorer, "Kids should prepare on their own."

"Too simplistic, did not cover material for the highest scores," says a student who scored 750 V, 760 M in evaluating his prep course. A Harvard-bound student of her school's prep course says, "It did me no good. I already knew or had heard all that

they told me." Of the six students who took a Princeton Review or Kaplan course, five said that the benefits were not worth the cost. (For extensive excerpts from high scorers who took Princeton Review and Kaplan courses, see chapter 7.)

While coaching courses were generally panned, the 1500s cited practice tests again and again as their single most important mode of preparation. "I took 10 practice SATs starting two weeks before the test, and it helped me take a look at all the things I was consistently missing," writes a 740 V, 780 M scorer who says his coaching course was not worth the cost. "Practice, practice, practice—the best way to become comfortable with the material," writes a Yale ED admit who scored 1510.

The following quote from a 1580 scorer will gladden the hearts of English teachers nationwide: "Cramming does not help at all for the SAT, but reading widely and looking up unfamiliar words is useful." No one should be surprised that many of the 1500+ scorers say that they are dedicated readers.

Mere mortals will be relieved to learn that the 1500 scorers do, like everybody else, have their challenges with the SAT. "Reading comprehension questions occasionally seem to have more than one or even no good answer depending on your opinion," says a Princeton-bound student, citing a common complaint among students of all ability levels. She says that practice "helps you learn what sort of answer the test is looking for." Another issue: high scorers frequently have trouble with basic math, especially geometry, that they may not have studied since eighth grade. Prone to overconfidence in their ability to resurrect that material, some high-scoring students learn the hard way that they need to brush up.

The clear message of the 1500+ scorers can be summarized in one word: self-reliance. In the words of a 800 V, 720 M scorer, "My mother and I considered a prep course but decided that, because of my limited time and good study and test-taking abilities, it was not the best option for me. The books allowed me to work at my own pace when I had pieces of time and to concentrate on what I knew I needed to work on rather than spending time on things I was already comfortable with."

Students Who Scored 1300–1490

At least these people show signs of being mortal. "I wanted to show colleges I was right for them, but was scared my scores wouldn't be good enough," says one student whose chances were probably not scuttled by her 1340. Another student writes that she disliked her SAT prep course for a surprising reason. "Everyone was comparing their scores, and even though mine were perfectly decent, I felt bad about how I had done…I wish I had done a couple of practice tests on my own," she writes. What were these "perfectly decent" scores? 760 Verbal, 630 Math.

> **"Students who aren't self-motivated and won't study alone benefit most from a classroom prep course. One-on-one tutoring should be for people who are perhaps behind or don't understand what to study. Self-motivated students should prepare on their own."**
>
> **—710 V, 720 M**

There is one difference between this group and the 1500s—attitude. The 1300 and 1400 scorers are more likely to take a test-prep course, more likely to spend hours on the preparation, and more likely to be feeling stress. Not that the stress is universal. "I didn't study much," crowed a student who scored 1450, "Studying is just making up for all the wasted time playing video games instead of doing homework and reading books." Touché.

As with the 1500 scorers, timed practice tests were considered crucial. "I took about six of the sample tests from the *10 Real*

WHEN A SCORE INCREASE ISN'T EVERYTHING

A student at a prestigious East Coast boarding school who scored 490 V, 600 M on her first SAT was determined to improve her verbal score. "I have never done well on standardized testing....The reading comprehensions scared me!" So she hired a tutor for once-a-week sessions. "I spent countless hours studying for vocabulary and devoting time to prepping for the test. After only going up 10 points, I was furious because I had put so much effort into it," she writes. Despite the fact that her score barely went up, this student rates her tutoring as more effective than her classroom course from Princeton Review. "I don't regret it because the tutoring has helped me in the long run, especially in school," she says.

SATs book in preparation for my second test and it helped me a great deal," says a Bucknell ED admit. His scores went from 600 to 650 on the Verbal and 710 to 780 on the Math.

As high scorers know, a test-taking state of mind is key. "Mental readiness is more important than academic," advises a 690 V, 780 M scorer, "It is the difference between good test-takers and bad ones." Or, in the words of a Bates-bound student, "Don't get psyched out about the damn test!" (He chose not to do a prep course.)

One student had an unusual 190 point jump in her scores on the third time she took the test—to 710 V and 680 M—after being mired at a combined 1200 on the first two. Reason? She took more practice tests before the third time, but she believes that her state of mind was the key. "The first two times I was anxious because so much pressure is put on this one test. The third time I went in very confident...I just

told myself it didn't matter and I could crush the test—and I did." (She also got in ED at Washington U. in St. Louis.)

There was plenty of diversity on the subject of coaching. "Human interaction, for me, is usually more fun and effective because books and software can't really change their way of explaining to suit my needs," writes a convincing advocate for test prep who scored 650 V, 710 M. Her other advice includes "get enough sleep, eat breakfast, do practice tests." A student who scored 1390 credits one-on-one tutoring with Princeton Review with raising her score 350 points. "We worked at a pace that was suited to my needs and therefore very beneficial," she writes.

"I think the SAT is a ridiculous, unfair system," writes a 1360 scorer who took Princeton Review and endorses its assessment of the test, "Although I felt that I was acquiring an unfair advantage because my family could afford to pay for the course, the course was effective." This girl identified practice tests as her most useful tool in preparing and estimated that her prep course—which cost about $1,000—raised her scores by 60–100 points.

One Princeton Review prepper found that a brand name is less important than the instructor. "Princeton was horrible. The prep class did nothing to make sure I was improving and when I had a tutor first from them she was flaky and late," writes the student, who nevertheless managed a 1330. An instructor with the right pedigree is not necessarily the solution. A 690 V, 700 M scorer reports that her course "was utterly boring, and our teacher, an MIT graduate with a major in nuclear engineering and a score of 1590 on the SAT, seemed as clueless half the time as we were."

One student who scored 680 V, 660 M voiced a common complaint about prep courses: "You had to go at the pace of people who did not understand things you did...I felt that if I used the prep book independently, I could do the same exercises at a pace that suited me," he writes. Says another student who scored 640 V, 740 M after one-on-one tutoring, "We used Kaplan books and I could have learned just as much without the tutor and just the book."

A 690 V, 710 M scorer says if he had it to do over again, he would skip his prep course and "have my parents force me to do practice tests."

Students Who Scored 1100–1290

If the 1300–1490 scorers were somewhat stressed, this group was positively manic. As a whole, the 1100–1290 cohort was the most stressed out in the survey. Students in this group scored in roughly the 62nd to 89th percentile nationally, yet in their high-powered schools, their scores were no better than average. "Because this is a standardized test, I get nervous thinking about the weight this has on my future," writes a 670 V, 520 M scorer. "I was nervous because I heard all the horror stories and forgot my calculator and I fell asleep," says a student who scored 580 V, 570 M despite these difficulties.

Does stress cause these students to score lower? Probably. Is the stress caused by anxiety about keeping up with higher scoring peers? Perhaps. These students were more likely to express negative attitudes toward standardized tests, but the comments had a different tenor than the nonplussed disdain of many 1500 scorers. "Keep in mind that the SAT is meaningless and a poor judge of one's person," writes a 1270 scorer who describes himself as "very anxious" before taking the test.

Lack of time was a major factor for many in this group. "It was the hardest trying to finish, and doing the problems under time pressure made me lose my train of thought a lot," says a 570 V, 530 M scorer. Students who prefer to deliberate over problems find themselves rushed, as do slow readers. "I find the reading comprehension questions the most challenging. I was very nervous and it is very tough to concentrate on long passages when your mind is wandering and thinking about other things," notes a student who scored 1160.

WHERE THE STUDENTS CAME FROM

Our survey included students at 67 schools in 29 states, as well as a handful of students who were clients of participating independent counselors. Our goal was not a representative sample of the nation as a whole, but rather a representative sample of students likely to consider SAT coaching. As a result, most of the students came from suburban public or private schools. The list consists of:

Albuquerque Academy (NM)	La Pietra Hawaii School for Girls (HI)	St. Andrew's–Sewanee School (TN)
The Athenian School (CA)	Lake Ridge Academy (OH)	St. Andrew's Episcopal School (MS)
Birmingham High School (CA)	Lakewood High School (CO)	St. Catherine's School (VA)
Bishop Brady High School (NH)	Los Angeles Center for Enriched Studies (CA)	St. Cecilia Academy (TN)
Brookfield Academy (WI)	Los Angeles Unified School District (CA)	St. John's Country Day School (FL)
Carol Gill Associates (NY)	Mandarin High School (FL)	St. Mary's Hall School (TX)
Carolina Friends School (NC)	McClure, Mallory & Baron (CA)	Salesianum School (DE)
Cherry Creek High School (CO)	Mercersburg Academy (PA)	San Ramon Valley High School (CA)
Cody High School (WY)	Milton Academy (MA)	Seven Hills School (OH)
The Colorado Springs School (CO)	Montclair High School (NJ)	Shaker Heights High School (OH)
Columbus School for Girls (OH)	Moravian Academy (PA)	Shawnee Mission South HS (KS)
Crystal Springs Uplands School (CA)	Newton North High School (MA)	Steinbrecher & Partners (CT)
Cypress Falls High School (TX)	North Central High School (IN)	Trinity Christian Academy (TX)
Deerfield Academy (MA)	Northfield Mount Hermon School (MA)	University of Illinois Laboratory High School (IL)
Durham Academy (NC)	Pace Academy (GA)	University Preparatory Academy (WA)
Dwight-Englewood School (NJ)	Peddie School (NJ)	The Urban School of San Francisco (CA)
Eaglecrest High School (CO)	Polytechnic School (CA)	Vail Mountain School (CO)
Episcopal School of Dallas (TX)	Providence Day School (NC)	Vermont Academy (VT)
The Gunnery (CT)	The Putney School (VT)	Webb School of Knoxville (TN)
Hathaway Brown School (OH)	Ravenscroft School (NC)	The Westminister Schools (GA)
Highland High School (ID)	Ridgewood High School (NJ)	Weston High School (CT)
Iolani School (HI)	Rockhurst High School (MO)	Wyoming Seminary (PA)
John Burroughs School (MO)	Rocky River High School (OH)	
Holy Innocents' Episcopal School (GA)	Rowland Hall–St. Mark's School (UT)	

Real academic weaknesses accentuated the test-taking difficulties for some in this group. Whereas higher scorers had trouble with their rusty geometry, this cohort was more likely to struggle with the algebra—a problem that will be accentuated when the New SAT adds additional Algebra II problems. On the verbal side, a number of students reported difficulty with vocabulary and word definitions.

> **“Studying beforehand seems to me less useful than pacing yourself and thinking clearly during the test itself.”**
>
> **—800 V, 710 M**

Some in this group also benefited from elementary test-taking techniques. A student who scored 990 on her first SAT bought a prep book and increased her focus. "My mistake on the first test was omitting too many questions instead of taking an educated guess," she writes. After studying five hours, her scores went up 160 points to 580 V, 570 M.

Assessments of test prep did not differ greatly from the 1300–1490 scorers. One student who took both a classroom course and tutoring from Princeton Review said she went up "only" 100 points. "I liked one-on-one because I needed someone to explain to me the answers I got wrong. If someone can understand the explanations in a book, go for it!" says this 650 V, 590 M scorer. A Kaplan student noted what many experts believe—that prepping for the math yields more results than for the verbal because vocabulary and reading are harder to improve in a short period of time. Another Kaplan prodigy who scored 510 V, 630 M said his course was "maybe" worth the cost and cautions that coaching is not a panacea. "When you take a course, you actually need to work on your own in order to get better. I only did what I was told to do inside the classroom and I didn't see results," says this student, who rates prep books as his most useful study tool. More so than the higher scorers, students in this range cite a lack of motivation as the reason why they took a prep course. "There needs to be structure and needs to be hand-holding," says a 580 V, 560 M scorer, "If my tutor hadn't checked my homework every time, I probably wouldn't have done it."

A Princeton Review student who said that her score had improved 100 points in verbal and math nevertheless said that her course was not worth the cost. "The company was helpful, but again, I didn't know when to apply their methods. With dozens of kinds of math tricks, it is difficult to know when to use what." This girl, who scored 1240, rates practice tests as her most important prep tool.

One student who did not take a prep

course devised a novel prep method. "I found that reading was a greater preparatory pastime than studying. The prep books and CD-ROM focus on 'beating the system' through strategy, but I found I used knowledge as a better weapon," she writes. Well enough to get a 1230.

Students Who Scored 1090 and Below

Though their scores place them near the national average for SAT test takers, students in this cohort were largely a dispirited and/or disengaged group. "I'm a horrible test-taker," says a 450 V, 400 M scorer, "I space out when taking a test such as the SATs." Another student who scored 470 V, 540 M says, "I did not want to take the test. I hate standardized tests," adding that students "should prepare for a long and pointless Saturday." A 540 V, 540 M scorer reports that the primary usefulness of his prep course was "to help me get the damned thing over."

Again and again, students in this cohort spoke of the clock as their primary nemesis. "Time pressure was my biggest problem. Other than that, the questions were not that hard," says a student who scored 540 V and 500 M. Adds a 520 V, 420 M scorer, "The time was the worst because no matter how confident you were it was always on your mind."

This cohort seemed to divide into two groups. The first, which generally did not take a coaching course, seemed to know little about the test and care less. "I wasn't concerned about getting a high grade because the colleges I applied to don't require a high SAT score," writes a student who scored 550 V, 440 M. A student who scored 1030 attributed his struggles to the fact that he was not taking a math course and had a demanding work schedule outside of school. A 970 scorer said that she "knew enough to get a high enough score, I just didn't prepare at all."

> **"I just felt stupid after I left the sessions because I hadn't remembered half that stuff we went over. I think preparing on your own is better because people can easily stress you out."**
>
> **—580 V, 520 M**

On the other side of the ledger were students who had a real commitment to improving their scores. Many of these took prep courses, though the results were often disappointing. One student who scored 450 V, 480 M says that his family spent $1,000 on a prep course. "When I was taking this prep course I felt my scores would improve, but they didn't." He identified

THE ENERGY DRINK STRATEGY

One energetic 590 V, 680 M scorer writes that the most important ingredient in SAT success is to "HAVE A LOT OF ENERGY!!!" His recommendation? Drink Red Bull, Spark, or Kmx. "Pick one of these and drink them before the test," he writes. The evidence? "The first time I made a 1270 and I had a Spark. The second time I didn't—1210." Evidence like this is hard to refute, but a word of warning: the stuff is nasty.

practice tests as his most important prep tool. Self-esteem issues cropped up for one student in her coaching course. "I took the prep course with very intelligent and competitive students. For this reason, I was embarrassed to ask questions and did not receive the attention that I needed," she says. This student scored 520 V, 530 M.

Of the twelve students in this cohort who said they had worked with Princeton Review, six estimated that their scores had gone up 50 points or less. "If I had their books, I could have done it on my own," says a 500 V, 520 M scorer. "The program forced me to study rather than sleep or waste time. I was able to survive the actual SAT without passing out at the end," reports a 500 V, 500 M scorer. She estimates that the course increased her score 60–100 points but was not worth the cost because "I was grouped with people who didn't

share my same problems and concerns." The most prominent Princeton Review backer in the cohort estimates that his scores went up 110–150 points, to a total of 500 V and 510 M, and says that a prep course is worthwhile "because you can talk to someone and get tips that no book can give you."

There was at least one ray of hope amid the general gloom of the many students who scored low in the context of their schools. "Don't worry! I got into every college I applied to even though my test scores were poor. There is so much more to a person than their testing abilities," she writes. This student scored 520 V, 460 M and was accepted by Alfred University, Hartwick College, Earlham College, Lesley College, and Warren Wilson College. Congratulations to her!

PREP COURSE CONCLUSIONS

Readers may draw their own conclusions from the responses we've cited. Here are the most important:

- Practice tests are the single most crucial element of any prep program. Students, particularly high scorers, say so again and again.

- High scorers tend to be much more confident than low scorers. They are more likely to prepare for the SAT on their own.

- Paying for test prep is an uncertain proposition at best. Many students are adamant that their coaching course was not productive; most are uncertain as to the benefits.

- The most commonly cited benefit of a coaching course is that it helps students who lack the initiative, discipline, or confidence to prepare on their own.

- Initiative, discipline, and confidence are among the most important ingredients of scoring high on the SAT.

Next, we make the case as to why preparing on your own is the best way for most students to tackle the SAT.

3

TAKING CHARGE OF YOUR SAT PREP

ANSWERS TO YOUR QUESTIONS

▶ What are the benefits of preparing on my own?

▶ When should I take the SAT?

▶ How many times should I take it?

▶ How do I register?

▶ How should I design my preparation program?

▶ What are the most important strategies for success?

How much would you pay for a spiffy SAT score? $500? $1,000? We recently saw a prep course advertised on the Internet for $1,775. That's a serious price tag for SAT tutoring, but with four years of tuition bills around the corner, a prep course suddenly may not seem so expensive.

Our problem with SAT coaching isn't the expense. We are reluctant to recommend coaching courses for most students because *we have come to believe, after doing our homework, that preparing on your own is likely to be more effective.* We say this not simply because so many of the students in our survey—particularly the high scorers—said coaching was a waste of time. Nor were we swayed merely by the fact that the students in our survey without coaching scored higher than the students who got it—maybe the uncoached students just didn't need the coaching.

The real issue is attitude. The students who prepare on their own do so because they have faith in themselves. They're self-directed and willing to get organized. They're independent. Students who seek coaching, whether they realize it or not, are making a tacit admission that they feel helpless. They want someone else to show them the way, or to give them the magic bullet. Over and over again, students will say things like "I needed the course to force me to study" and "I could never have done it on my own."

> **"I am a firm believer that it is more beneficial to prepare to take the test than it is to study the material."**
>
> **—690 V, 690 M**

But if the SAT is really so important, why can't you do it your own? And why, if you aren't motivated to do it on your own, do you think attending a course will help? If the subject were Calculus or AP Physics, you might need somebody to guide you.

But the SAT isn't like a class in school where the goal is to master new or hard material. The "stuff" is easy. You've already learned it. The hard part is getting yourself accustomed to a new test-taking process.

Forget the idea that there is a mysterious secret to acing the SAT that someone else must teach you. There is only an obvious secret: *practice*. Think about the way you learn any new skill, like singing, dancing, drawing, writing, skateboarding, throwing a Frisbee, or playing a new game on your Xbox. The first step is to get familiar with the basics. If you're on a skateboard, you fall down a lot. If you're drawing or writing, a lot of paper gets tossed in the trash. If you're throwing a Frisbee, your first toss will start off straight and then hook at a crazy angle and crash-land in the neighbors' tulips. Only after hours, days, months or years of practice do you get the feel of what you're doing. Only then can you begin to master advanced techniques. You learn fore-shortening to make your drawings appear 3-D. You master the art of beginning your essays with an anecdote. You start doing tail-whips or curb-stalls on your skateboard. And how do you learn all this? Practice. Along the way, it helps to get some advice on the finer points—that is why we've written this book. But advanced information is useful only when you know how to use it.

By preparing on your own, you can construct your own strategy for taking the test rather than trying to ape someone else's.

You can weigh various techniques and choose the ones that work best for your learning style. You'll develop far greater mastery than if you merely tried to copy the latest guaranteed plan. By trusting yourself, you'll begin to build the confidence that will be a crucial element of your success. Is doing it on your own a challenge? Of course! That's why it has the potential to raise your score.

We know all this may sound scary, and we sympathize. Fear and procrastination are powerful enemies. We know you'll probably think of a million reasons to put off focusing on the test. Does that mean you should go running to a tutor? We think not. A tutor may provide a temporary security blanket, but until the day when the College Board and ETS allow them in the test center, the effects of tutoring will usually wear off about the time you blacken your first oval. The SAT is all about you— alone with the test—and your preparation should be the same.

When Should I Take the SAT?

Left to their own devices, some parents would start their kids on SAT prep in about seventh grade. Easy there, mom. Better take a chill pill if you feel those thoughts coming on.

The main risk from starting too early goes something like this: mom and dad are nervous about the SAT. Mom and dad transmit their nervousness to son or daughter. Instead of helping, test prep simply makes son or daughter more nervous.

A second pitfall is nearly as destructive as the first. It follows a basic law of parenting: when mom or dad exert a force in one direction, son or daughter exerts an equal and opposite force in the other direction. Let's say mom wants son to start preparing for the SAT. That means son probably wants to do anything but start preparing for the SAT. Not to be outdone, mom forces son to start preparing. To get back at mom, son goes through the motions of preparing but never really tries.

Given the crucial importance of a positive attitude, we think the student should make the call about when to start preparing—though we don't rule out periodic parental nudges. That said, there are several advantages to starting early for top students. A number of higher scorers in our survey recalled taking the SAT in middle school as a positive experience. (Most did so in preparation for "Talent Search" summer programs based at Duke, Johns Hopkins, Northwestern, or University of Denver.) These students said that a good score in seventh or eighth grade gave them confidence that they would do well in eleventh grade.

We suspect, however, that this dynamic might work the opposite way for a student who is not so advanced. A poor score in middle school doesn't help anyone. Also, the New SAT will include math from Algebra II, which few students get until ninth grade. It remains to be seen whether the Talent Search programs will continue to ask applicants to take the New SAT, but even if they do, we would recommend that only students who typically score in the top 1st–3rd percentile on standardized tests consider this option. SAT prep for middle schoolers is over-the-top and likely to fuel anxiety and frustration.

> **"Practice, practice, practice— the best way to become comfortable with the material."**
>
> **—800 V, 710 M**

A second early-bird option is becoming more popular among top scorers: taking the test in tenth grade. Several of the high-scoring students in our survey suggested this option. There are two rationales:

The math is fresher. "The most challenging thing for me was just that I hadn't done any of this type of math since about seventh grade," said a Pomona ED admit who scored 770 V, 680 M. Another student with 760 V, 680 M described the math section as "hard to do when you're in a calculus frame of mind." These comments were echoed by many, many students who told us that the hardest part of the math was overcoming rustiness.

The pace of school is slower. "Since school course work is more difficult junior year, there is more free time to study for the SAT sophomore year," says a 700 V, 800 M scorer who recommends taking it in March of grade ten. He adds that students can begin studying vocabulary as soon as ninth grade. Though most students will probably take a pass on that, it is true that eleventh grade is when everything hits the fan in the life of a high school student, including AP courses, varsity sports, and leadership positions.

Most students wait until at least the summer after tenth grade to prepare, usually before the PSAT or their first SAT. Though some students seem to need the experience of bombing their first SAT before they get serious for the second, the best strategy is to get it right the first time. Below are some pros and cons of preparing for and taking the SAT on the various possible test dates. We recommend that students in the Class of 2006 take the New SAT. Many colleges will require the New SAT because of the Writing section, and we think it would be too stressful to prepare for and take both versions. We also believe that preparation can make the biggest difference on the New SAT.

October SAT—Too early for eleventh graders. Get the PSAT under your belt. Twelfth graders can consider this date as the last one definitely in time for early decision or early action.

October PSAT—In 2004, this test will be the first preview of the material on the New SAT. Prepping before this test makes particular sense for students who are gunning for recognition in the National Merit Scholarship competition. Students with busy school schedules may choose to do a chunk of their work in the summer, then maintain a moderate pace in September before ramping up in early October. The main pitfall to the PSAT strategy is the fact that summer is a long time from mid-October, and work done then may be a distant memory. In addition, some students are simply not ready to cope with major test prep so early in eleventh grade.

November SAT—Eleventh graders who prepped before the PSAT can take their first SAT on this date as part of a kill-two-birds-with-one-stone strategy. Since the date is only two to three weeks after the PSAT, the material should still be fresh. Early November is not a bad time in the school calendar—mid-semester exams are over but the end-of-term crunch has not yet hit. The timing is also good for athletes: fall sports are generally over and winter sports have not yet begun. The

Class of 2006 should wait until March and the New SAT.

December SAT—An unlikely choice except for last-minute twelfth graders who want one last shot. Not near any major breaks and too close to first-term exams. Not for the Class of 2006.

January SAT—Students with school exams in December should seriously consider this one. Winter break is not a time that most students would prefer to prepare for the SAT, but busy superachievers must take time where they can get it. The results from the October PSAT will arrive before the break, and students can generally get their test booklets from the guidance office and go over every question they missed. Two weeks of leisurely study in late December can be followed by another two or three weeks in early January, when school work is light because the new term has just begun. In 2005 only, this date will probably not be a good one because of the debut of the New SAT in March. This date may not be appropriate for those who play winter sports and those who have exams in January.

March SAT—The long-awaited New SAT debuts on this date in 2005. A hint for those taking it on that date: *register early*. The College Board will probably make provisions for a log jam of test-takers on that date, but some test centers may fill up. This is a reasonably good date for many students, though it often arrives before spring break. In some years, this administration of the test is given in late March or even in the first week of April. Mid-March fits well with the sports season; winter sports are generally over but spring ones are not yet in full swing.

May SAT—March test-takers in the Class of 2006 would be well-advised to sign up for this date as well. If anything is askew with the March scores—a distinct possibility with a new test—the College Board will try to get the kinks out by this date. In normal years, May is a dubious choice for students with AP courses because their exams hit in the first half of the month. On the plus side, students who have spring break in April can use that time to ramp-up their preparation. Year-end academic demands will not have reached a crescendo, especially at schools that continue through early June.

June SAT—Applicants to highly selective institutions will want to reserve this date for SAT II: Subject Tests. For students not taking SAT IIs, this date may fit well for students who get out of school in late May.

After taking the SAT I once or twice in grade eleven, most students will want to take it again in grade twelve, generally in October or November. A second pass at the SAT II: Subject Tests may also be on the agenda, usually in November or December.

How Many Times Should I Take It?

The standard advice has always been to take the SAT twice in eleventh and/or twelfth grade—and a third time if you have a particular reason to want one more crack at it. But that was the old SAT. The New SAT has three sections, and since colleges generally add the highest scores in each category, our hunch is that students are going to want every opportunity to increase all three scores.

Like all standardized tests, the SAT has a built-in margin of error. This is because the SAT does not test all the knowledge out there, but only a small sample of it. One test might have "scrupulous"—a word you happened to learn in English class last year—while another might have "apocryphal," a word you've never seen in your life. (Scrupulous means "honest" while apocryphal means "of questionable origin or authenticity.") Because of differences like this from exam to exam, the score you get on a particular test may vary from your "real" score—the average score you would get if you took the test a large number of times.

Score jumps caused by random variations are amplified by events in the life of the student who takes the test. Maybe you didn't drink enough water on the morning of the test, got dehydrated, and got a headache. Maybe you drank too much water, got nervous, and got the runs. For a hundred different reasons, your score can fluctuate depending on whether you had a good day or a bad day.

THE COLLEGE BOARD'S FEE MACHINE

When it comes to finding clever ways of extracting cash from the pockets of high school students and their families, nobody does it better than the College Board. In 2003–2004, a few of its fees were as follows:

Taking the SAT I	$28.50
Taking three SAT II: Subject Tests, including Writing	$48.00
Late registration	$18.00
Standby registration	$30.00
Score reports after the test date	$6.50 per college
Rushed score reports	$23.00 plus $6.50 per college

It doesn't take a genius to figure out why the College Board can charge such inflated prices. The people who decide that you must take College Board tests—the colleges—are not the ones who pay for it (you do). Though students can theoretically take the ACT as an alternative to SAT I and II, in reality students in many parts of the country feel little choice but to take the SAT.

One of the most egregious examples of College Board money-grubbing occurred several years ago when it hatched the idea of making students pay for the privilege of viewing their scores "early" via its website. Though scores would be made available to everyone on the Web about three weeks after the test date, the College Board charged $13.00 to those who wanted to see their scores seven to ten days ahead of time. Though the College Board billed the scheme as a way to ease student anxiety, critics charged that the Board was attempting to profit from that anxiety. The College Board has since quietly dropped the fee to view scores online, though students can still pay $8.00 to get their scores early by phone.

Look for more price hikes with the advent of the New SAT. As long as the colleges and the College Board have a stranglehold on standardized testing, there is little to restrain future fee increases. The paying customers (you) have no leverage.

Of the 815 students we surveyed, 137 or 17 percent, increased their combined score by at least 100 points from their first SAT to their second, third, (and in a few cases) fourth SAT. Like the colleges, we looked at only the highest verbal and math scores. For instance, if a student scored 600 Verbal and 650 Math on the first SAT, then 670

Verbal and 630 Math, we counted that as a 70 point increase despite the 20 point decline in Math. If on the third time the student scored 650 Verbal and 680 Math, the combined score increase from the first test to the third would be 100 points.

There is a distinct possibility of increasing your score significantly on the second or third try, and that possibility will be magnified on the New SAT. Our advice to the Class of 2006: plan on taking the SAT I in both March and May of 2005. You may substitute the June date if you are not planning to take SAT II: Subject tests on that day.

Registering for the Tests

This part should be simple. Right?

Guess again. Registering for the SAT is a maze with enough twists and turns to confuse even the savviest applicant. The key is to get on top of it early. Each year's dates are listed on the College Board's website and in the annual registration bulletin mailed to high-school guidance offices. The registration deadline is about 35 days ahead of each test date. There is no sense in procrastinating—go ahead and register. In addition to all the usual personal information, you will need the following:

Your high school's code—This six-digit number will ensure that your school gets a copy of your scores. Many schools report SAT scores on the back of your transcript.

Your social security number—Another milestone on the road to adulthood. You probably have no clue what your social security number is, and now is a perfect time to memorize it.

Your choice of test center—Your best move is to consult current twelfth graders (or your counselor) about the best place in your area to take the test. You want a test center with big desks instead of those narrow ones that are an extension of the armrest—especially if you're left-handed. You also want a center where the heat works without making the room 90 degrees. The most popular test centers sometimes fill up. Register early for the best shot at your first choice.

A list of colleges to receive your scores—Students are always leery of this one when they take the test for the first time. Most would rather see their scores before they send them to the colleges. We understand. It doesn't really matter if you designate colleges to receive scores until the last time you take the SAT I or II, when you must send scores to all colleges that require them. Designating these colleges when you register will save you money since College Board lets you send scores to up to four colleges for free if you do so at registration. If you wait, you'll need to send in an Additional Score Report Form with a per-college fee.

WON'T SOME STUDENTS DO BETTER WITH A TUTOR?

Possibly. If a student has trouble with the subject matter on the SAT—particularly the math—a tutor may be the best choice. If a student has a learning disability, or is motivated but simply can't get organized, a tutor may provide a helpful touchstone. Too often tutors are hired simply because a student is anxious or has low self-confidence. This is exactly the kind of student who would benefit most from working through the test on his or her own rather than developing dependence on an adult. Some students say that they learn better through human interaction, and we don't doubt it. But taking the SAT is not about learning subject matter. It is an individual process that is best mastered through experience. The best a tutor can offer is a structured and encouraging space for the student to do the same things they could do on their own.

> **"I regret waiting too long to take practice tests, and I would tell tenth and eleventh graders to start practicing months before the test, even if it's once a week."**
>
> **—690 V, 770 M**

Along with the nuts and bolts information, the registration form features the SAT Questionnaire. It includes everything from your family income and religious preference to your own assessment of your scholastic ability. Is your mathematical ability "Highest," "Above Average," "Aver-age," or "Below Average?" The Questionnaire asks about your experience with computers, and what you intend to major in, and whether you have a disability.

Why all the questions? The College Board explains, "The SAT Questionnaire allows you to provide information about your academic background, activities, and interests to help you in planning for college and to help colleges find out more about you." Translation: the College Board wants to sell your address to colleges who are interested in recruiting students with your characteristics. It will also use your responses in evaluating the test. To keep adding to your pile of college mail, choose "yes" on the question that asks if you would like to participate in the Student Search Service.

If this is your second or third time taking the test, there is no reason to bother with the Questionnaire. If you do fill it out, you can always leave any questions blank that you choose.

As you complete the registration form, you'll also have an opportunity to sign up for SAT I Answer-Reporting Services. If you take the test in October, January, or May, you can get the Question-and-Answer Service, which gives you all the questions and whether you got them right or wrong. On other test dates, you can get the Student Answer Service, which offers a breakdown of the types of questions you answered right and wrong and their level of difficulty. In a recent year, these services cost $14 and $6, respectively. Dates and costs may change, but these services are worthwhile if you plan to take the test again.

Late Registration and Score Reporting

If you space out and miss the registration deadline, don't have a conniption. The College Board can still accommodate you—for a fee. For a week or two after each deadline, students can register late. If you miss the boat entirely, you can still show up on test day with a shot at getting in as a standby. There are no guarantees with standby registration. You must show up at a test center with a completed registration form in hand and a check for the registration fee plus an additional $30 or so. If you are thinking of doing standby, we recommend that you call

FINDING THE RIGHT STUDY SPACE

This may sound like a mundane detail, but it is really make or break. To get the maximum effect from your work, you should find a spot that simulates the testing conditions as exactly as possible. For practice tests or extended study sessions, we recommend a place outside of where you live your normal life that tells you "This is where I am preparing for the SAT." One option would be to stay after school if you can find study space there, or to go to mom or dad's office during non-business hours. A nearby library is another possibility. For routine study sessions, choose a space at home away from clutter and confusion. Silence is essential. If all your studying is done with music in the background, you will recall less on the real SAT when there will be no music in the background. (Research shows this—we're not making it up.) One other hint: make sure you have a good stopwatch. If you're like most students, you get nervous at the idea of timing yourself. All the more reason to use that stopwatch.

WHY YOU DON'T NEED A PHONEBOOK-SIZED PREP BOOK

You know we recommend *10 Real SATs* as a valuable resource. What about other books? By all means try them if you have the time and energy, but don't get too bogged down. This book is relatively short because we don't want to take too much time from your main job: taking practice tests. Instead of throwing everything but the kitchen sink at you, we've boiled it down to our most essential insights about the SAT. Some books drone on forever, mixing a few important points with page after page of information you already knew or don't need to know. Let real SATs be your guide as to what you need to focus on, and don't waste too much time trying to wade through a massive prep book.

your test center of choice on Monday or Tuesday before the test. Ask to speak to the SAT Coordinator. He or she may be able to tell you whether there is likely to be space. In most cases, there will be.

A variety of issues can crop up related to reporting scores to the colleges. First, be aware that the report sent to you and your school is not considered "official." Even though your college application may ask you to fill in your scores—and even though your high school transcript may include your scores—most colleges ask that you have the College Board send scores directly to them.

Unlike the ACT, which allows students to send scores from a particular date, the SAT I and II operate on a send-one-send-them-all system. Suppose you take an SAT I in April, two SAT IIs in June, and another SAT I in October. If you want to send the October score to Middlebury, the report will automatically include the June and April scores.

It hasn't always been this way. When Big Sis took the SAT IIs, she may have had the option of withholding the score under a program called Score Choice. Alas, College Board abolished Score Choice in 2002. That said, most students are more worried about the colleges seeing bad scores than they need to be. Remember: your highest scores will be what they look at. The same goes for SAT IIs—if you bomb one, you can always take it again and the first score is unlikely to count against you.

If you have a nervous breakdown while taking the SAT I or II, there is one recourse. Until the Wednesday following the test, you can cancel your scores—meaning that your scores will disappear forever and no one (including you) will see them.

The most common issue with score reports is getting them to the admission office fast enough. Reports are generally sent to the colleges about three weeks after the test date. So if you're applying with a January 1 deadline and take the test in December, your score will arrive in plenty of time at the colleges you designated to receive your scores. The hitch: sometimes students decide to apply to a college after they have taken their last SAT. In this case, students must use an Additional Score Report Form (or go to www.collegeboard.com) and pay a fee to get the scores sent. Under normal circumstances, additional reports take a poky three to five weeks to arrive at Most Desirable U. That's a problem if your deadline is next week. Not to worry. For the incredible low price of $23.00—plus $6.50 per college—the College Board will rush your scores within two business days to all the schools on your list. (Prices subject to increase every year.) We should hasten to add that rush reporting will not speed initial scoring but only helps after you have received your scores.

Students should always make every effort to have their scores arrive by the application deadline. But generally speaking, scores that arrive within a few weeks of the deadline are in time for consideration. For early decision, scores from the October date are always in time and scores from November often are. For regular decision, if you bomb your Math II subject test in December and want one more crack at

it, January will probably work.

Students who are concerned about their scores being reported in time should contact the college. An admissions officer may be able to advise you as to whether you really need to rush a score, or whether a particular score will arrive in time for consideration. If your school already has a copy of the score report, your counselor may be able to report the score pending arrival of an official report.

Students with Disabilities

As this book makes clear, the ability to cope with time pressure can be a major factor in determining your score. Why fight it if you don't need to? Students with diagnosed physical and learning disabilities have the right to take college admissions tests with special accommodations, most notably extended time, large print, or an audio version of the test. In 2003, the College Board discontinued its long-time practice of "flagging" the scores of students who tested with disabilities. Since such scores are no longer identified in any way, there is no down side to testing with accommodations if you qualify.

Schools file the paperwork with College Board, and there are two basic requirements:

- A diagnostic evaluation and recommendation for extended time by a qualified professional. In cases where

WHAT ABOUT ELECTRONIC PREP MATERIALS?

Despite all the hi-tech gadgetry crowding the lives of today's students, the vast majority still prepare for the SAT using books rather than CD-ROMs or the Internet. As long as the SAT is administered on paper, books will offer the nearest facsimile of the real thing. Books also allow students to scan several dozen questions on the same page while computers typically have a narrower field of view and must be scrolled up and down.

But technology has its advantages. A CD-ROM, or programs available on the Internet, can immediately tell students how many questions they got right on a practice test and identify areas where they are weak. Some programs will also adjust their degree of difficulty automatically based on questions answered right and wrong. Others offer video instruction segments that spice up the routine. "The CD-ROM kept me engaged and I was less likely to get bored or distracted," says a student who scored 660 V, 690 M. Our electronic program of choice is the College Board's "One-on-One with the SAT," available on CD-ROM, for the simple reason that all of its questions are from real SATs.

Along with software available for use or purchase on the Internet, students can also opt for online courses that include live chat with an instructor. Only a handful of students in our survey paid for such a course, and most who did were disappointed with the results. One little gem on the Internet that might be worth a look is Number2.com, a site that offers a free test-prep tutorial. For building word power, try thefreedictionary.com, a comprehensive source where the definitions of synonyms, antonyms, and related words are one click away.

the original diagnosis was made more than three years ago, follow-up testing must confirm the original diagnosis.

- Evidence that the school has acknowledged the disability and is granting the same accommodations in day-to-day work that are being requested for the SAT.

For students in public schools, this generally means having an Individualized Education Plan (IEP) that is the product of at least one meeting between parents, teachers, and the student. A comparable plan is necessary for private school students. If you have been diagnosed with a disability or are thinking of having an evaluation, do it as soon as possible. Speak to your high-school counselor to get the ball rolling. The best time to ask the College Board for accommodations is at the end of ninth grade—before your first PSAT—at which time your school accommodations must already be in place.

KNOWING WHAT YOU NEED TO DO

Scoring for the SAT is straightforward. Your raw score equals the number you get right minus a fraction of those you get wrong. The raw score is then converted to a score on the venerable 200–800 scale. As we explain below, it is generally to your advantage to answer every question. Assuming that you do, the chart below tells you roughly how many questions you need to get right and wrong for various scores. The data is based on a version of the test given in May 2000.

Target Score	Number Right	Number Wrong	Percent Right
Verbal			
800	74	4	95
700	69	9	88
600	60	18	77
500	51	27	65
Math			
800	58	2	97
700	63	7	88
600	44	16	73
500	39	21	65

Exact figures fluctuate slightly from test to test and may change further with the New SAT. In school, 88 percent is a B+—a disappointing grade for many ambitious students. But on the SAT, 88 percent means a score of roughly 700, outstanding by almost anyone's standards. The bottom line: you can probably miss 5–10 questions and still get the score you are looking for. Don't come undone if there are a few that you have no clue how to solve. Focus on getting the ones that you do know how to solve. (Computations based on data from *10 Real SATs*, Third Edition.)

A last-minute rush to get accommodations may increase your likelihood of getting denied. College Board has begun to clamp down on perceived abuses by students who seek extended time based on a questionable diagnosis, and a student who suddenly petitions for accommodations in eleventh grade may raise red flags. A high proportion of the students who seek special testing come from wealthy areas, and the College Board recently implemented a School Compliance Review that is aimed at schools with a suspiciously high percentage of students seeking extended time.

Students who are approved for testing with up to 50 percent additional time generally take the SAT at national test centers on the same day as other students. Students needing more than 50 percent additional time take the test at their home schools during a four-day window of time beginning on the national test date.

Making Your Own Prep Course

There are many things in life that are less than pleasant—but which must be done anyway. Like eating broccoli, going to the dentist, or sitting beside mom and dad at a college night presentation.

Add SAT prep to the list. But like most challenges, preparing for the SAT is also an opportunity. With you in control of the process, you'll learn more while boosting your confidence.

It is no easy task to shoehorn SAT prep into the hectic schedule of an eleventh grader, and planning ahead is essential. *First, students should figure out how much time they want to spend.* In as little as ten hours, students can take two full-length practice tests and have another four hours of study—a minimal review but better than nothing. A

fuller commitment of about forty hours will allow students to do half a dozen or more full-length tests along with plenty of work focused on particular areas of strength and weakness. Anything more than fifty hours is probably overkill, though if a student is motivated and has the time to spend, there is no reason not to keep going. Students who need significant brush-up on SAT math or grammar may want to do a more extended review, as will students who want to take a long-term approach to building their vocabulary.

Generally speaking, we recommend starting about 45 days, more or less, before your exam date. If your life is hectic, two months ahead might be better. If you have a break from school or plenty of free time, one month may do. Though you don't need to plan every minute of your prep regimen ahead of time, it is helpful to have a clear sense of your path from the beginning. We recommend that you do a tentative schedule at the outset to give yourself a clear idea of where you are going. You can always revise your plan as you go.

Often, the biggest hurdle is getting started. Here are some tips:

Begin with a bang—Starting in dribs and drabs may make it more difficult for you to build momentum. The best way to get your head around SAT prep is to find a weekend or school break where you can begin with

CONSIDER EAR PLUGS

Do you ever get distracted when the person behind you has the sniffles? Consider ear plugs. They're cheap and easy to use. Try them out on a practice test and see if they help you focus. One potential hitch: make sure you can hear the proctor when time is called.

at least five hours of focus in the span of a day or two.

Don't make your sessions too long— Once you get started, it is better to do four 45 minute study periods per week than one that lasts 3 hours. This is a flaw with most SAT prep courses, which are built for the convenience of the instructor, not you. The longer you focus on your task, the lower your efficiency will be. The more frequently you study, the more you will learn.

Schedule downtime afterwards— Research suggests that there is a period after focused thought when the knowledge sinks in—literally. Try to wind down after you study. Vegetate in front of the TV. Read *Cosmo* or *Sports Illustrated* for twenty minutes and then go to bed. Take a break before studying something else.

Make sure that at least 75 percent of your work is practice—You may need to look up words or go back to your tenth grade math book to learn about a specific type of problem. But don't stray too far from doing actual SAT problems.

Schedule practice tests for Saturday mornings—As test day approaches, nothing gets you ready better than taking practice tests at 8:00 a.m. on the Saturdays before your SAT. We recommend that you find a quiet place like a library or office. Simulate the real thing as closely as possible.

> **"I would say buy a prep book, don't pay $900 for a prep course.... My friends who took courses were bored and did worse than me. I learned the same techniques for $17.99 from a nice paperweight."**
>
> **—800 V, 770 M**

Aside from buying this book, your first move should be to get the latest edition of the College Board's *10 Real SATs*. This is the only book in which every question is a real question. Since the Board does not allow others (like us) to publish complete SATs, the practice tests in other books are cobbled together by authors trying to mimic the real thing. (You should know that we designed the sample problems in this book for illustration purposes.) To be sure your practice material is exactly like what you'll see on the test, get *10 Real SATs* and use it in combination with this book.

Getting started with SAT prep is like sizing up an ice-cold swimming pool. Some people stick a toe in the water and then procrastinate. Others wade in cautiously—and begin yelping when the water reaches their knees. But a few hardy souls avoid all the nonsense and simply take the plunge.

This is the strategy we recommend with SAT prep. A full-length, timed practice test is a good way to start. If you are using *Real SATs*, turn to the answer key and tally your score. This is your first benchmark of where you are and offers a realistic idea of the score you can shoot for as you prep. Compare your score on the practice test with your PSAT score(s). If they are close, you have an excellent indication of where you stand. Go back and look at how many you got right and wrong in each section. What are the patterns?

Even before blackening their first oval, most students will have a clear idea of what they need to work on. After a prac-

tice test or two, we advise students to focus on the types of problems that give them the most difficulty. You may feel uncertain about the subject matter on the test—especially the math—but resist the temptation to go running for your ninth grade geometry book. You've had the material before; use practice problems rather than non-test-related material to re-sharpen your skills. "Actually doing test questions was far more effective than rote memorization of vocabulary words or math formulas" says a Princeton-bound 800 V, 800 M scorer.

After reaching a minimum comfort level with each kind of question, your attention should turn to one of the most important issues of SAT prep: how to pace yourself to avoid anxiety and make sure you spend the right amount of time on each kind of question.

Beating Anxiety and Time Pressure

Why do you fear the SAT? If you're like most students, it isn't because the grammar is too hard or because you can't handle a few multiple-choice tricks. You're probably taking trigonometry, pre-calculus, or calculus in math—are you really going to get worked up over an exam that ends with Algebra II?

We know what scares you: time pressure. We read about it over and over again in our surveys:

BUILDING YOUR PREP COURSE:
A SAMPLE TIMELINE

Eight Weeks
Total Time: Approximately 45 hours

The following is merely a guideline. If you have a break from school near your test date, you can follow a more concentrated schedule. If this pace seems too intense, you can spread out your prep over 9–12 weeks.

1. Full-length practice tests:
Time frame: 1–2 weekends

Do two of these on your first weekend, one more on the following weekend if necessary. Get the feel of the test. Diagnose strengths and weaknesses.

2. Practice each problem type:
Time frame: 3–4 weeks, 4–6 sessions per week

Begin 45-minute sessions after your first weekend of practice tests. Develop a strategy for each kind of problem. Experiment with various approaches. Do subject-matter review if necessary. Target areas in need of improvement.

3. Sections under timed conditions:
Time frame: 3–4 weeks, 4–6 sessions per week

Fine-tune your pace on each type of section. Do two sections per session (45–50 minutes total). Accelerate your speed and examine the impact on your accuracy. Experiment with skipping and guessing. Get a feel for the clock.

4. Whole test under timed conditions:
Time frame: 2–3 weekends

Do two to four full-length, timed tests in the last two weekends before the test. Work on staying focused in the last two sections of each test. If overly fatigued or stressed, experiment with resting during the last several minutes of each section rather than checking work. Learn to pace yourself.

- "Whether or not you are a fast or slow test-taker, time is always attacking you," writes a 730 V, 720 M scorer.

- "Time pressure really affects the way my brain processes things," writes a student who scored 550 V and 590 M.

- "The time pressure is exhausting. I know I could do better if I had fifteen more minutes to do each section," says a student with 670 V and 700 M.

The vicious cycle goes like this: time pressure causes anxiety, and anxiety increases susceptibility to time pressure. Students get anxious because of the fear that they won't have time to finish. Anxiety slows their processing speed and they fall behind the pace necessary to finish—which makes them even more anxious. Most students gamely fight through their stress, and many earn a good score. Nevertheless, these students will score far below what they could have gotten had they been stress-free.

One of the most striking findings of our survey was the extent to which the highest scorers—those who scored a combined 1500 or above—were able to remain stress-free. In most cases, they were relaxed because they did not feel time pressure. It is no doubt true that many of these students possess outstanding academic skills that allow them to excel. But the charac-teristic that defines them more than any other is their relaxed, clear-headed approach. The students who scored 1200–1400 were much more stressed out, and we suspect that many of them had the skills but not the temperament to score even higher. Had the 1370 scorer quoted above not been so exhausted by fighting the time pressure, he might not have needed those additional 15 minutes at the end of each section, and he might have scored 1470 or 1570.

> **"Don't worry, calm down, pay attention in class, read the TI-83 manual."**
>
> **—650 V, 720 M**

Another thing we learned is that a clear head is more important than preparation. "The SATs test my emotional state more than anything else," says a student who scored 760 V, 680 M. She reports that she improved her verbal score by 90 points on her second SAT simply because she was more relaxed. Another student who admitted to being very nervous before his first SAT scored 540 V, 550 M. He prepared less for his second test, was less nervous, and improved to 650 V, 670 M.

Your Game Plan

Perhaps the best way to lower the pressure is to be familiar with the test, and specifically, to know what lies ahead. This chapter lays out a complete game plan for beating SAT stress that can be executed with a month or two of preparation.

Step One: Getting Comfortable

Telling students to relax before taking the SAT is like telling them to ignore the pink elephant floating in the corner of the room. It won't work. Relaxation comes only with mastery and a feeling of control. Students must conquer their fear of time pressure by proving to themselves, again and again if necessary, that they can finish the test.

If you're preparing to take the SAT, consider yourself in training. Throughout this book, we have spoken of timed practice tests as the single most important way to condition your mind for the rigors of the SAT. After your first practice test or two—which should act as an overall diagnostic of your strengths and weaknesses—turn your attention to the sections that make up the test. Which ones are the toughest for you? Focus on the most difficult, but don't ignore others that you may already be good at. Use your stopwatch. Subconsciously, you probably won't want to time yourself because timing causes stress. That's the main reason why you need to time yourself. Get used to it.

As you work through your practice sections, record your observations for later review, either in a notebook or a Word file on the computer. A student who scored 750 V, 790 M used this approach for learning grammar. She did numerous practice sections, and for every question she missed, she typed the error and the corrected sentence—along with an explanation of the error in her own words. By the time test day neared, she had accumulated 25 pages of problems that she reviewed every 48 hours.

> **"Don't let yourself be pulled into the test-taking hysteria. The most important thing is to have the confidence to believe that you can figure things out and to believe in your abilities."**
>
> **—760 V, 630 M**

Learning From Your Mistakes

Look for patterns in the questions you get right and wrong. In College Board's *10 Real SATs*, the answer key for each test rates the questions on a scale of 1–5, with 1 being the easiest and 5 being the hardest. One of the most important secrets to doing your best on the SAT is to get the easy questions right. You should be acing the 1s and 2s, which generally account for between 25 and 30 percent of the test. You might miss a handful of 3s—which generally make up about 40 to 45 percent of the questions—and even more of the 4s and 5s, which together comprise an additional 25 to 30 percent of the test.

After you take a practice test or section, go back to look at the ones you missed. Did you really not know the answer? Or did you make a bonehead mistake? Nothing is more important than getting the ones you *should* get—either because ETS defines them as easy, or because you know you should have gotten them after seeing the answer. The fix might be as simple as reading more carefully, or checking alternative answers even after you think you've found the right one. Maybe you're forgetting to do the final step in too many math problems and falling for distracters. Keep doing practice problems and review the strategies in this book.

Part of the problem may be that you are putting too much pressure on yourself to finish the entire test. Since speed is at a premium, our first advice is to push yourself to see how fast you can go. But if the thought of trying to finish makes you break out in a cold sweat, maybe you shouldn't try. For students who have particular difficulty with time pressure, the best strategy may be to aim for completing the first two-thirds or three-fourths of the questions of each type—and doing the rest only if there is time. An alternative strategy, skipping problems, is discussed below.

Step Two: How the SAT is Different

Forget everything you've learned about taking tests in school. The SAT is different. In school, you learn a unit of material and then take a test on it. If you get all or almost all of the questions right—say, 90 percent of them—you do well. Get 65 percent and you're staring at a D. Let's say you get 65 percent of the questions right on your SAT Math section. That means you score about 500—roughly the national average. But most students probably aim higher—say 650 or so. To reach that goal, you'll need to get about 49 out the 60 questions—82 percent. Even if you're shooting for an 800, you can still generally miss two or three on the math section and three or four on the verbal.

The point is simple: hardly anyone gets them all right. Too many students take the SAT as if it were a normal school test—and stress themselves out trying to get 100 percent. The right approach is to come into the test with a mindset of cool efficiency, knowing that you probably won't get them all. The SAT has more questions on it than a typical school test, and in every section, each one is worth the same amount. Get the easy ones right, don't sweat the hardest ones, and have a strategy to deal with the ones in-between.

Each time you approach an SAT problem, there are four possible outcomes:

1. Solve the problem and move on
2. Can't solve the problem—skip and come back
3. Can't solve the problem—guess and move on
4. Linger and try to solve the problem

Obviously, you hope that most problems fall into the first category. The key issue is what to do with problems that you do not know immediately how to solve. On school tests, the natural tendency is to grit your teeth and hang in there. Giving up quickly isn't in the nature of most good students. You'll think a little harder, try a different approach, redo your calculations one more time, and...Grrrrr. Before you realize it, five minutes have passed. If you don't get the problem after spending all that time, you're going to be demoralized and stressed-out. Even if you do get it, you'll be playing catch-up for the rest of the section. A hard-won victory over a difficult problem is not worth the cost if you miss an easier one later because you are hurrying to finish, or if you can't get to two problems at the end because time runs out. We cannot emphasize enough: *committing more than two minutes to one problem is almost never a good strategy unless you have finished everything else in the section.*

Step Three: Are You a Skipper or a Guesser?

Since you're too smart to fret and pull your hair out over a tough problem, there are two options. You can either skip it and come back, or you can guess. Our survey included many advocates of skipping. "I took practice tests and found out a target score and the number I could skip to get the score," says a matter-of-fact student who got 700 V, 690 M. According to a 770 V, 800 M scorer, "It's better to get all the easy questions done that you can, so you aren't rushing through them later and making stupid mistakes." Another student was not satisfied with her 690 V, 710 M on her first SAT. "I knew I could do better because I hadn't managed my time very well, so I taught myself to skip hard questions. (It really does help, even though it feels wrong after taking too many tests in school where you had to answer every question.)" With the new strategy, her score jumped to 760 V and 740 M.

Despite widespread praise for skipping, there were some dissenting voices. One student who scored 610 V, 630 M writes that skipping "misleads an average student into thinking that he or she cannot do a question." Another potential drawback: skipping means that you must read the question twice, and you may need to remind yourself of its context. This can be especially damaging in the Reading Comprehension, where students who skip are forced to reacquaint themselves with an entire passage. Says a Princeton-bound 730 V, 770 M scorer, "Too much jumping around can be discouraging and/or time-consuming rather than time-saving." There is also the nightmare scenario of skipping a problem in the test booklet but forgetting to skip on the answer sheet.

If you do skip, watch your oval blackening with extra care. Write some quick notes in the test booklet next to the problem if you have a thought worth remembering when you come back. If you can eliminate possible answers before moving on, leave a mark to remind yourself which ones you have eliminated.

Students should experiment with the amount of questions they skip. Between three and five is a reasonable number. If you find yourself skipping more than ten, you may need to start trying harder to get an answer before you skip, or making a few more guesses before moving on.

> **"By rehearsing a musical piece, you get better as you get accustomed to the sound and rhythm. The same goes with taking the SAT."**
>
> **—640 V, 680 M**

Students who are generally unable to finish the test—but who also get distracted by skipping—can try a modified version of this strategy. Because test questions of each type go from easy to hard (with the exception of Reading Comprehension), some students may prefer to answer every question through the first two-thirds or three-quarters of each section, and then skip around among the hard questions at the end. This strategy allows unbroken concentration at the beginning while limiting time-pressure anxiety. After completing most of the test, students can use the remaining time to decide which of the relatively hard questions at the end of the section they will answer. This method is preferable to working straight through until time runs out because it is always possible that an easy question or two—or perhaps a "hard" question to which you happen to know the answer—will be lurking near the end.

In lieu of skipping, your second alternative for a stumper question is to guess. Which option is best? It depends on the question. If your gut feeling is that more thought will give you a chance to solve the problem, skip it. If you size it up and conclude that more thinking is not going to help, make a guess and move on. As you take your practice tests, ask yourself: Do you often skip a problem and then come back to it, only to make a guess because you still can't figure it out? If so, you would have been better off to guess the first time and put the question out of your mind.

One thing you should never do is leave a question blank. On the multiple-choice questions that form the majority of the test, ETS awards one point for each question you get right and subtracts one-quarter of a point for every one you get wrong. That means that if you randomly guess at five, the odds are that you will get one right and miss four—with no affect on your score. The idea is to ensure that on average, random guessing will neither hurt nor help you. But guesses on the SAT are rarely random. In most cases, you can eliminate at least one bonehead response. On questions where you have any clue, no matter how faint, a guess is better than no answer.

To gauge the effectiveness of your guessing, we recommend that you monitor how many of your guesses are right and wrong when you take your practice tests. You can do so by making a mark beside each response that is a guess, then checking to see if you got them right. "Taking timed practice tests and making educated guesses sort of go hand-in-hand," says a student who scored 730 V, 800 M, "By taking mock SATs, I was able to get used to the answers that the test-makers were looking for, and was thus able to reason out answers on the actual test." Another student who scored 800 V, 730 M says that practice tests "help you find out how good of an 'educated guesser' you are so you'll know how much to trust that skill."

Step Four: Speed, Speed, Speed

By the time you get to Step Four, you should be reasonably comfortable with the SAT. One student who scored 710 V, 800 M described the importance of getting "into the groove of test-taking, to go with the flow." If you have done enough practice tests to develop a "feel" for the test, it is time to push yourself even harder.

As part of their training for track meets, distance runners increase their speed by running intervals. A person who runs the 1600 meters, for instance, might do ten consecutive sprints of 200 or 400 meters. The person will probably never sprint like that in competition, but speed drills help to build capacity by forcing runners to go faster in practice than they do in a meet.

The SAT is the testing equivalent of a distance run, and speed work can pay big dividends. Can you finish a section in five minutes less than the time allowed? Ten minutes less? See how fast you can go before your efficiency drops. If you get your mind accustomed to finishing every section five minutes before time is called, you'll have plenty of time on the real test.

You may not think it is possible to save that much time. Try it and see. Perhaps you already take all the right shortcuts. But if you're a good student, you may be the kind who listens to the teacher when she says to show all your work, and not to skip steps. Maybe you always set up problems according to the formula, and carefully double-check each answer. Great strategies for school, lousy strategies for the SAT.

The SAT rewards people who live on the edge, get the test done, and don't stress out. So if you usually read the whole passage, experiment with skimming. Don't bother reading all the other answers if you are sure that (A) is the right one—move on. If you can solve a math problem with a quick estimate, don't bother doing the computations to confirm that you are right. Trust yourself and get to the next problem.

Even the highest scorers can benefit from accelerating their pace. Says one such student, "I tried to play it safe by spending more time making sure my answers were correct. I didn't have enough time to answer the hard ones and got a 740 [on the math]. On my second SAT, I strategically raced through the test to get to the hard questions." The result: a sparkling 800.

Another obvious benefit of moving faster is more time to go back to the problems you have skipped and/or to check your work. Students who have finished can breathe a sigh of relief and come back with a clear head. See how many skipped problems you can get on the second time around. If a skipped problem is a lost cause, five more minutes of puzzling over it will be a waste. Make a guess and move on. Your time might be better spent checking the ones you think you got right—especially if you can catch a blunder or two. We recommend that you experiment with how best to use your time at the end of a section.

As you ramp up your speed, keep an eye on your score. If you start to miss problems you'll need to slow down. But we wager that most students can go faster than they think. Speed will help you triumph over fear of the clock and give you a clearer head throughout the test.

Step Five: Stamina and Focus
With the advent of the New SAT, testing time will balloon to a whopping three hours and forty-five minutes—more than an hour longer than the world's best runners take to run a 26-mile marathon. Talk about exhausting. Even the best students can hit a wall about two-thirds of the way through. They lose focus. They slow down. They start looking out the window. "My problems were never a problem of knowledge, but of making dumb mistakes and losing focus, something that is easy on such a long and boring test," says a Dartmouth ED admit who scored 700 V, 760 M.

In the final weeks before the exam, students should return to taking full-length, timed practice tests. We recommend at least three. Just as preparing for a marathon requires running long distances, so too taking the SAT requires practice of sustained mental focus. Take a look at how well you do on your last section—the one you do when you're the most tired. Are you missing a few that you should get? If so, pay special attention to staying sharp on that section when you take your next practice SAT.

If you are one of those students who has persistent trouble with exhaustion at the end, we have two possible strategies. First, if you finish some sections early, consider resting instead of checking your work. Close your eyes, clear your head, and relax as much as possible. Over the course of three and a half hours, a few breaks like this may make a difference.

Another possibility is that you are running out of gas due to a lack of food. Though food is prohibited in test centers, you can probably get away with eating a small piece of candy or two if you bring it already unwrapped. Keep it in a tissue and pop it in your mouth when the opportunity arises, preferably between sections.

One of your last items of business before test day is to get a clear sense of your preferred pace so that you can stick to it. On a Math section with 20 questions and 25 minutes, where do you want to be when 15 minutes are gone? Question 12? 15? Since the section lengths vary, it may be impractical to try to memorize the exact place you want to be when there are, say, fifteen minutes remaining. But students should have a well-honed sense of roughly where they ought to be as time winds down.

Of the numerous testimonials to taking timed practice tests, we found particularly noteworthy a young man who scored 600 V, 710 M on his first SAT but was not satisfied.

He did six of the practice tests from *10 Real SATs* and went up to 650 V, 780 M. "The one most important bit of advice I can give to potential test-takers is to keep taking timed practice tests," he says. A second student had taken a number of practice tests but had never timed himself and had generally gone over. "The second time around, I limited my work to the allotted time and found I was much more successful on the actual exam," he writes. How much more successful? He improved 160 points, from 670 to 750 on Verbal and from 640 to 720 on Math.

No matter how much you prepare, the SAT is bound to bring a few anxious moments. But with focused practice, you can teach yourself what to expect and thereby increase your comfort level. The best SAT takers are proactive about staying calm. They attack the test with cool efficiency and preempt anxiety by getting to the end quickly. "The key is to stay smooth and avoid letting any difficulty lead to indecision or nervousness," says a 710 V, 800 M scorer.

The Zen of Test Day

Test day is all about being relaxed and focused. On the night before, do what will make you feel comfortable at 8:00 a.m. the next morning. Go to a movie. Hang out with friends. Watch mindless TV. If you're the type who feels more comfortable thinking about the test, go over a few last-minute details in your head. But don't do a full-blown cram session. Relax.

Go to bed at your regular time for a school night. This is the wrong night to experiment with going to bed early. If you try to hit the sack at 8:00 p.m.—and you're not tired—you may find yourself tossing and turning in bed until 2:00 a.m. If you do fall asleep, you'll be in bed ten hours instead of your usual eight and risk being groggy all day.

It should come as no surprise that staying up late is also a bad idea. Even if you're 100 percent convinced that your brain can function just as well on six hours sleep as it does on eight, we guarantee that you're wrong. Trust us—and get your normal amount of sleep.

On test morning, don't cut anything close. Get up in time for a leisurely breakfast. Leave the house in time to get there a little before 8:00 a.m. If you don't know exactly where you're going, make sure you have a map. Leave extra time once you arrive to find the room where the test will be given. At all costs, bring:

- **Your admission ticket.** Even if you registered via the mail, you can print a copy of it from www.collegeboard .com.
- **A photo ID.** Usually a driver's license or passport. If you don't have an ID, your school can make you one. See your counselor.
- **Your calculator.** The one you use in school, with fresh batteries.
- **At least three No. 2 pencils.** Make sure they are slightly dulled to better blacken those ovals.
- **A watch or stopwatch.** You never know if you'll be sitting near a clock. Make sure the alarm is turned off.

TEST DAY ADVICE FROM THE EXPERTS

Our survey participants were full of test-day advice. Here is some of the best:

"Put together all your materials the night before so you don't forget anything like a calculator or ID card." —660 V, 690 M

"SLEEP is the most important thing to get a good score. Also, knowing that it is not the end of your life if you don't get a good score helps you relax." —660 V, 730 M

"Keep the date well-marked on a calendar so that it doesn't sneak up on you. Eat a good breakfast so that your stomach doesn't growl, but not too many liquids. Know how to get to the testing center and where to park. Bring a jacket and dress in layers."—730 V, 670 M

"Arrive early at the test center—it takes away anxiety to be one of the first to show up." —700 V, 640 M

"Make sure you go to the bathroom before the test." —710 V, 720 M

4

WRITING

TOTAL TESTING TIME: 60 MINUTES

Sections:

▶ 1 of 35 minutes
▶ 1 of 25 minutes

Question Types:

▶ **Student-Produced Essay**
▶ **Identifying Sentence Errors**
▶ **Improving Sentences**
▶ **Improving Paragraphs**

Writing will be added to the SAT I in March 2005. We begin with it because the College Board promises that the essay will come at the beginning of each SAT when students are freshest. The multiple choice questions, which will be similar to those on the PSAT and SAT II: Writing Test, come in three varieties. Identifying Sentence Errors problems test grammar, word choice, and knowledge of idiomatic English. Improving Sentences problems focus on grammar and modification of sentences to improve their flow and make them more concise. Improving Paragraphs questions highlight how sentences fit together to form a coherent whole.

The Essay

As if regular college essays weren't stressful enough, along comes the New SAT and its new essay. At least the agony of this essay will be over quickly. Regular college essays inflict their stress for weeks and even months. With the New SAT, the torture is compressed into 25 gut-wrenching minutes. Lucky you.

You may be wondering how anybody can expect you to write a decent essay in a mere 25 minutes. A lot of people are asking the same question. The College Board's response is that the essay is not supposed to be perfect. "At the College Board, we recognize that an essay written in a short amount of time will not be polished but represents the initial phase of the writing process: the first draft," says a brochure describing the new test. The brochure reminds students that essays can get a top score with some errors in spelling, punctuation, and grammar.

But let's get real. Even if readers are instructed to overlook a limited number of syntactical errors, essays that do not have such errors are likely to make a better impression than those that do. On the more important issues of organization and marshaling evidence to back up your opinion, you will have less margin for error.

There is no sugar-coating the fact that the SAT essay is a race against the clock. The challenge is to learn how to write an essay in 25 minutes that looks similar to one you could produce in two hours. Sound impossible? The trick is to come to the test with a blueprint in mind. The subject matter of your essay will be dictated by the question, but the structure of the essay should already be in your head. You'll need to master—or re-master—the art of writing a five-paragraph essay in which you state an opinion and back it up with evidence. After fine-tuning your approach with plenty of practice under timed conditions, you should be able to go on autopilot when you sit down to write. You'll be in trouble if you don't. With only 25 minutes, there will be no time to experiment or ponder your approach. For this reason, preparation is more crucial for the essay than any other section of the SAT. Come in cold and you may draw a blank. Practice, and you can ace it.

The most common type of question asks you to respond to an excerpt or quotation. Typically, the excerpt expresses an opinion on an issue that does not have one correct answer. It doesn't matter whether you agree or disagree with the statement. You may think the excerpt is completely true, partly true, or totally false. The test-makers want to know how skillfully you can back up your opinion with relevant evidence.

Here is an example:

Directions: Think carefully about the issue presented in the following quotation and the assignment below.

People are always blaming their circumstances for what they are. I don't believe in circumstances. The people who get on in this world are the people who get up and look for the circumstances they want, and, if they can't find them, make them.
From *George Bernard Shaw,* Mrs. Warren's Profession *(1893)*

Assignment: What is your view of the idea that people make their own opportunities in life and are not controlled by their circumstances? Plan and write an essay in which you develop your point of view on this issue. Support your position with reasoning and examples taken from your reading, studies, experiences, or observations.

DO NOT WRITE YOUR ESSAY IN YOUR TEST BOOK. You will receive credit only for what you write on your answer sheet.

The first order of business is to demonstrate that you understand the meaning of the passage and can restate it in your own words. From there, you need to take a position on whether and to what extent the statement is true. Finally, you must back up your opinion with specific evidence from the subject areas listed in the question. The finished product should be about 300–400 words.

Sounds easy enough, right? OK, maybe it's not so easy. Let's take a closer look at the writing process.

Getting Your Brain in Gear

Before you sit down to do practice essays, get familiar with the kind of thinking you will be required to do. Your task: link the excerpt to something in "your reading studies, experiences, or observations." The quotation above suggests that people can control their circumstances rather than their circumstances controlling them. Let's say you agree with this proposition—your first step is to think of evidence and anecdotes to back up your view. In literature, Anne Frank comes to mind, the girl who wrote a world-famous diary about hiding from the Nazis during World War II. She faced horrible circumstances and rose above them. In the performing arts, Ludwig van Beethoven composed many of his greatest works while battling deafness. Science? Thomas Edison was so persecuted by his teacher at an early age that his mother pulled him out of school. Then he later endured repeated failures before inventing the electric light.

These are all good possibilities that could be expanded upon. But you could just as easily think up evidence to support the other side. Suppose you have just finished reading *Manchild in the Promised Land* in English class, a novel about life in Harlem in the 1940s and '50s. Though the narrator, Sonny, manages to escape from his world of violence and mayhem, virtually all the other characters in the book fail to escape from their situations. Circumstances obviously play a huge role in the lives of those characters. The same applies to characters in *The Autobiography of Malcolm X, The Grapes of Wrath*, and hundreds of other books, fiction and nonfiction, that students study in school.

Evidence can also come from the world of current events. Consider the rising cost of a college education. With tuition climbing and government grants falling, fewer low-income students can afford to go to college—a circumstance beyond the control of those born into poor families. In politics, the family dynasties of Kennedy and Bush suggest that not everyone has an equal chance at a career on the national stage, or of being president, and that circumstances (family connections in this case) play a significant role in who gets elected.

How are you supposed to know all of this? Relax—you're not supposed to know any particular facts to write your essay. What you do need is some practice in connecting facts that are in your head—whether from the classroom or your own reading—to quotations such as the one above. Trust us—you've got plenty of useful information in your brain. The trick is to pull it out at the right time.

The next ingredient is an anecdote from your life. As above, most essay questions leave open the possibility of citing evidence from your own experience to back up your opinion. Occasionally, you may see a question that asks you to write primarily about your personal experiences. We recommend that you take the opportunity to write about your life or your perspective as often as you feel comfortable. A personal angle, especially when combined with references to academic topics, will give your essay extra breadth. When you cite William Shakespeare or Maya Angelou, you demonstrate that you can think like a professor. When you offer an anecdote from your own experiences, you show the ability to connect abstract issues to your personal life. Doing both demonstrates that you can combine analytical insight with personal reflection.

WHO ELSE MIGHT READ YOUR ESSAY?

Sending your essay to the College Board is scary enough. But there might be someone else who reads it: an admissions officer at Most Desirable U. The College Board's plan is to make an electronic copy of every essay and send them via the Internet to graders in remote locations. But the Board will also allow admissions officers at particular colleges to access the essays of students who have designated those colleges to receive their scores. Not only will colleges be able to evaluate your essay for themselves; they'll also have a chance to compare your SAT essay with the ones on your application. Make sure the same person—you—writes all of them.

Some students are afraid to use the first person in the essay because teachers have said that the use of "I" is a no-no. It is true that the first person is not appropriate for some kinds of writing. But you definitely should use "I" in the SAT essay. Look again at the question. It begins with "What is *your* view?" and goes on to give advice on how to support "your position." The best way to respond to a "you" question is with an "I" answer. In fact, students who do not use "I" generally come off sounding stilted and are often forced into using the passive voice.

The First Paragraph

Picture one of the hapless English teachers recruited by the College Board to read SAT essays. There she sits with bloodshot eyes, slogging through her 247th essay on how people make their own opportunities in life and are not controlled by their circumstances.

That essay could be yours, and if it is, you'd better have a strong first paragraph. The impression from the first sentence or two can last throughout the essay. If your essay tails off at the end, the reader's attention may also be tailing off. Whatever the case, you'll get a good score if the opening shows that you can write.

Your first paragraph should be about three to five sentences, and there is a reliable formula. You need to do three things:

1. Rephrase the main idea of the quotation, preferably with new information or in a new context.
2. Take a position on the main idea that can be backed up in the rest of the essay.
3. Provide a roadmap for the rest of the essay.

Before we go further, a word of warning. This chapter includes some sample paragraphs and sample essays that we have designed to set a high standard for you. A few of them are pretty good, but most are downright sick. Don't let it bother you. We don't expect you to write essays this good, but we do want to you to aim high and get as close as you can.

And finally, a procedural note: SAT essays are graded on a 1–6 scale by two separate readers for a combined scale of 2–12. When readers disagree by more than two points, the essay is referred to a third reader and reassessed. A student's essay score is combined with his or her score on the multiple choice questions in the Writing section before being converted to the 200–800 scale. For the details of the grading standards, see the chart at the end of this chapter.

Let's get started. Below is a reminder of the assignment, then a reasonably good opening that restates the excerpt's main idea:

> Assignment: What is your view of the idea that people make their own opportunities in life and are not controlled by their circumstances?

Abundant evidence shows that people make their own opportunities in life regardless of their circumstances. History is full of people who were born humble but seized opportunities and developed into leading figures. Examples such as Andrew Carnegie and John D. Rockefeller come to mind of people who began with nothing and rose to the top. Though not everybody can become as rich as these two men, everyone can succeed if they work hard.

This looks like the beginning of a "3" essay, possibly a "4." In the first sentence, the author demonstrates understanding of the excerpt with a competent paraphrase of it. There is no clumsy sentence like "I believe this statement is true." Instead, the author *shows* what she believes in the process of restating the main idea of the excerpt. Yet the first sentence lacks sparkle and does not expand on the quote. The second sentence is OK but vague; only in the third sentence does the author use specifics. As we will see below, strong writers are capable of integrating specific examples into their general statements that can help guide the entire essay. This author's references to Carnegie and Rockefeller are not particularly convincing because the lives of these two men were not typical of late nineteenth-century America. She helps her cause by acknowledging as much in her final sentence, but better examples would not need to be qualified in this way. Grammar hawks will note the minor agreement error in the last sentence ("everyone" should be followed by a singular pronoun). Overall, this opening is competent but flawed.

A better opening paragraph is as follows:

The idea that people have the power to make their own destiny is a thoroughly modern notion. Had Shaw been writing 400 years earlier, in the time of William Shakespeare, he would almost certainly have had a different view. In the Shakespearean world, human life was controlled by the vagaries of Fate. I believe that the truth lies in the middle. Human beings can change some of their circumstances, but much of life is still controlled by the happenstance of birth, location, and social class.

This opening paragraph is superior to the first on a variety of fronts. It rates at least a "5" and perhaps a "6." Note how the first sentence goes beyond merely restating the main idea of the excerpt. By telling the reader that the idea of free will is a "modern notion," the writer signals that he or she understands the question and gives the impression of having thought about it before. The ability to contrast the excerpt to a major theme in Shakespeare's works is impressive and on target. For his thesis, the author takes a middle ground between the two, and his task will be to cite evidence on both sides of the issue. A weakness is that he fails to differentiate between the part of life controlled by circumstance and that

which human beings can change. He will have the rest of the essay to do so, but his focus would be clearer if he had taken care of business in the beginning.

We don't want to give the impression that there is a right answer to this question, so here is a fine opening paragraph that takes the other side:

In Mrs. Warren's Profession, George Bernard Shaw restates a classic tenet of modern enlightenment rationalism. It is not circumstance, Fate, or birth that dictates life's path, says his character, but the free will of every human being. Though the modern world cherishes this view, the realities of race, class, and gender limit our prospects far more than most of us realize. And modern science, far from liberating us, has highlighted the extent to which our genes may foreshadow our life outcomes. In a world where both nature and nurture conspire to rein us in, we humans have less real freedom than we think.

This essay looks like a "6" in the making. In the first two sentences, the author gives a clear restatement of the excerpt's main idea while placing it in the context of the development of Western civilization. But rather than supporting the excerpt, the author challenges it, suggesting that though we like to think we have free will, in reality our parents and our

FINDING YOUR VOICE

Funny things happen when students begin to write essays for a grade—or for the SAT. Remember the Professor on Gilligan's Island? Some students begin to sound like him, using stilted and distant language that makes them sound clumsy. SAT essay readers look for a range of vocabulary, including big words where appropriate but also simple and direct ones where appropriate. On the other hand, some students seem to think that all manner of slang and street talk will pass muster. Think again. Direct language is good; sentences that include words such as "dude," "phat," and "da bomb" should be avoided. Your best bet is to write the way you would talk to your English teacher—naturally but not too informally.

genes have much to do with who we are. The range of vocabulary is superb—words like foreshadow and conspire show strong mastery of language without being unnecessarily stilted. The paragraph also provides a quick outline of the body of the essay, which could include a paragraph elaborating on each of the last three sentences. The author demonstrates creativity by suggesting that nature and nurture "conspire," a creative twist on the more commonly referenced tension between nature and nurture. Most of all, this student shows independence of mind in challenging a statement that most students will probably go along with.

We have already given you the two primary keys for a good opening paragraph. Here are two corollaries:

Be specific. Many students mistakenly believe that any mention of specifics should wait until the body of the paper. Nothing could be further from the truth. The opening paragraph should be an examination of broad themes, but it should also be as specific as possible. Getting specific early allows you to probe more deeply in the body of the paper. Vagueness at the beginning shows that you lack clarity. Essays that begin vaguely have a meandering quality as the author uses the process of writing the essay to figure out his main point. Only at the conclusion do such essays arrive at insights that ideally should be made in the introduction.

Use complex sentences. A simple sentence has only one clause. "I went to the store" is a simple sentence. So is "I was hungry." But "I went to the store because I was hungry" is a complex sentence. See the difference? The two simple sentences express disconnected thoughts that don't say anything about the cause of the action. The complex sentence joins the two and establishes a relationship between motive and action. Without complex sentences to connect thoughts, there is no way to deal efficiently with ideas that must be modified, qualified, and fine-tuned to achieve just the right meaning. To put it another way: weak writers use simple sentences and strong ones use complex sentences.

This is not to say that you can never use a simple sentence. Everyone should sprinkle them in for variety if nothing else. If you use mainly complex sentences, the occasional simple one will be eloquent in its simplicity.

In suggesting that you use sentences with more than one clause, we are not advocating that you pad your prose with unnecessary verbiage. Each clause should be as lean as possible. The trick is to express the relationship between ideas as simply as possible while still doing justice to their complexity. Be precise, but also be concise.

Simple sentences can also be put to good use at the beginning of an essay to reach out and grab the reader. For most students, we recommend beginning with a conventional complex sentence that restates the main idea of the quotation while putting it into perspective. Pithy zingers are not easy for most writers to think of under time pressure, and there is no reason to get hung up on stylistic wizardry when straightforward competence will do just fine. But maybe you're one of those gifted writers

THE RHYTHM OF THE OPENING PARAGRAPH

Since practice makes perfect, we offer three more excerpts below that are typical SAT Writing fodder. Your assignment: write the first paragraph of an essay that takes a position on the excerpts with reference to "reasoning and examples taken from your reading, studies, experiences, or observations." Once you have written your three opening paragraphs, turn to the box on page 88 for our suggested opening paragraphs on these three topics:

• No one should underestimate the power of heartbreak to sharpen and motivate the human mind. Happiness may soothe us, but grief grants us wisdom.

• It is safe to say that no other superstition is so detrimental to growth, so enervating and paralyzing to the minds and hearts of the people, as the superstition of Morality.

• I have thought about it a great deal, and the more I think, the more certain I am that obedience is the gateway through which knowledge enters the mind of the child.

who always do it with style. Here's how your opening might look:

George Bernard Shaw obviously never read Shakespeare. At least his character in Mrs. Warren's Profession *never did. Shakespeare's enduring relevance is due to his skill in chronicling how human lives are ruled by forces we can neither comprehend nor control. Has human nature changed in 500 years? I am skeptical of neat and tidy theories about human nature that gloss over issues of identity, power, and hierarchy. Not everybody has an equal chance to control their circumstances.*

The first sentence of this essay has real flair. The detour into Shakespeare takes most of the first paragraph but is worth the trip. This writer also highlights the not-so-subtle political implications of the excerpt, which, by suggesting that everyone has the power to control his circumstances, implicitly downplays the concerns of minorities and others who may get a raw deal from society. By taking exception to the quotation on these grounds, the author has set himself up to defend the perspectives of those who are bypassed or left out. With the second-to-last sentence, the author has left open the possibility of devoting the three paragraphs of the body to identity, power, and hierarchy. Just to make you feel better, note a few flaws. In the second sen-

tence, the author mixes the third and first person with "human lives" and "we." The repetition of "human nature" is slightly awkward, and technically the last sentence should read "to control his or her circumstances." But all in all, this is a great opening paragraph.

To recap: your first sentence should generally be a complex sentence that restates the main idea of the excerpt but also sheds new light on it. Move directly to your best insights in as much detail as you can muster in two or three sentences. As you summarize your position, introduce topics that will be followed up on in the main body.

The Body and the Conclusion

If you do the first paragraph right, everything else should be a piece of cake. We recommend that you make your essay five paragraphs: one of introduction, three of main body, and one of conclusion. Don't forget the paragraph breaks. Each of the three paragraphs in the body should be focused on developing an example from "your reading, studies, experiences, or observations" to back up what you said in the first paragraph. Our preferred strategy is to choose topics from two of the many possible academic topics and then to offer a personal experience or observation in the third and final paragraph of the main body. It is always possible to devote more than one paragraph to the same piece of evidence, but without a supply of facts at hand, students will find it difficult to do so except in the case of personal experiences that can be written about from memory.

On the following pages, we offer two complete essays with comments.

CLEANING UP THAT NASTY HANDWRITING

SAT essay readers are under strict orders not to allow handwriting quality to color their assessment of an essay. Will they succeed? Probably not. Readers are under pressure to read a huge number of essays, and they have little time to puzzle through chicken-scratch. Even in cases where hand-writing is legible, a subtle advantage may go to the essay with immaculately formed letters as opposed to the one that looks like it was written during an earthquake. If you are among those who have offending handwriting—and you know who you are—we recommend that you pay special attention to penmanship as you practice. You may get a better score—and you'll definitely make your second-grade teacher proud.

Directions: Consider carefully the following excerpt and the assignment below it. Then plan and write an essay that explains your ideas as persuasively as possible. Keep in mind that the support you provide—both reasons and examples—will help make your view convincing to the reader.

The human mind cannot stand prosperity. The solution to one problem often contains the seeds of the next, and today's dream can easily turn into tomorrow's nightmare. As an ancient sage once said, "Be careful what you wish for—you may get it."

Assignment: What is your view of the idea that successes and achievements often create more problems than they solve? In an essay, support your position by discussing an example (or examples) from literature, the arts, science and technology, history, current events, or your own personal experience or observation.

DO NOT WRITE YOUR ESSAY IN YOUR TEST BOOK. You will receive credit only for what you write on your answer sheet.

The ability to plan for the future is among the traits that distinguish human beings from the rest of the animal kingdom. At least since the time of Moses, people have looked beyond the troubles of the present toward a new beginning—a promised land. Yet as the Israelites were to learn, sometimes achieving a goal can create new and unexpected problems.

The early settlers of New England learned just such a lesson. In the early 1600s, the Puritans landed in Massachusetts, seeking the freedom to practice their particular brand of Protestantism. They were tired of being pushed around in England and wanted a new start. They got what they wished for—a safe place, far removed from the long arm of the Church of England. Yet they failed in their mission of creating a model religious community, the fabled "city upon a hill." Freed from persecution, they had less need to stick together. With vast stretches of fertile land extending to the horizon, the Puritans drifted apart and lost their sense of shared purpose.

In more recent times, the growth of technology offers a second example of this phenomenon. Modern people seem to have an insatiable desire for new gadgets that will make life easier. First, we invented computers. Then cell phones and the Internet. Have these wonderful inventions eased our stress? Quite the contrary, people today work harder than ever partly because these new inventions have extended the time we can work. It is laughable to think that in the 1970s, many people believed that new technology would result in everybody working four-day weeks. We wished for new inventions and got them—along with more anxiety, stress, and over-work.

When I was in elementary school, I always dreamed of what it would be like to be a big kid. Now I am in high school and feeling stressed about homework, college admission, and the question of what to do with the rest of my life. I look forward with great anticipation to the time when I will be an adult and will finally be able to do what I please. Hmmm. On second thought, maybe being a teenager is not so bad after all.

This essay is definitely a "6." Don't let it stress you out. We use it to illustrate what to shoot for (and you may note that it contains a few minor errors).

Let's focus on the body—a paragraph about history, a paragraph about technology, and a personal insight. Each is an illustration of why we should be careful what we wish for. The paragraph on New England begins with a seamless transition from the opening. The first sentence is not a conventional thesis for the paragraph but a segue (transition) reaching back to the introduction. After two sentences of factual background, the author echoes the excerpt with a note that the New Englanders "got what they wished for" but failed in their mission.

The middle paragraph examines the paradox of technology that is supposed to make our lives easier. The subject matter in this paragraph is slightly less complex, allowing for simple sentences to provide a punchy break from the multi-clause ana-lytical ones. The author asks a rhetorical question in the fifth sentence, an effective device in a persuasive essay (and one that you will see throughout this book).

The first use of "I" comes in the fourth paragraph, where the author relates an anecdote which shows that she understands the proposition on a personal level. Though students may cite personal experiences at various points in the essay, first-person insight is often best placed at the end. Beginning with too many personal experiences can undermine your credibility in talking about other topics. You may use "I" in your opening paragraph, but we generally recommend that you build your case with academic or current-events facts and then use a personal anecdote as your clincher.

The essay ends with a flourish of humor that will help make it memorable.

To make you feel better, the following is a not-quite-so perfect essay in response to the same question:

I agree that successes and achievements often create more problems than they solve. There are many instances in history in which a scientific "advance" actually caused unintended consequences. The problem is that while people often focus on short-term goals, they fail to see the long-term consequences of their actions.

The prevalence of genetically modified foods is a good example. The U.S. and other countries have produced large quantities of genetically modified foods to feed hungry people and put money in farmers' pockets. But there has been too little consideration for the long-term impact on the environment and on people. People may get resistance to antibiotics, for instance. The people who defend genetically modified foods are the ones making a profit from it.

Another good example is all the famous people who become drug addicts and even die. So many people want to go into show business. Yet once they achieve it, many stars seem desperately unhappy. The number who have committed suicide is large. It includes people like Kurt Cobain and Ernest Hemingway. All of these people chose to try to become famous artists, but once they achieved their goal they still weren't happy.

When I was in middle school, my life's goal was to be a cheerleader. In eighth grade, my best friend and I both tried out. I was chosen for the squad but my friend was not, and to make a long story short, I gained a spot as a cheerleader but lost my best friend. By the time the season ended, I had had enough of cheerleading but I was never going to get my best friend back.

"Be careful what you wish for" is a good motto. Many of the world's problems come after people get what they want.

We give this essay a "3" or "4." On the plus side, it is well organized with an opening, a closing, and three paragraphs of body. The examples are generally well-conceived, and the essay is competently written for the most part.

But there are still plenty of issues. The first sentence is weak. Words such as "I agree with" or "I think that" are unnecessary in an essay like this. Your writing should be strong enough to show what you agree with and what you think. The rest of the first sentence is a mere restatement that does not convey any new insight—we would recommend cutting it if the writer were to do a second draft. The rest of the first paragraph includes good ideas but lacks the specifics necessary to give the essay a strong focus. The writer talks about scientific advances, discussed in the first paragraph of the main body, but does not do a good job of setting up the last three paragraphs.

The first paragraph of the main body contains good insight but is flawed in execution. The first sentence of the paragraph is OK but could elaborate more on what, exactly, genetically modified foods are an example of. The third and fourth sentences could be combined, as in an Improving Paragraphs question, and the last sentence is an assertion that lacks evidence to back it up. Note also the clumsy repetition of the word "people."

In the second body paragraph, the author's discipline breaks down with awkward word choice and simple sentences. She needs to be *clearer* about whether she is writing about a universal irony of human nature or a problem specific to rock stars.

In the third body paragraph, talking about herself, the author regains her rhythm and tells a nice story, followed by a straightforward one-sentence conclusion. Overall, this essay is good but not stellar.

THE RHYTHM OF THE OPENING PARAGRAPH II

Back on page 81, we asked you to write an opening paragraph for essays on the following excerpts with reference to "reasoning and examples taken from your reading, studies, experiences, or observation." Here again are the questions along with a sample opening paragraph from us. How does yours compare? There are many possibilities for an excellent opening paragraph and we offer only one. Our hope is that you can use these models to sharpen your own ideas.

■ ■ ■

"No one should underestimate the power of heartbreak to sharpen and motivate the human mind. Happiness may soothe us, but grief grants us wisdom."

It is no coincidence that grief has touched the lives of so many luminous figures in history. From statesmen such as Abraham Lincoln and Theodore Roosevelt to creative geniuses like Charles Dickens and Virginia Woolf, great lives seem to go hand in hand with great tragedy. I believe that we learn lessons about ourselves in failure that we cannot learn from success. Those who have always been successful may try hard, but those who have known failure generally try harder.

The first sentence restates the main idea while placing it in historical perspective. The second cites four examples that might be addressed in the main body. The author shifts to first person for the last two sentences and develops the link between wisdom and motivation. The rest of the essay will fall neatly into place. The first paragraph of the main body can be devoted to Lincoln, Roosevelt, and other public figures. The second paragraph will probably deal with literary figures and perhaps delve into some complexities. For instance, while Charles Dickens's early grief seemed to feed his creative energy, Virginia Woolf was ultimately overwhelmed by her creative demons and committed suicide. Personal perspectives in the fourth and/or fifth paragraph will round out the essay.

■ ■ ■

continued

"It is safe to say that no other superstition is so detrimental to growth, so enervating and paralyzing to the minds and hearts of the people, as the superstition of Morality."

Morality is a convenient whipping boy for liberal intellectuals. Yet we should not be so fast to dismiss the importance of a moral code. From scandals on Wall Street to lies in the White House, we see everywhere the breakdown of morality. It is true that excessive moralizing can lead to oppression, as recent hate crimes against gays and lesbians amply demonstrate. But true morality affirms humanity rather than limits it, and our democratic society cannot function without a moral code.

This quotation comes from a turn-of-the-century radical, and the first sentence of the opening paragraph shows excellent awareness of who might make such a seemingly outlandish statement about morality. The author does a fine job of weighing the pros and cons of morality, with specific evidence on both sides, but also takes a strong position as the paragraph ends. The main body of the essay can mirror this structure with the first body paragraph devoted to the problems caused by a lack of morality and the second to the dangers of excessive moralizing. The author does not include a first-person element in this paragraph but the door is open for a personal anecdote in the fourth and/or fifth paragraph to tie the two strands together.

■ ■ ■

"I have thought about it a great deal, and the more I think, the more certain I am that obedience is the gateway through which knowledge enters the mind of the child."

Since the beginning of time, adults have been imposing their will on children while rationalizing it as being "for their own good." But real learning is never the product of slavish obedience. To truly learn, children must have the freedom to make their own mistakes—impossible if they spend all their time obeying their elders. Thomas Jefferson once said that "a little rebellion is a good thing." Anyone who works with children should heed these words.

This opening is not as strong as the two above, mainly because it includes fewer pieces of concrete evidence that can be expanded on in the body of the essay. Although the quotation from Thomas Jefferson does have the potential for elaboration, ideas from the author's head dominate the paragraph. As a result, there are fewer topics that can be developed in the body of the essay. That said, this is still a fine opening paragraph that argues cogently.

The Nitty-Gritty of How to Prepare

There are three keys to doing your best on the SAT essay:

- Good writing
- Good examples
- Speed

You've got the first of these—at least we hope so. The basics of good writing are no secret: organization, vocabulary, word choice, and variation of sentence structure are the biggies. If you need a refresher, the criteria are spelled out in the grading standards for the SAT II: Writing Test, printed on pages 124–125.

While you can't teach yourself to write in a month or two, you can definitely make headway on your ability to think of and use examples. Many students develop a working list of examples that they can call upon in a pinch. You won't know the exact subject of your SAT essay question until you crack open your test booklet, but there are variations of certain themes that pop up over and over again. A few of them include:

- overcoming obstacles or failure
- encountering people from other cultures or backgrounds
- dealing with peer pressure and social expectations
- maintaining individual values and a sense of self
- being underappreciated or ignored

- balancing relationships with others and commitment to oneself

These are general topics, but for how many of them could you identify a theme that relates to "reasoning and examples taken from your reading, studies, experiences, or observations"? Let's take peer pressure and social expectations. Can you think of an historical figure who defied them? Henry David Thoreau comes to mind. Or Margaret Sanger, who crusaded for birth control in the early 1900s. In the arts, consider Oscar Wilde, the homosexual playwright, or Spike Lee, the African American filmmaker. The technology figure could easily be the contrarian Albert Einstein, though you might also choose Galileo, who was condemned by the Roman Catholic Church in the 1600s for saying that the Earth revolved around the sun. Lastly, can you think of a time in your life when you confronted harmful social expectations? What happened?

Some coaching firms advise students to spend hour upon hour perfecting several essays covering themes such as this before taking the SAT. When the students sit for the actual exam, the thinking goes, they can adapt their essay from memory to the particular question they encounter.

This approach seems to have worked at least part of the time for the SAT II: Writing Test, and if you want to try it, here's how: write several generic essays on the themes

THE GRADERS: WHO ARE THEY?

In the years before the launch of the New SAT, College Board materials describing the test included a sales pitch: "If you are a teacher who would like to become more involved in the New SAT, think about becoming a reader for the New SAT essay. Teachers of English, writing, or language arts courses are particularly welcome."

above, then crack open your copy of *10 Real SATs* and see if your essays give you an edge on a random selection of the ones therein. If it works, you'll have a tool to carry with you to the SAT.

However, we are leery of advising you to spend too much time crafting generic essays. The College Board and ETS are aware of this little game, which has been widely reported in the press, and they are tinkering with the format of the essay section. We suspect that they will try to make the New SAT essay more resistant to generic essays by crafting questions with a narrower focus. For instance, a practice question circulated in 2003 asked students to respond to the idea that appreciation of the arts "may actually worsen us, diminishing our ability to respond to actual situations…" An unexpected question—and not the sort likely to be addressed by boilerplate material. We fear that students who spend a lot of time perfecting a few generic essays may get blindsided by a question that does not fit what they prepared. The result will be frustration, panic, and probably, a lower score.

We recommend a more flexible approach. Instead of focusing huge energy on perfecting a few generic essays, think broadly about the themes listed above and think about figures in literature, the arts, science and technology, history, politics, and current events who may relate to these themes. You can think of events or social trends, too, but since most SAT essay themes apply to the human condition, the life experiences of people tend to be the most useful. You may want to brainstorm four or five people in each area, or choose areas such as history or literature with which you are familiar, and then concentrate mainly on them. Pick people that you already know about and if necessary, remind yourself of their life stories by reading a few encyclopedia entries. Generally, you will only need to write about two to four figures per essay, preferably from different walks of life, to get the job done.

Once you have a pool of potential evidence in mind, tackle some of the essays in *10 Real SATs*. Writing essays will help you master factual details about your examples that may come in handy when you take the actual SAT. Practice integrating anecdotes from diverse people and subject matter with perspectives drawn from your own life. Write your first several essays untimed so that you can get the feel of writing a good one.

Know Your Audience

Your high school English teacher has probably taught you the importance of knowing your audience. How fitting that your audience on the SAT essay will be...high school English teachers. What do we know about them? They're intellectual, they're liberal, and they're female. The minority of males sprinkled in will generally be cut from the same cloth. Like any other group, English teachers have their preferences and pet peeves. Here are some themes that will resonate with them.

The world is complicated. The SAT is not the best time to dust off your essay about how self-discipline is the key to success, or how persistence always pays off. Save that for the American Legion essay contest. English teachers want to hear about conflict, complexity, and alienation. Instead of writing about black-and-white issues, probe some gray areas. Don't forget the complex sentences.

The road less traveled. English teachers love the unexpected. On many questions, there is an obvious direction that most stu-

dents will take their essays. For instance, most students would probably agree with the proposition that "the best things in life are free." A student who disagrees with this statement—and proposes that the best things in life must be earned—is likely to stand out. Don't be afraid to go a different direction or add a new twist. We are not advising that you go against your own instincts, but if you see multiple ways to approach a question, consider choosing the unconventional route.

Respect for diversity. Your ability to see things from the perspective of others is always solid gold, especially if the others are different from you in important ways. If you are from a minority group, don't be shy about tapping into that experience. Minority or not, show that you can learn from interactions with others, and don't be afraid to question or redefine your own sense of self in light of these interactions.

Lest there be any doubt, we are not suggesting that you concoct a phony essay based on what you think an anonymous reader wants to hear. English teachers can spot nonsense a mile away. These are general themes that may—or may not—be appropriate for any particular essay.

Hitting the Fast-Forward Button

Got your track shoes on? You'd better. Twenty-five minutes is precious little time. After mastering the art of writing your essay, you'll need to learn how to get it done before time is called. The only way to do it is with practice. By repeating the process, over and over if necessary, you can develop a sense of how much time you should spend on each phase.

When you hear the magic words—"open your test booklet and begin"—your first impulse may be to begin writing frantically. Think again. Too many students get caught up in the pressure of the moment and cut loose with the first thing that pops into their heads. Consider making a brief outline. This might include two or three major examples and at least one personal anecdote that could be covered in the body of the essay, and then some secondary points related to each. Not everybody functions best with an outline, but even if you're not accustomed to making one, try it and see for yourself.

From there, experiment with how much you can put on the page before time is called. If you're consistently getting caught before you finish, cut down your introduction or consider going to a three or four paragraph format rather than five paragraphs. Find out how much detail you can give on one example while still having time to get to one or two others. Always try to have a conclusion, or at least a coherent way to finish. The beginning is more important than the end, but the end matters.

A final strategy: do at least several practice essays in only 20 minutes. If you find that your writing remains just as coherent despite the fact that you are moving faster, that's a sign that you could probably speed up, cover more ground, and have an even better essay. When you get accustomed to writing an essay in 20 minutes, having 25 minutes will be a luxury.

Keys to Success

1. Find a comfort level. We've loaded you up with advice, but your first priority should be to write a coherent essay with sentences that flow with a reasonable range of vocabulary. Use practice to figure out what you can—and cannot—accomplish in 25 minutes. Find a rhythm with your practice tests that you can repeat on the exam.

2. Get more specific. Your English teacher has told you over and over again—concrete detail is what makes an essay sing. See how specific you can make your first paragraph, and use complex sentences to express shades of meaning. An opening paragraph with specifics will give your essay focus and allow you to develop your analysis in the main body.

3. Longer is better. English teachers are constantly telling their students that longer is not necessarily better, and students never believe them. In this case, the students' gut feeling is right. A lot of bad writing won't get a good score, but the more fully you can develop your essay with specific examples, the more likely that you will get a high score. Practice the art of finishing as close as possible to when time is called without getting caught by the clock.

4. Forget the "right" answer—go for the interesting answer. Repeat after us: *There is no right answer to the SAT essay.* Pick what you think is the "right" answer and you'll end up belaboring the obvious along with thousands of other students. Oddball questions deserve free-wheeling responses. Any answer is right as long as it is backed up by logic and examples.

5. Lose your perfectionism. Are you the kind of writer who sweats over every word? You can afford to do it on a term paper—but not on a 25 minute essay. We're not suggesting that you write a sloppy essay or one that is full of mistakes. But perfectionism is one of the major inhibitions to writing an excellent essay. Let your writing flow. Pause over key phrases, but don't sweat them all. You can't write a perfect essay in 25 minutes, and trying to do so may prevent you from writing an excellent one.

Identifying Sentence Errors

Studying grammar is nobody's idea of a good time. Even English teachers hate the stuff—a big reason why so many students can analyze a Victorian novel but have never heard of the subjunctive mood and think that a gerund is a small furry animal found in pet stores. Even if you didn't know that a gerund is an "-ing" form of a verb that functions as a noun—as in "I did the cleaning for Mom"—you know perfectly well how to use one. And if your ability to define the objective case is a little fuzzy, your ear will tell you that "Paul and me are going to the store" is incorrect. (The sentence needs the nominative "I" in that spot.)

If you don't learn this stuff in school, where do you get it? This is part of what the College Board calls "developed ability." It comes from reading, from conversations at the dinner table, and from listening to correct English. If your parents are college professors, you're in good shape. If you come from a home where grammar is not a priority, you may need to devote a little more practice to this kind of question.

A few students may want to do a formal grammar review, though we suspect that this would be a waste of time in most cases. While we have no doubt that learning about modifiers, antecedents, and idioms would be highly entertaining, a better approach is to take practice tests that will identify trouble spots within these categories. You don't need to know fancy grammar terms; you merely need to know a mistake when you see one.

Identifying Sentence Errors is all about your ear for correct grammar. Most of the rules should be second nature. But there are a few tricky spots where the words that feel right may not be technically correct—and you can count on the SAT to dredge them up. The sixteen questions that follow are intended as examples of the problem areas that students most often encounter. The answers are in the paragraph immediately following the questions—don't peek until you've given them a good shot.

SAMPLE TEST

Directions: The following sentences test your knowledge of grammar, usage, diction (choice of words), and idiom.

Some sentences are correct.
No sentence contains more than one error.

You will find that the error, if there is one, is underlined and lettered. Elements of the sentence that are not underlined are always correct. When choosing answers, follow the requirements of standard written English.

If there is an error, select the one underlined element that must be changed to make the sentence correct and fill in the corresponding oval on your answer sheet.
If there is no error, fill in answer oval E.

1. Everyone <u>who is</u> interested <u>in going</u> to
       A   B
the game should <u>proceed to</u> the front
             C
door with <u>their</u> hat and coat. <u>No error</u>
        D   E

2. If Grandma <u>was</u> still able <u>to feed</u> herself,
            A   B
she <u>would not</u> need to consider
       C
<u>moving into</u> a nursing home. <u>No error</u>
    D   E

3. Neither the teacher <u>nor</u> the principal
                A
<u>were</u> <u>willing to forgive</u> Ben's absence
   B   C
because it <u>was</u> his third since the
         D
beginning of October. <u>No error</u>
              E

4. Steve <u>observed</u> that the novels of Jane
        A
Austen, <u>unlike Dickens,</u> <u>did not rise</u> to
         B   C
the level of literary masterpieces in the

eyes of <u>contemporary</u> critics. <u>No error</u>
      D   E

5. Although he <u>earned</u> a lower grade than
            A
Sally and Joy, John firmly <u>believed that</u>
                   B
he <u>was</u> the <u>better</u> of the three at
     C   D
writing essays. <u>No error</u>
           E

6. Amy proposed a plan <u>where</u> we
                        A
<u>would split up</u>, go dancing <u>with</u> our
   B   C
respective partners, and then <u>meet back</u>
                                   D
at the ranch. <u>No error</u>
                   E

7. The team, <u>which</u> consisted of ten-year-
               A
olds and nine-year-olds who

<u>had never played</u> the game,
        B
<u>were assembled</u> for the <u>purpose of</u>
        C   D
learning the rules. <u>No error</u>.
                        E

8. The orange signs <u>entreat</u> motorists
                       A
<u>to drive</u> <u>slow</u> as they <u>come near</u> the
   B   C   D
construction zone. <u>No error</u>
                       E

9. If I <u>had known</u> that she <u>was going</u> to
        A   B
the show, I <u>would</u> have suggested that
               C
we <u>share</u> a cab. <u>No error</u>
      D   E

10. As she <u>turned from</u> the chalk board,
               A
Ms. Jones <u>shot</u> a disapproving glance at
              B
<u>Tony and I</u> and asked that we stop
    C
<u>talking</u>. <u>No error</u>
    D   E

11. <u>Uncomfortable with</u> our plan
        A
<u>to drive via</u> Atlanta, my father
    B
<u>suggested</u> that <u>Tony and I</u> consider
    C   D
changing our route. <u>No error</u>
                        E

12. Tomatoes and carrots <u>are</u> <u>an example</u>
                          A   B
of <u>the kind of</u> food that Americans
       C
should <u>eat</u> in larger quantities.
          D
<u>No error</u>
    E

13. Media coverage and alumni <u>support of</u>
                              A
the university <u>has increased</u> rapidly
                      B
since the <u>hiring of</u> a new president
              C
<u>about</u> four years ago. <u>No error</u>
      D   E

14. The novel, <u>written by</u> Jules Verne,
                    A
<u>follows</u> the <u>exploits of</u> Phineas Fogg as
   B   C
he <u>circumcises</u> the globe in 80 days.
          D
<u>No error</u>
      E

15. <u>Located in</u> eastern Utah, Delicate Arch
        A
<u>is</u> one of the <u>most unique</u> landforms
 B   C
in the continental United States, and

also one of the <u>most photographed</u>.
                        D
<u>No error</u>
      E

16. <u>Be they</u> adjectives or adverbs,
        A
modifiers <u>should</u> always <u>be placed</u> as
              B   C
near as possible to the words

<u>they modify</u>. <u>No error</u>
      D   E

The answers: 1.(D) 2.(A) 3.(B) 4.(B) 5.(D) 6.(A) 7.(C) 8.(C) 9.(E) 10.(C) 11.(E) 12.(B) 13.(B) 14.(D) 15.(C) 16.(E). Got 'em all? If so, feel free to skip to the next section. These are typical of the toughest sentence error questions, so don't feel bad if you missed some or even most of them. Here are the explanations:

1. **Can't We All Agree?**
   This question illustrates the exalted principle of subject-pronoun agreement. With ordinary nouns and pronouns, this is a snap. Depending on whether the subject is singular or plural, you make an easy pronoun adjustment. I get my coat and they get their coats. But there are a few renegade pronouns—such as everybody, everyone, somebody, someone, nobody, no one, anybody, and anyone—that are singular but an awkward mate to third-person singular pronouns. "Somebody needs to get their act together!" yells mom from the upstairs bathroom after finding a wet towel in the middle of

the floor. Tell her that technically speaking—and especially on the SAT—it should be "somebody needs to get his or her act together." Answer: (D).

2. The Moody (Subjunctive) Blues

"If I were the Grammar Guru," said Tess testily, "I would abolish the subjunctive mood." SAT-takers everywhere would heartily agree. The subjunctive connotes a conditional situation that would, could, or should happen if some other condition were to prevail. All well and good. The problem comes in the first- and third- person singular, where "were" is the correct usage in the "if" part of the sentence instead of the more normal-sounding "was." If Tess were the Grammar Guru, you would not need to waste your time learning this stuff. Answer: (A).

3. Agreement, Take II

"Neither...nor" and "either...or" are examples of singular constructions masquerading as plural ones. Since the teacher and principal are both mentioned in the beginning of the sentence, it would be easy to conclude that they are part of a compound subject with a plural verb, as in "Neither the teacher nor the principal were willing to forgive." But "neither" and "either" refer to only one of them. A hint: substitute the word "one" for

"the teacher nor the principal." The sentence would now read, "Neither one were willing to forgive"—an obvious error. The singular "was" is the correct verb form. Answer: (B).

4. The Importance of Parallelism

Parallelism is the idea that things being compared should correspond logically to one another. Were everything spelled out, the passage would read, "The novels of Jane Austen, unlike the novels of Charles Dickens..." There is nothing wrong with avoiding repetition of the word "novels," but a place-holder pronoun must remain because comparing the novels of Austen to Dickens himself does not make sense. The correct form: "The novels of Jane Austen, unlike those of Dickens..." Answer: (B).

5. Comparatives and Superlatives

This one is a no-brainer but students can miss it because the incorrect usage does not stand out. A not-so-subtle hint: think good-better-best, bad-worse-worst, easy-easier-easiest. Got the idea? In comparing quantities, the –er form refers to the amount or degree when comparing two. The –est form refers to three or more. There are a few variations, like "worse" instead of "worser" and the fact that "lesser" drops its -er in many situations. In the question, "the better of the three" does not sound awful, but "the best of the three" is correct. Answer: (D).

6. **Idiot's Guide to Idioms**

Talk about sneaky. This sentence looks perfectly fine except for the fact that "where" is not the right preposition to go with "proposed a plan." The right usage is "in which." Questions of this type test your knowledge of idioms. Idioms are preferred combinations of words that sound right together. Often, but not always, they are a verb and preposition combination. You know most of them instinctively: "talk with," "go to," "flee from," "recommend that," and so on. Idioms only get dicey occasionally, as with "different from" rather than the incorrect "different than." Answer: (A).

7. **Subject-Verb Agreement**

This one is such a dirty trick that it makes us blush. The sentence starts with a collective subject that is singular even though it has more than one part. The sentence proceeds with a diversionary clause designed to make the reader forget that the subject is singular. On subject-verb agreement questions such as this, the key is to edit out the modifying clause. "The team was assembled" is correct. Answer: (C).

8. **Adjectives and Adverbs**

Call this "the –ly rule." A word that modifies a noun is an adjective, and a word that modifies a verb is an adverb. A person may have a *soft* voice, but that person speaks soft*ly*. Likewise, a driver may be *slow*, but only if he or she drives slow*ly*. Adverbs are often beside the verbs they modify. If your first glance at a sentence does not reveal an error, take a look beside the verb to see if there is an adjective that needs an –ly. Answer: (C).

9. **The Subjunctive Shakedown**

There's nothing like puzzling over a past-perfect subjunctive to brighten your day. Did you figure out immediately that this sentence had no errors? Or did you keep looking and looking until a phantom error surfaced? This is exactly the kind of conundrum ETS loves to create. At least they're not tearing the wings off butterflies. Answer: (E).

10. **Getting On Your Cases**

This question takes us back to the nominative and objective cases. When it comes to "I" and "me," students tend to remember the nominative. As everyone knows, "Me and Pauline are going to the store" doesn't cut it. Me and Pauline are the subject, so the correct usage is "Pauline and I." But question 10 includes Tony and I as the object of Ms. Jones's action. Correct wording: Tony and me. Answer: (C).

11. **Nominative and Objective Again**
If you've been paying close attention, you know the difference between this and question 10. This time, "Tony and I" has its own clause that is linked to the sentence by a conjunction, "that," rather than a preposition, which would mean the objective case. The father is suggesting that they take an action, and "Tony and I" is the subject of the last clause. Hence, the nominative case is correct. Answer: (E).

12. **More Issues With Agreement**
This problem involves agreement between three entities: the subject, a "to be" verb, and the object of the sentence. A prepositional phrase with a singular collective noun, "the kind of food," is inserted to distract students from the necessity of matching the plural subject and verb. Tomatoes and carrots are plural "examples" of foods within the category of the kind of food that should be eaten in larger quantities. Answer: (B).

13. **And Another Dirty Trick**
Like problem 12, this sentence has a compound subject. If the sentence included only "media coverage of" or "alumni support of" as the subject, "has increased" would be a correct usage. But together, media coverage and alumni support are a compound subject, which requires a plural verb, "have increased." Answer: (B).

14. **How's Your Diction?**
OK, this one is comic relief. But it does illustrate what the College Board calls a "diction error." These generally occur when the writer is searching for one word and incorrectly uses another. In this case, "circumnavigate" is the word the writer was looking for. Another example: "Regretfully, he was absent on the day I gave my presentation." Correct word: "regrettably." Answer: (D).

15. **Can't We Both Be the Best?**
This is a diction error of a different sort than that of 14. According to *American Heritage*, "unique" means "the only one of its kind." Therefore, one thing cannot be more unique than another or most unique among a group of three or more. Substituting "unusual" for "unique" or eliminating "most" would make this sentence correct. Answer: (C).

16. **Sick of the Subjunctive?**

Sorry, you don't have a choice. In addition to its use with "if...would" statements, the subjunctive applies to present-tense statements of what should be. For example, "I recommend that all students be exempted from taking final exams" uses "be" without "should." Another example: "The teacher insisted that Sheila do her homework." Since the present subjunctive form is identical to the base form of the verb, the subjunctive is noticeable only in the third person singular. In problem 16, the sentence is correct with the subjunctive form "be" in the first clause. Answer: (E).

Verb Tenses

There are two ways to learn a language: you can either memorize the rules, or you can start using the language and develop a feel for it. Good language instruction emphasizes the latter. As in most other areas of learning—including test prep—true mastery comes not from memorizing abstract rules, but from developing a working knowledge through practice.

That said, there is one area of grammar where a bit of review may be in order. Verb tense is the most important subject area in Identifying Sentence Errors. Though most of the questions related to it are easy, some students may need to brush up. There are six tenses and each has a variation to indicate progressive action. Each form conveys a specific meaning that is relevant to particular situations. At the risk of insulting your intelligence, here is an example of each:

Present:	She climbs the mountain.
Progressive:	She is climbing the mountain.
Past:	She climbed the mountain.
Progressive:	She was climbing the mountain.
Future:	She will climb the mountain.
Progressive:	She will be climbing the mountain.
Present Perfect:	She has climbed the mountain.
Progressive:	She has been climbing the mountain.
Past Perfect:	She had climbed the mountain.
Progressive:	She had been climbing the mountain.

Future Perfect: She will have climbed the mountain.

Progressive: She will have been climbing the mountain.

Between these twelve forms, a speaker of English can place climbing the mountain in any imaginable time frame. For Identifying Sentence Errors, make sure that the verb agrees with the nouns and pronouns in the sentence. As you may be aware, there are six pronoun variations that must match the verb form:

1st Person Singular: 1st Person Plural:
        I   we

2nd Person Singular: 2nd Person Plural:
        you   you

3rd Person Singular: 3rd Person Plural:
    he, she, it, one   they

If none of this makes sense, or if you simply want to relive your seventh grade language arts class, you may want to do a grammar review. Most students will be able to iron out the kinks with more practice problems. Here are three that focus on some of the toughest cases:

Since June had not <u>been climbing</u> Pike's
                          A
Peak since 1996, she <u>was</u> nervous about
                          B
<u>getting</u> back on the mountain,
    C
particularly because

three hikers <u>had been</u> lost
                   C
there in the past year. <u>No error</u>
                              B

<u>Answer</u>: A. The phrase "been climbing" is an incorrect usage of the past-perfect progressive form because the action is not continuing at the time of the main clause. Instead of "been climbing," the correct usage is "climbed." A correct usage of the past-perfect progressive would be, "June had been climbing Pike's Peak for four hours when she encountered a snake."

When June and Joe <u>have reached</u> the
                        A
summit, they <u>will have been</u> climbing for
                      B
six hours and <u>will</u> probably
                  C
<u>be fighting</u> dehydration. <u>No error</u>
     D   E

Answer: A. The main clause of the sentence includes phrases in the future and future-perfect. The past-perfect is inappropriate for the first clause because the past and future do not make sense in combination. Instead of "have reached," the correct form is the present "reach."

Everyone in the group <u>will be</u> an expert
                         A
hiker, even <u>those</u> who <u>have struggled</u>
              B   C
thus far, when <u>they have climbed</u> the
                      D
mandatory total of eight 14,000-foot

peaks. <u>No error</u>
          E

Answer: D. We couldn't resist throwing in another shifty pronoun agreement question. The action in the sentence takes place in the future and present-perfect tense.

The middle clause is a curve ball, designed to distract attention from the singular subject "everyone." Therefore, "they have climbed" should be replaced by "he or she has climbed."

Keys to Success

1. Listen for the answer. As with the sentence completions, we recommend that you read the questions while listening to the voice inside your head, and if necessary, moving your lips. In most cases, you will "hear" the incorrect word or phrase.

2. Use practice to identify weaknesses. This kind of question does not take long to answer, so you can do lots of them in a short period of time. Make a list of the kinds of questions you miss, categorizing them in a way that makes sense to you. In most cases, simple repetition will help you make the necessary adjustment.

3. Make sure your mind doesn't play a trick. You know ETS is trying to sucker you, but sometimes your own head helps ETS do it. It happens when you read a sentence that has an error in it, yet somehow your eye slides over the mistake as if it were correct.

Most of the sentences you read in your life are correct, so your brain somehow substitutes a correct usage for the incorrect one—and you never notice your mistake. Weird how that works. If you have this problem, it is possibly a sign that you are reading too quickly. In problems in which the first reading shows no error, do a second one, reading more slowly to make sure you do not bypass the error.

4. Work through the "no error" dilemma. If you're stuck after two readings, ETS is probably trying to camouflage the error beneath a phrase that might pass muster in informal speech but is technically wrong. Unfortunately, students commonly miss these questions and choose "no error" when there really is an error. On the flip side, students who fear that they have answered "no error" too many times may convince themselves that there is an error where one does not exist. The solution: keep track of the questions in which you do not see an obvious error after the first reading. Do you tend to get these questions right when you choose "no error"? Or are you more likely to get them right if you choose a response that you think may be an error but you're not sure? Each person has different tendencies. Some students need to have more trust in themselves and believe that when they don't see an obvious error, there isn't one. Other students tend to miss errors and need to look more carefully if their initial reading reveals no error. Use practice tests to find out which tendencies you have.

Improving Sentences

There is one universal rule for Improving Sentences: shorter is better. Some people wish to do their writing with lots of clauses, putting many participles in their prose, and having lots of repetitiveness, and generally mucking things up. Others get right to the point. Some people try to show their perspicacity by elucidating their ideas with erudite words that would look good in an analogy question but don't fit their sentence. Others write hard-hitting prose. Some writers subscribe to the more-is-better theory, thinking that because there are many words on the page as well as many pages, that people won't notice a certain convoluted quality that may begin creeping into their writing because they can't seem, no matter how hard they try, you know, to get to the freakin' point.

Your job in Improving Sentences is to clean up this mess. Here's an example:

Directions: Choose the option below that changes the underlined phrase to make the sentence better. If no change is best, choose (A).

Jane wrote <u>stories and they capture</u> the feeling of alienation that she felt in her youth.

(A) stories and they capture
(B) stories, capturing in them
(C) stories, which were designed to capture
(D) stories, being the explanations of
(E) stories that capture

The correct answer is (E) because that response says in three words what the others say in four, five, or six words. This pattern repeats itself over and over. Of course, ETS knows you know that the short answer is generally best, so there will be some cases when a longer answer may be the right one. But incorrect short answers are often obvious. They tend to leave out important facts or change meanings, whereas too-long answers are plausible in their meaning but include unnecessary clutter. When in doubt, always choose the shortest answer.

As powerful as the shortest-is-best technique may be, it is not a substitute for knowing the relevant grammar. Improving Sentences questions include the grammar topics in Identifying Sentence Errors, plus some additional ones related to writing style. We covered verb tenses, a major topic, in detail on pages 102–103. Here is a quick review of other key grammar topics. The correct form is in parentheses.

Noun-Pronoun Agreement—A first-person singular noun, called the antecedent, must be referred to later in the sentence by a first-person singular pronoun. The same goes for second-person plural, and so on. Third-person singular accounts for most mistakes.

Common mistakes:
• No one should take *their* pencils. (*his* or *her* pencils)
• The team used a secret ballot to choose *their* captain. (*its* captain)
• Neither of them remembered *their* pencils. (*his* or *her* pencils)
• Each promised *they* would bring a friend. (*he* or *she* would)

Subject-Verb Agreement—Nouns and verbs must match in every sentence according to whether they are singular or plural, and whether they are first, second, or third person. Many subject-verb problems are easy. The tough ones generally have to do with singular subjects that look plural and plural subjects that look singular.

Common mistakes:
• A fleet of one hundred ships *sail* tomorrow. (*sails* tomorrow)

- Neither John nor Susan *visit* their old home anymore. (*visits* their old home)
- Tanya, Jeff, and George, the dynamic jazz trio in town, *plays* at the club on Saturday. (*play* at the club)

Subjunctive Mood—The subjunctive expresses a condition that does not reflect reality but would or could if some other condition prevailed. The subjunctive is also used to describe actions done "as if" or "as though" a condition prevailed. First- and third-person "was" changes to "were."
Common mistakes:
- If I *was* gone, you would be sad. (If I *were* gone)
- He acted as though he *was* a king. (as though he *were* a king)
- If I *would have* noticed the frog, I would have tried to avoid stepping on it. (If I *had* noticed the frog)

Comparisons—Adjectives and adverbs generally have two forms by which to make comparisons: comparative (i.e., bigger, stronger) and superlative (i.e., biggest, strongest). The comparative form should be used when there are two items; the superlative applies to three or more.
Common mistakes:
- She is the better of the three. (*best* of the three)
- He is the best of the two. (*better* of the two)

Parallelism—The toughest of these questions tend to be comparisons. In everyday speech, many people use shortcuts when making comparisons, as in "I thought Lincoln's speech was better than Douglas," rather than "better than that of Douglas" or "better than Douglas's." To preserve parallelism, you must refer to the thing being talked about with at least a pronoun in the second half of the comparison.
Common mistakes:
- The defense attorney's closing argument was more effective *than the* prosecutor. (more effective than *that of* the prosecutor)
- The skiing in Colorado was *better than Vermont*. (was better than *that in* Vermont)

Idioms—These make foreigners pull their hair out. There are no rules; just a pattern that everybody follows. Why should people "lace up" shoes but "shut down" a computer? Why should a boat be "dead in the water" instead of "dead on the water"? The toughest problems with idioms on the SAT are generally related to verbs and their propositions. Unfortunately, there is not much advice to give other than to suggest you look for phrases that sound slightly wrong.
Common mistakes:
- Vince is qualified *for joining* the tennis team. (qualified *to join*)

- She lives *at* Chicago.
  (lives *in* Chicago)
- I remember the chapter where Harry meets Ron. (*in which* Harry meets Ron)

"Don't spend your time memorizing every vocab word and trick. It is more useful to get used to the sorts of questions and time restrictions as well as the format of the test than to memorize."

—620 V, 620 M

Style and Sentence Structure

Improving Sentences questions cover more terrain than Identifying Sentence Errors questions. The latter require students to identify a word or two that violate the rules of grammar in the context of a sentence.

Improving Sentences questions require students to examine the effectiveness of a sentence as a whole. While some questions hinge on a single offending word, many offer more than one grammatically correct answer choice. The key is to evaluate the overall fluency of the sentence. Is it concise? Is the meaning clear? Is there a more effective way of conveying the meaning of the sentence? Errors that must be corrected include:

- Fragments and run-on sentences
- Misplaced adjectives and adverbs
- Wordiness and awkwardness
- Passive voice

The following are some sample questions that include commonly missed concepts. Answers and explanations follow.

Directions: The following sentences test correctness and effectiveness of expression. In choosing answers, follow the requirements of standard written English; that is, pay attention to grammar, choice of words, sentence construction, and punctuation.

In each of the following sentences, part of the sentence or the entire sentence is underlined. Beneath each sentence you will find five ways of phrasing the underlined part. Choice A repeats the original; the other four are different.

Choose the answer that best expresses the meaning of the original sentence. If you think the original is better than any of the alternatives, choose it; otherwise choose one of the others. Your choice should produce the most effective sentence—clear and precise, without awkwardness or ambiguity.

1. Kimberly wanted to meet with Mrs. Stone to review the material on the test, <u>but she did not have a free period.</u>

   (A) but she did not have a free period.

   (B) but she does not have a free period.

   (C) but she will not have a free period

   (D) but Mrs. Stone did not have a free period.

   (E) but Mrs. Stone was not having a free period.

2. <u>The students were told repeatedly by Mrs. Shaw</u> not to use the passive voice, but her advice went unheeded.

   (A) The students were told repeatedly by Mrs. Shaw

   (B) Repeatedly, the students were told by Mrs. Shaw

   (C) Mrs. Shaw told the students repeatedly

   (D) Mrs. Shaw, repeatedly telling the students

   (E) The students, repeatedly told by Mrs. Shaw

3. Because he told the students to remain seated until the end of class, Mr. Peterson was angry when they left before the bell rang.

   (A) Because he told the students to remain seated until the end of class,

   (B) Telling the students to remain seated until the end of class,

   (C) Because the students were told to remain seated until the end of class,

   (D) He told the students to remain seated until the end of class, and as a result,

   (E) After telling the students that they would remain seated until the end of class,

4. Requests for transcripts should be given to the main office they will be processed within three days.

   (A) to the main office they will be processed within three days.

   (B) to the main office; they will be processed within three days.

   (C) to the main office, they will be processed within three days.

   (D) to the main office and within three days is when they will be processed.

   (E) to the main office since they will be processed within three days.

5. After encountering a fierce thunderstorm near St. Louis, the trip was delayed by two hours.

   (A) After encountering a fierce thunderstorm near St. Louis, the trip was delayed by two hours.

   (B) Encountering a fierce thunderstorm near St. Louis, we took two hours longer than expected to complete the trip.

   (C) A fierce thunderstorm encountered near St. Louis delayed us by two hours longer than we expected.

   (D) Delayed by a fierce thunderstorm near St. Louis, our trip encountered a two hour delay.

   (E) We encountered a fierce thunderstorm near St. Louis that delayed our trip by two hours.

6. For people who commit their lives to community service, helping others is more important than being well paid.

   (A) helping others is more important

   (B) to be helpful to others is more important

   (C) there is more importance in helping others

   (D) helpfulness to others has more importance

   (E) help for others is more important

7. The highway bill had strong support, and Congressman Smith did not believe that the House of Representatives would fail to approve it.

(A) Congressman Smith did not believe that the House of Representatives would fail to approve it.

(B) Congressman Smith had been convinced that the House of Representatives would approve it.

(C) Congressman Smith did not believe that the House of Representatives would approve it.

(D) Congressman Smith believed that the House of Representatives would approve it.

(E) Congressman Smith believed that the House of Representatives would not approve it.

8. Catharine Beecher was less radical than other reformers of her time and she believed that women should take a lead role in educating the young.

(A) Catharine Beecher was less radical than other reformers of her time and she believed

(B) Catharine Beecher had been less radical than other reformers of her time and she believed

(C) Catharine Beecher was less radical than other reformers of her time, believing Catharine Beecher disagreed with other reformers of her time and she believed

(D) Catharine Beecher disagreed with other reformers of her time and she believed

(E) Catharine Beecher, less radical than other reformers of her time, believed

The answers: 1.(D) 2.(C) 3.(A) 4.(B) 5.(E) 6.(A) 7.(D) 8.(E). We wager you found these a bit easier than the Identifying Sentence Errors questions because hair-splitting grammar rules are not quite so important here. But you probably missed at least a couple of these, so here are the explanations:

1. **When Your Antecedent is Unclear**
   This question tries to trick you into looking for a tense error. But Kimberly wanted the meeting in the past and <u>did not have</u> is correct. The problem with the original sentence is an unclear antecedent for <u>she</u>. Does <u>she</u> refer to Kimberly or Mrs. Stone? Response (E) clarifies that issue but with an incorrect progressive form. Answer: (D).

2. **Don't Be Passive**
   Nothing is more crucial to improving sentences than eradicating passive voice. Passive voice weakens prose by burying the subject in a prepositional phrase or even editing it out. With passive voice, "we published the book in 2004" becomes "the book was published by us in 2004" or even simply "the book was published in 2004." Accurate, but hardly dynamic. There are occasions when the passive voice is acceptable, usually when the subject is unknown or unimportant. In this sentence, (C) is the only response that makes the sentence active while also making sense.

3. **Being Direct With Directions**
   Nobody listens to poor Mr. Peterson. The facts are clear from the original sentence: Mr. Peterson told the students to remain and was angry when they left. Response (B) uses an incorrect present progressive form to explain the situation and response (C) uses the passive voice. Response (D) includes an extra phrase, <u>as a result</u>, that slows down the sentence, and response (E) features a misplaced use of the subjunctive. The original version is the best. Answer: (A).

4. **When a Sentence Won't Quit**
   This sentence is a classic example of a run-on. It has two main clauses that express separate (if related) ideas. Response (C) makes the sentence into a comma-splice, (E) creates a falsehood, and (D) is full of gobbledygook. The College Board says that it does not test spelling and punctuation, but semicolons are an exception. Use them to divide run-on sentences when the second half flows from the first. Answer: (B).

5. **Stamp out Dangling Modifiers**
   Whenever a sentence begins with a clause that modifies a subject but does not name it, that subject must come

immediately after the clause to avoid confusion. The trip didn't encounter a fierce thunderstorm—we did. "The trip was delayed" is a passive construction, adding to the woes in this sentence. The best fix is to say who was delayed—"we" were—and to describe what happened with the storm as directly as possible. Answer: (E).

6. **Putting Participles to Work**
Though you should always be suspicious of –ing forms, sometimes they are correct. In this case, <u>helping others</u> parallels <u>being well paid</u> and does a reasonable job of conveying the sentence's meaning. None of the other responses parallel being well paid, and (B), (C), and (D) are also more wordy than the original phrase. Response (E) makes help a noun and thereby creates uncertainty as to who is doing the helping. Answer: (A).

7. **Don't Want No Double Negatives**
This one includes a double negative, though not a blatant one such as, "We didn't get no beans for dinner." "Would fail to approve" is another way of saying "would not approve," but there is already a "not" earlier in the clause because the Congressman "did not believe that the House of Representatives would fail to approve it." In other words, he believed that

the House would approve it.
Answer: (D).

8. **A Blast From the Past**
In the immortal words of Henry David Thoreau, "Simplify, simplify." The first step is to consolidate the comparison of Catharine Beecher to other reformers into a separate clauses set off by commas. By doing so, you can cut out a weak "to be" verb, a redundant pronoun, and an unnecessary conjunction. The correct response, (E), is the shortest.

Keys to Success

1. Shorter is better. Picking the shortest answer to questions in this section is one of the most reliable strategies in this book. After reading the sentence, glance down and read the shortest answer first—even if that answer is shortest by only a hair. Then read the other responses to see if any of them beats it. The shortest answer won't always be correct, but use it as a measuring stick. If you must guess, always pick the shortest response. Be especially skeptical of the longest responses.

2. Watch for "to be" verb clutter. We're talking about forms like "is," "are," "was," "were," "has been," and "had been." These are sometimes necessary, but often they are a sign of passive voice. The play was written by me. (I wrote the play.) She has been told by the teacher. (The teacher told her.) The ball had been kicked by Mia Hamm. (Mia Hamm had kicked the ball.) Whenever possible, make sure the actor in the sentence is in front of the verb instead of hiding behind "by" at the end of the sentence.

3. **Watch for –ing words at the beginning of sentences.** These are often bad news. Be especially on guard for convoluted "to be" expressions, for example: "Being tired, I decided to take a nap." (I was tired and took a nap.) And those dangling modifiers can be a real headache: "Diving into the water, the rock hit my head." (I dove into the water and hit my head on the rock.) Not all –ing words are bad, but you'll often find more concise ways to make a point.

Improving Paragraphs

The difference between Improving Sentences and Improving Paragraphs boils down to this: instead of only one sentence to improve, you now have 10–15 sentences. All of the errors you corrected in Improving Sentences are also fair game in Improving Paragraphs. But here, the emphasis is on the way sentences connect to one another.

Improving Paragraphs also has a lot in common with Reading Comprehension. The material is presented in passages that are about 200 words long—twice as long as the shortest Reading Comprehension passages but only a fourth as long as the longest ones. Most of what we say about Reading Comprehension also applies here. Some students may choose to read the passage before answering the questions, others may skim the passage, and still others may dispense with reading and go straight to answering the questions. (See Chapter 5.)

The questions come in five categories:

Correcting Grammar Errors—The topics highlighted earlier get a workout here, including passive voice, run-on sentences, noun-pronoun agreement, dangling modifiers, and verb tense agreement. The questions typically ask you to correct an underlined portion of a sentence.

Paragraph Context—Many questions will ask you to revise a sentence to make it clearer in light of the paragraph context. For example, a pronoun might have an unclear antecedent, as in, "The workers lost their jobs after the enactment of stricter air quality regulations. This is unfortunate." If the passage is about recent trends in employment, you can correct the sentence to reflect the fact that the author means the job losses were unfortunate, while the enactment of stricter air quality regulations might or might not have been unfortunate.

Connecting Sentences—Passages often include simple sentences that can be combined to clarify the meaning of the passage or improve its flow. For instance, your task might be to combine the following two sentences: "The region is experiencing a prolonged drought. Dry conditions have made trees more vulnerable to beetle infestation." Answer: "A prolonged drought has made trees more vulnerable to beetle infestation."

Adding Sentences or Paragraphs—You may be asked to choose the most appropriate among five sentences that might be added to the passage, or to choose the best topic for a paragraph that might be added. To do so, you must understand the passage's tone and main idea and be able to identify other topics related to that idea.

Reading Comprehension—To make sure you understand the passage, ETS throws in an occasional question that has more to do with the meaning of the passage than fixing it. Such questions may deal with topics such as: Which sentence best states the main idea of the passage? What is the function of a particular sentence? What strategies has the author used to back up his/her opinion?

"Take a year of Latin, or even a summer course. I could approximate many difficult vocabulary words I didn't know by considering its Latin roots. More effective than studying vocab words one at a time."

—660 V, 730 M

If there is such a thing as an easy section of the SAT, this is it. The questions offer more context to get the answer than do Identifying Sentence Errors or Improving Sentences questions and are generally not as challenging as those in Reading Comprehension. Some sample questions follow.

SAMPLE TEST

Directions: Each of the following passages is an early draft of an essay. Some parts of the passage need to be rewritten. Read each passage and answer the questions that follow. Some questions are about particular sentences or parts of sentences and ask you to improve sentence structure and word choice. Other questions refer to parts of the essay or the entire essay and ask you to consider organization and development. In making your decisions, follow the conventions of standard written English. After you have chosen your answer, fill in the corresponding oval on your answer sheet.

Questions 1–6 are based on the following passage.

(1) One of the most powerful storms ever to hit the U.S. mainland was Hurricane Camille, which roared ashore on the night of August 17 near Port Christian, Mississippi. (2) Camille began as a tropical disturbance on August 9 in the Atlantic Ocean about 500 miles east of the Leeward Islands. (3) It reached hurricane strength on August 14, at which time its location was about 100 miles south of Cuba. (4) Turning north, the storm brushed past Cuba's western tip before emerging into the open waters of the Gulf of Mexico, quickly intensifying to a huge Category 5 storm on the Saffir-Simpson Hurricane Scale and began moving north-northwest at about 15 miles per hour.

(5) The eye of the storm hit the coast of Mississippi on the night of August 17. (6) Camille destroyed all weather instruments in its path, but its winds are estimated to be about 200 miles per hour at the time of landfall. (7) The most deadly aspect of Camille was its storm surge, estimated at 24 feet. (8) In the area of landfall, nearly 150 residents were killed. (9) In addition, 5,000 homes in the area were destroyed and 40,000 were damaged. (10) Camille's path of destruction continued north to St. Louis before the storm veered east to Virginia, where over 100 people were killed by flooding.

1. The tone of the passage is best described as

(A) skeptical
(B) sorrowful
(C) matter-of-fact
(D) sensational
(E) wistful

2. Of the following, which is the best version of sentence 4 (reproduced below)?

Turning north, the storm brushed past Cuba's western tip before emerging into the open waters of the Gulf of Mexico, quickly intensifying to a huge Category 5 storm on the Saffir-Simpson Hurricane Scale and began moving north-northwest at about 15 miles per hour.

(A) (As it is now)

(B) Turning north, the storm brushed past Cuba's western tip before emerging into the open waters of the Gulf of Mexico. Following a quick intensification to a huge Category 5 storm on the Saffir-Simpson Hurricane Scale, it began moving north-northwest at about 15 miles per hour.

(C) Turning north, the storm brushed past Cuba's western tip before emerging into the open waters of the Gulf of Mexico. It quickly intensified to a huge Category 5 storm on the Saffir-Simpson Hurricane Scale and began moving north-northwest at about 15 miles per hour.

(D) The storm brushed past Cuba's western tip before emerging into the open waters of the Gulf of Mexico, turning north, and quickly intensifying to a huge Category 5 storm on the Saffir-Simpson Hurricane Scale and began moving north-northwest at about 15 miles per hour.

(E) Turning north, the storm brushed past Cuba's western tip before emerging into the open waters of the Gulf of Mexico. Quick intensification to a huge Category 5 storm on the Saffir-Simpson Hurricane Scale followed, and it began moving north-northwest at about 15 miles per hour.

3. In the context of the second paragraph, which of the following is the best revision of the underlined portion of sentence 6 (reproduced below).

Camille destroyed all weather instruments in the area of landfall, but its winds are estimated to be about 200 miles per hour at the time of landfall.

(A) (As it is now)

(B) but its winds were estimated to be about 200 miles per hour at the time of landfall.

(C) but its winds had been estimated to be about 200 miles per hour at the time of landfall.

(D) but its landfall winds had been estimated to be about 200 miles per hour at the time of landfall

(E) but its winds are estimated to have been about 200 miles per hour at the time of landfall.

4. To connect sentence 7 to the rest of the second paragraph, which is the best word or phrase to insert after "The most deadly aspect of Camille" (reproduced below)?

The most deadly aspect of Camille was its storm surge, estimated at 24 feet.

(A) , surely,
(B) , however,
(C) , by contrast,
(D) , therefore,
(E) , as a consequence,

5. In context, which is the best way to revise and combine sentences 8 and 9 (reproduced below)?

In the area of landfall, nearly 150 residents were killed. In addition, 5,000 homes in the area were destroyed and 40,000 were damaged.

(A) In the area of landfall, nearly 150 residents were killed, 5,000 homes destroyed, and 40,000 homes damaged.
(B) In the area of landfall, nearly 150 residents were killed, 5,000 homes in the area were destroyed and 40,000 were damaged.
(C) In the area of landfall, nearly 150 residents were killed, while an additional 5,000 homes were destroyed and 40,000 damaged.

(D) In the area of landfall, nearly 150 residents were killed, and 5,000 and 40,000 homes were destroyed and damaged, respectively.
(E) In the area of landfall, nearly 150 residents were killed, and additionally, 5,000 homes in the area were destroyed and 40,000 were damaged.

6. Which of the following is the best revision of sentence 10 (reproduced below)?

It reached hurricane strength on August 14, at which time its location was about 100 miles south of Cuba.

(A) It reached hurricane strength on August 14, locating it about 100 miles south of Cuba.
(B) It reached hurricane strength on August 14, about 100 miles south of Cuba.
C) On August 14, it reached hurricane strength about 100 miles south of Cuba.
(D) On August 14, it reached hurricane strength when it was located 100 miles south of Cuba.
(E) It reached hurricane strength on August 14, maintaining a location about 100 miles south of Cuba.

The answers: 1.(C) 2.(C) 3.(E) 4.(B) 5.(A) 6.(C). There's nothing here you can't handle. Hurricanes are more interesting than ETS's typical fodder, but we think the questions are of about average difficulty. The explanations:

1. **Don't Be Tone Deaf**
   This is one of those questions designed to make sure you understand the whole passage. A quick read shows that the passage is crammed full of facts and does not express any emotions or judgments. We'd call that matter-of-fact. Answer: (C).

2. **Coping With A (Sentence) Disaster**
   There are two problems with this sentence: it is a run-on, and it includes a verb ("began") that messes up the parallel structure of the clauses. You need to break this into two sentences, and (C) offers the most concise way of doing so. Answers (B) and (E) include awkward usage of "intensification," a verb masquerading as a noun. Always aim to make the verb as strong and active as possible—in this case, "intensified." Answer: (C).

3. **Tricky Tenses**
   Back to those aggravating tenses. You might have been tempted to choose (B), but this sentence suggests that the estimates of wind speed were made at the time of landfall. The estimates are actually being made today—and therefore should be in the present tense. That makes the present perfect "to have been" the only possible companion to the present "are estimated," and (E) is the correct response. Notice that the shorter-is-better rule does not apply in this case because answer (B) does not get the tense right. Answer: (E).

4. **Smoothing the Transition**
   Sentence 7 says, "The most deadly aspect of Camille was its storm surge, estimated at 24 feet." Since the previous sentence focused on wind speed—and since most people envision hurricane winds as doing most of the destruction—it may come as a surprise that the storm surge was actually Camille's most deadly aspect. Of the possible answers, (B) best expresses the idea that the logic of sentence 7 runs counter to what most people probably believed after reading sentence 6. "However" is a better response than "by contrast" because sentences 6 and 7 do not present a contrast, but rather two facts that might not seem at a glance to go together. Answer: (B).

5. Concise is Nice

This is one is a no-brainer. Apply your "shorter-is-better" rule and move on. (A) is correct, though a few people might be tripped up by the omission of "were" for the houses damaged and destroyed. In this instance, "were" is understood and it is not necessary to repeat. (B) is wrong because of the unnecessary repetition of "were" and "in the area." The words "additional" and "additionally" are not necessary— the latter is not even a real word. Answer: (A).

6. When Phrases Are Out of Order

The awkwardness in this sentence comes from the fact that the action in the sentence, "reached hurricane strength," is separated from "about 100 miles south of Cuba," the place where it happened. The problem with response (B) is that "about 100 miles south of Cuba" does not modify "August 14." Solution: move "August 14" to the beginning. Therefore, the "shorter-is-better" rule applies. Answer: (C).

■ ■ ■

Questions 7–12 are based on the following passage.

(1) *Recreation in wilderness areas has increased dramatically in recent years, and as a result, the number of encounters between humans and bears has also been rising.* (2) *The thought of coming face to face with a bear may sound terrifying, but the vast majority of such situations pass without incident.*

(3) *Since bears generally try to avoid humans, make plenty of noise.* (4) *Many outfitter stores sell bear bells that can be strapped to a backpack.* (5) *Try to minimize food odors.* (6) *Store your food and garbage in air-tight containers.* (7) *Campers should never bring food into a tent.* (8) *If you encounter a bear while hiking, come to a stop and then back away slowly.* (9) *Look in the direction of the bear but do not make eye contact, which the bear might perceive as threatening.* (10) *Talk softly to let the bear know that you are human, and definitely not prey, but also not a threat.* (11) *Never consider running from a bear, as this may spark a chase instinct in an otherwise non-aggressive bear.*

(12) *Thousands of people encounter bears every year, but bear attacks are exceedingly rare.* (13) *You are far more likely to be injured in an automobile accident on the drive home than by a bear during an excursion into the outdoors.*

7. Which of the following best states the main idea of the passage?

(A) People should not be concerned about a bear attack in wilderness areas.
(B) Though bear attacks are rare, people should take simple precautions when they are in bear country.
(C) People should avoid wilderness areas where they are likely to encounter bears.
(D) A few simple precautions can eliminate the danger of bear attacks in wilderness areas.
(E) The frequency of bear attacks in wilderness areas is increasing rapidly.

8. Which of the following would be the most suitable sentence to insert immediately before sentence 3?

(A) Most people underestimate the dangers of bears in the back country.
(B) Readers should not be concerned about encountering a bear in the back country.
(C) Only outdoor experts should venture into bear country.
(D) A few simple precautions can help maximize your safety in bear country.
(E) Most people will encounter a bear at some time during their lives.

9. In context, which is the best way to revise and combine sentences 6 and 7 (reproduced below)?

Store your food and garbage in air-tight containers. Campers should never bring food into a tent.

(A) Store your food and garbage in air-tight containers; you should never bring food into a tent.
(B) Food and garbage should be stored in air-tight containers, and food should never be brought into a tent.
(C) Store your food and garbage in air-tight containers, and never bring food into a tent.
(D) Store your food and garbage in air-tight containers, and campers should never bring food into a tent.
(E) Store your food and garbage in air-tight containers, never bring food into a tent.

10. Inclusion of a paragraph on which of the following would most strengthen the passage?

(A) the mating habits of bears
(B) places where bear encounters are most likely
(C) techniques used by bear hunters
(D) the diet of bears
(E) a comparison of bears to cougars

11. Which of the following best replaces the word "definitely" in sentence 10?

(A) therefore
(B) you are
(C) unquestionably
(D) usually
(E) as a result

12. In the context of the passage, which of the following is the best revision of the underlined portion of sentence 11 (reproduced below)?

Never consider running from a bear, as this may spark a chase instinct in an otherwise non-aggressive bear.

(A) Always think twice before running from a bear,
(B) Avoid running from a bear you encounter,
(C) You should never consider running from a bear,
(D) Running from a bear is not very wise,
(E) Never run

The answers: 7.(B) 8.(D) 9.(C) 10.(B) 11.(A) 12.(E). Our passage on bear attacks allows us to continue the disaster and mayhem theme (and hopefully keep you at least mildly entertained). The explanations:

7. **Getting the Main Idea**
Like many others, this passage is not black and white. It doesn't tell you to forget about bear attacks and neither does it suggest that you should live in fear of them. The danger can never be eliminated but neither should it be overstated. Answer: (B).

8. **That's An Insert**
The second paragraph outlines strategies for minimizing the likelihood of encountering a bear, such as making plenty of noise and minimizing food odors, and strategies for lessening the likelihood of a violent confrontation if you do encounter a bear. Since both emphases fit nicely under the heading of safety, (D) is the correct answer.

9. **Be Concise But Be Clear**
We may have gotten a few of you on this one. Answer (A) is not correct because the two sentences express independent thoughts not appropriate for joining with a semicolon. (And besides, it includes an unnecessary "you should.") Answer (E) is the shortest of the bunch, but without a conjunction it is a comma splice. Response (B) is burdened with passive voice. Response (D) has an unnecessary "campers should" for an imperative sentence in which the subject (you) is understood. Answer: (C).

10. Strengthening the Sentence

The major theme of the passage is how to prepare for encounters with bears. Part of being prepared is knowing where you are likely to see one. Answer (B) is the only one that relates directly to encounters with bears. 'Nuff said.

11. Making the Logic Flow

Sentence 10 suggests that the reason people should talk softly when encountering a bear is "to let the bear know you are human." (The soft part relates to the idea that you are "not a threat.") A human by definition is not prey, and answer (A) is the response that best establishes the idea that "not prey" follows from "human."

12. Brevity is the Soul of Wit

Repeat after us: short is good, shorter is better, shortest is best. Responses (A) to (D) fiddle around before getting to the point. At first glance, you might be put off by the fact that (E) says merely "Never run" as opposed to "Never run from a bear." But look at the context again. The whole passage is about bears, and there is no ambiguity about what "never run" refers to. Answer: (E).

Keys to Success

1. Experiment with reading the passages vs. going straight to the questions. The passages in Improving Paragraphs are easier to skip around in than those in the Reading Comprehension. While reading comprehension passages are numbered at five-line intervals, every sentence in Improving Paragraphs is numbered. The language is generally easier to understand and the selections are relatively short. We think the case for going straight to the questions is at least as strong as in Reading Comprehension. You decide for yourself.

2. Shorter is better—most of the time. After pounding away at shorter-is-better, perhaps we should remind you once again that ETS knows you know that shorter is better. Watch for short responses that omit key information or distort meanings, as in question 3. In the absence of errors like these, shorter is still definitely better.

3. Answer sentence-specific questions before answering comprehension questions. If you decide to dive straight into the questions before reading, skip comprehension questions such as 1 and 7 until you have answered the ones that focus on particular sentences. In the process of answering those, you will pick up more about broad issues such as the passage's main idea and tone.

HOW THE ESSAYS WILL BE SCORED

Below are the College Board's scoring guidelines that the essay graders will use. The essays will be graded holistically, meaning that the overall impression conveyed by the essay will be the basis of the score:

Score of 6

An essay in this category is *outstanding,* demonstrating clear and consistent mastery, although it may have a few minor errors. A typical essay:
- Effectively and insightfully develops a point of view on the topic and demonstrates outstanding critical thinking, using clearly appropriate examples, reasons, and other evidence to support its position;
- Is well organized and clearly focused, demonstrating clear coherence and smooth progression of ideas;
- Exhibits skillful use of language, using a varied, accurate, and apt vocabulary;
- Demonstrates meaningful variety in sentence structure; and
- Is free of most errors in grammar, usage, and mechanics.

Score of 5

An essay in this category is *effective,* demonstrating reasonably consistent mastery, although it will have occasional errors or lapses in quality. A typical essay:
- Effectively develops a point of view on the topic and demonstrates strong critical thinking, generally using appropriate examples, reasons, and other evidence to support its position;
- Is well organized and focused, demonstrating coherence and progression of ideas;
- Exhibits facility in the use of language, using appropriate vocabulary;
- Demonstrates variety in sentence structure; and
- Is generally free of most errors in grammar, usage, and mechanics.

Score of 4

An essay in this category is *competent,* demonstrating adequate mastery, although it will have lapses in quality. A typical essay:
- Develops a point of view on the topic and demonstrates competent critical thinking, using adequate examples, reasons, and other evidence to support its position;
- Is generally organized and focused, demonstrating some coherence and progression of ideas;
- Exhibits adequate but inconsistent facility in the use of language, using generally appropriate vocabulary;
- Demonstrates some variety in sentence structure; and
- Has some errors in grammar, usage, and mechanics.

Score of 3

An essay in this category is *inadequate*, but demonstrates developing mastery, and is marked by one or more of the following weaknesses:

- Develops a point of view on the topic, but may do so inconsistently, demonstrating some critical thinking, but using inadequate examples, reasons, or other evidence to support its position;
- Is limited in its organization or focus, but may demonstrate some lapses in coherence progression of ideas;
- Displays developing facility in the use of language, but sometimes uses weak vocabulary or inappropriate word choice;
- Lacks variety or demonstrates problems in sentence structure; or
- Contains an accumulation of errors in grammar, usage, and mechanics.

Score of 2

An essay in this category is *seriously limited*, demonstrating little mastery, and is flawed by one or more of the following weaknesses:

- Develops a point of view on the topic that is vague or seriously limited, demonstrating weak critical thinking, providing inappropriate or insufficient examples, reasons, or other evidence to support its position;
- Is poorly organized and/or focused, or demonstrates serious problems with coherence or progression of ideas;
- Displays very little facility in the use of language, using very limited vocabulary or incorrect word choice;
- Demonstrates frequent problems in sentence structure; or
- Contains errors in grammar, usage, and mechanics so serious that meaning is somewhat obscured.

Score of 1

An essay in this category is *fundamentally deficient*, demonstrating very little or no mastery, and is severely flawed by one or more of the following weaknesses:

- Develops no viable point of view on the topic, or provides little or no evidence to support its position;
- Is disorganized or unfocused, resulting in a disjointed or incoherent essay;
- Displays fundamental errors in vocabulary;
- Demonstrates severe flaws in sentence structure; or
- Contains pervasive errors in grammar, usage, or mechanics that persistently interfere with meaning.

5 CRITICAL READING

TOTAL TESTING TIME: 70 MINUTES

Sections:
- 2 of 25 minutes
- 1 of 20 minutes

Question Types:
- Sentence Completion
- Reading Comprehension
- Paragraph-Length Critical Reading

Both types of Critical Reading questions, Sentence Completion and Reading Comprehension, appeared in the old Verbal section. Budget most of your time for the Reading Comprehension, where plowing through the passages is the main chore. The new wrinkle: shorter paragraph-length passages will also be included. The biggest change is that the dreaded analogies have been axed. For old time's sake—and for those who will take the test before March 2005—we offer a brief rundown on strategies for these beginning on page 130.

Sentence Completion

Many students consider Sentence Completions to be the easiest kind of question on the SAT. Part of this has to do with the fact that these questions can be answered quickly. But statistically, there is a higher proportion of the hardest questions among the Sentence Completion than there is in the Reading Comprehension. Why? Because the Sentence Completion place greater emphasis on vocabulary. If you don't know the words, you have little chance of getting the answers.

The College Board divides Sentence Completion questions into four types. Here are some relatively easy examples of each.

One-Blank Vocabulary-Based

1. The ____ countryside stretched out before her, cool and quiet in the morning mist.

   (A) raucous
   (B) placid
   (C) lively
   (D) jaded
   (E) disquieted

Two-Blank Vocabulary-Based

2. The dog sat forlornly beside the door; he had been ____ and ____ since his master left.

   (A) electrified..content
   (B) excited..bemused
   (C) morose..listless
   (D) eager..disappointed
   (E) dilatory..joyous

One-Blank Logic-Based

3. Although most people tend to be resistant to change, they are also quick to ____ new technology when it proves useful in daily life.

   (A) embrace
   (B) eschew
   (C) enact
   (D) empower
   (E) dislike

Two-Blank Logic-Based

4. Because Peter ____ to finish his homework, the teacher ____ him in front of the class.

   (A) hastened..ennobled
   (B) decided..berated
   (C) neglected..admonished
   (D) disdained..circumscribed
   (E) elected..alienated

For anyone who is curious, the answers are: 1.(B) 2.(C) 3.(A) 4.(C). Got 'em all? Don't get too pleased with yourself. They get a wee bit harder as you go along.

The distinction between vocabulary- and logic-based questions is a fine one. Sometimes the hard part is knowing the words (vocabulary-based questions), and sometimes the hard part is following the analytical reasoning that dictates the answer (logic-based questions). So goes the theory anyway. In our informal review, we found that vocabulary-based questions were generally one-blank and logic questions were generally two-blank. As with all sections of the SAT except Reading Comprehension, the questions get harder as you go. The first three or four questions are generally easy, the next few get harder, and the last one is often a nasty vocabulary-based mind-bender.

The secret to solving the sentence completions may have as much to do with listening as thinking—listening, that is, to the little voice inside your head. "Say the problem to yourself without looking at the answers and often the right answer will pop into your head," says a Cornell admit who scored 710 V, 800 M. If you are lucky enough to have an epiphany of this sort, glance down to see if it is in the answer choices. If so, and you are doing a two-word question, see if the second word fits. If yes again, glance at the other choices, and if nothing seems equally plausible, blacken your oval and move on.

You come out ahead when you solve problems this way because a) you save time, and b) you don't get bogged down in the tricks that ETS has cooked up to throw you off track. But alas, many questions won't be so easy. Don't lose heart. If your initial read does not reveal the answer, look deeper and you'll see patterns that can offer important clues. These patterns are best described as tendencies rather than rules because there are always exceptions, but more often than not these patterns will lead you to pay dirt.

WHEN THE CLAUSES CONTRADICT

A favorite tactic of ETS is to build sentences out of two clauses that express ideas or conditions that seemingly do not go together. To spot this kind of question, look for any and all of the following words and phrases: *although, but, despite, however, nevertheless, rather than, though, while, whereas, yet*. When you encounter one of these, the sentence will generally express a contrast or contradiction.

The majority of sentence completion questions share a common structure. They consist of two clauses connected by punctuation such as a comma, semicolon, or colon, or connected by linking words such as *although*, *but*, *despite*, *since*, *that*, and *whereas*, to name a few. (If you want to get technical, these linking words are generally conjunctions or conjunctive adverbs.) In one-blank questions, or in two-blank questions where both blanks are in the same clause, the right answer is generally defined by its relationship to the most important phrase in the opposite clause—what we call "the key phrase."

Confused? Don't be. Look back at Question 1. A comma divides the sentence into two clauses. *Cool and quiet in the morning mist* is the key phrase that determines the correct response: *placid*. In Question 2, the key phrase is *forlornly*, which has nearly the same meaning as the combination of *morose* and *listless*. Problems like these, in which a colon, semicolon, or comma joins the two clauses—and in which there is no linking word—are the least complicated. In such problems, the correct answer generally has the same meaning as the key phrase, as in questions 1 and 2.

The presence of a linking word—either in the middle of the sentence or at the beginning—complicates the relationship between the key phrase and the answer. Look again at Question 3. The sentence begins with *although*, a word used to explain how two conditions that seem contradictory can coexist. The key phrase is *resistant to change*, but the word *although* implies that you should look for an answer that means the opposite of *resist* or *resistant*. Which response is most clearly the opposite of these two? The correct one: (A) *embrace*.

Most two-blank questions present a variation on this theme. Typically, these sentences have a blank in both clauses. The clauses are generally connected in the same way as in the one-blank questions, that is, by punctuation and/or by a linking word. The absence of a key phrase without a blank can be a challenge, but you may also find that having two blanks in different parts of the sentence can be an advantage because you have two chances to find the correct answer.

Go back to Question 4 above. Begin with the word *because*, a word that shows that the first blank will be the cause of what happens in the second. Next, plug in the pairs of words and see which one makes the most logical cause-and-effect sentence. Responses (A) and (D) are out because the second word in the pair does not make sense in the context of *teacher ____ him*. The teacher could have *berated* him, but not because he *decided* to do his homework. Nor would the teacher have *alienated* him because he *elected to finish* his work. The correct answer is (C) *neglected..admonished*.

For all we have said about patterns and tendencies, we should stress again that the best way to solve sentence completion problems is by ear. When in doubt, go with the response that sounds the most fluid and/or expresses the clearest logic. See how you fare on the following ten questions, then consult the answers and explanations below. (No peeking.)

SAMPLE TEST

Directions: Each sentence below has one or two blanks, each blank indicating that something has been omitted. Beneath the sentence are five words or sets of words labeled A through E. Choose the word or set of words that, when inserted in the sentence, *best* fits the meaning of the sentence as a whole.

1. As big as the United States and Mexico combined, the continent of Antarctica is a ____ place, with little vegetation and temperatures that average about –60° Fahrenheit.

   (A) reflective
   (B) forbidding
   (C) awesome
   (D) predominate
   (E) dauntless

2. After tons of waste had been dumped at the landfill, a ____ smell emanated from the site.

   (A) lurid
   (B) doleful
   (C) putrid
   (D) turgid
   (E) despicable

3. Dorothy has been quietly effective since her promotion to plant manager; though ____ with her employees, she has already ____ productivity on the assembly line.

   (A) jovial..promoted
   (B) strident..momentous
   (C) direct..enlarged
   (D) soft-spoken..increased
   (E) scrupulous..elongated

4. Many drivers ____ this road on their way through the county because its sharp curves and blind intersections make it ____.

   (A) bypass..deleterious
   (B) dislike..risky
   (C) encompass..disjointed
   (D) enjoy..engaging
   (E) avoid..hazardous

5. In *Their Eyes Were Watching God*, Zora Neale Hurston makes ____ use of dialect to portray the ____ of African American Southerners in the 1930s.

   (A) excessive..alienation
   (B) consistent..foibles
   (C) innovative..cadences
   (D) inappropriate..speech
   (E) intemperate..rage

6. Atmospheric pressure, a ____ measured by barometers, is an important ____ of developing weather systems.

   (A) mechanism..effect
   (B) process..agent
   (C) forecast..precursor
   (D) phenomenon..outgrowth
   (E) condition...predictor

7. The story of buried treasure on the island was ____, based as it was on unsubstantiated rumors.

   (A) phlegmatic
   (B) apocryphal
   (C) uninformed
   (D) distasteful
   (E) unknown

8. While the lieutenant demanded that his men act ____, he also insisted that they not be ____ to danger.

   (A) bravely..intrepid
   (B) affirmatively..dubious
   (C) courageously..oblivious
   (D) lively..incredulous
   (E) flatulently..impertinent

9. Critics describe the new novel as ____, even ____; it excoriates the rich and powerful and sounds a call for the disempowered to mobilize.

   (A) controversial..offensive
   (B) belligerent..mocking
   (C) salacious..blasphemous
   (D) iconoclastic..revolutionary
   (E) disturbing..malevolent

10. Usually ____ to criticism, Mr. Smith showed surprising ____ at his negative reviews from the critics.

   (A) impervious..pique
   (B) immune..volubility
   (C) hostile..truculence
   (D) disgruntled..dismissiveness
   (E) derisive..rage

Did you get all ten? Don't feel bad if you didn't; these are typical of the hardest ones you'll see. The answers: 1.(B) 2.(C) 3.(D) 4.(E) 5.(C) 6.(E) 7.(B) 8.(C) 9.(D) 10.(A). Explanations follow:

1. **A Forbidding Place**

   This problem is relatively easy, the kind that students should expect at the beginning of a section. The blank modifies *place*, thereby eliminating *reflective*, which applies to people, and *predominate*, a verb that means *larger in number*. *Dauntless*, meaning *invulnerable to fear*, is a distracter that calls to mind *daunting*. The key phrase, which comes immediately after ___ *place*, is *with little vegetation and temperatures that average about –60° Fahrenheit*. A place like that is forbidding and the answer is (B).

2. **What's That Smell?**

   Technically, this is a logic-based problem. The linking word *after* sets up a cause-and-effect relationship between *tons of waste* and ___ *smell*. You know that smell is nasty, but we've turbo-charged the problem with tough distracters. For instance, you might be tempted to choose *turgid*, a word that sounds stinky but really means *bombastic* or *ostentatious*. Likewise, *lurid* means

   shocking or *sensational* and is obviously inappropriate. These are diversions from the real answer, (C) *putrid*, the smell of stuff rotting.

3. **Key Phrase Follow-Up**

   A sentence divided by a semicolon (or colon) virtually always consists of two clauses that express a similar meaning. The key phrase in this problem is *quietly effective*. The first blank after the semicolon calls for a synonym of *quietly* while the second should be filled with a word that means *effective*. Response (A) is typical of distracters that include words that convey some of the right meaning but don't quite fit. *Jovial* means lighthearted but not quiet, and if a form of promote were in the answer, the right choice would be *promoting* instead of *promoted* since her work is ongoing. The closest synonym to quiet or quietly among the answers is *soft-spoken*, and *increased* also fits better than any of the other second words in the pairs. While her job of promoting productivity is continuing, it is appropriate to say that she *has increased* productivity since any measurement must be based on past results. Answer: (D).

4. **When a Distracter Is Response (A)**

In two-blank problems, a common trick is to include a wrong answer in which the first word in the pair looks right. This is the case with *bypass..deleterious*. Often, a distracter such as this comes before the right answer so that students moving too quickly will pick it as the right answer and move on. Though *bypass* appears to be appropriate, *deleterious* connotes something that is harmful or negative in its nature. (A road is not deleterious in itself, but an accident can have a deleterious affect on one's health.) *Dislike..risky* is another choice that might appear possible at first glance, but the timeframe of *on their way through the county* rules out this one because the dislike would not be limited to this period. Answer: (E).

5. **Feeling the Positive Vibes**

Even if you've never heard of Zora Neale Hurston, you can guess that she is an African American woman because ETS takes every opportunity to write about people of color. We're glad that the bad old days of the white male SAT are over, but we also cannot fail to note that the test's statements about women and non-whites are predictable and therefore can give you an advantage. (See Political Correctness and the SAT, page 17). Since virtually every reference to persons of either group is positive, you can solve some questions without knowing the meanings of every word. In this case, the first word in the pair is unlikely to be *excessive*, *inappropriate*, or *intemperate*. Once you spot the most positive word among the five, *innovative*, you can be fairly sure that (C) is the right choice even if you have no idea what *cadences* means. If you do know the word *cadences*, you recognize it as the closest synonym for *use of dialect* among the second words in the pairs. *Speech* would also be a plausible answer were it not paired with *inappropriate*. Answer: (C).

6. **A Different Kind of Pressure**

The key phrase in this problem is *atmospheric pressure*. The hard part is figuring out exactly what sort of thing atmospheric pressure really is. A *mechanism*? A *process*? A *phenomenon*? ETS hopes that you will pick one of these without thinking it through, but atmospheric pressure is actually a weather *condition*. Even if the first blank stumps you, think about the weather reports you see on TV and use a little logic. Barometers exist because they can help predict weather conditions. Answer: (E).

7. **Dealing With 50-Cent Words**

This question is typical of the hardest vocabulary-based problems, the kind that generally comes at the end of a section. The key phrase is *unsubstantiated rumors*. Let's suppose you don't know that *apocryphal*—the correct answer—means "of questionable or dubious authenticity." You do know the definition of *uninformed*, *distasteful*, and *unknown*. None of them are an exact fit. Faced with the choice between a word they know that doesn't exactly fit and a word that they don't know, too many students choose the simpler word just because its definition is familiar. For many students, the best approach will be to guess between *apocryphal* and *phlegmatic* (meaning *unemotional*). Answer: (B).

8. **A Logical Contrast**

Although the odds are remote that you'll see so much as one question with a military theme, we thought it would be nice to put at least one question in the book for the guys. Joined by the linking word *while*, the two clauses express a contrast in the lieutenant's demands: his men should act ____ but not ____. *Bravely* is a perfectly acceptable possibility but is revealed as a distracter because *intrepid* (*fearless*) does not fit the second blank. Answers (B) and (D) do not present a logical contrast, and if you don't know what *flatulently* means…er, look it up. *Courageously..oblivious* captures the idea that the soldiers should be brave but not reckless. Answer: (C).

9. **Two Blanks, Heightening Intensity**

The word *even* is your clue that the second blank will be an intensified version of the first. The semicolon is a tip-off that the first clause and the second will probably express similar ideas, and the entire second clause is the key phrase. *It excoriates the rich and powerful* parallels the first blank, while *sounds a call for the disempowered to mobilize* approximates the meaning of the second blank. *Controversial, belligerent, salacious*, and *disturbing* are all plausible responses for the first blank, but none comes as close to *excoriates the rich and powerful* as does *iconoclastic*. Even if you don't know the meaning of *iconoclastic*, the *call for the disempowered to mobilize* is a perfect match for *revolutionary*. Answer: (D).

10. **Saving the Toughest for Last**

We have noted that in sentences divided by a comma without a linking word, the meaning of the

SHOULD I CRAM VOCABULARY?

Probably not. Trying to cram word definitions a month or two before the test is one of the biggest time wasters in SAT prep. In the words of a 720 V, 690 M scorer, "I studied approximately 500+ SAT words in my English class and there were only three or four words that were the same. Instead of wasting all this time on learning words it would be more useful to practice problems." Says another student who got 630 V, 630 M, "I studied as many vocab words as Kaplan had to offer and saw only one of those words on the test." With the demise of the analogies, studying vocabulary will become an even more dubious proposition. The one possible exception is if you have a long period of time—like six months to a year—in which you can learn words gradually. Several students in our survey suggested making a vocab notebook, in which you record words from reading or prep books. Leave about four lines between each word—enough space to write a definition and use the word in a sentence. You'll need to do 1,000 words—and preferably 2,000 or more—to have much hope of making an impact. If you're determined to build your word power, a better strategy may be to work on prefixes, suffixes, and word roots. These will help you figure out a word even if you've never seen it before.

second clause generally parallels that of the first. But there are exceptions. In this case, there is an implied linking word—*though*—that does not appear. By reading the first clause as *Though usually ____ to criticism*, you can quickly gather that the second clause will present a contrast or contradiction. *Immune..volubility* is a nasty distracter because *immune* is a logical choice and many students don't know the meaning of *volubility*. Though it looks like *volatility*, it actually means *fluency* or *articulateness*. Scratch that one. Responses (C), (D), and (E) have some tantalizing words, but none present

an adequate contrast. But *impervious to criticism* works nicely and *pique*—a relatively difficult word—is a synonym of *irritate*. Answer: (A).

Keys to Success

1. **Watch for distracters**. These get more ornery as the questions get harder. In two-word questions, the first word of the distracter looks suspiciously like the first word in the correct answer. And since the sneaky test-makers often put the distracter before the real answer, students unwittingly pick the distracter and blissfully move on without realizing their mistake. In a

two-blank question, make sure that both words fit.

2. **Don't get stuck when you don't know the vocab.** You can waste valuable time puzzling over questions with incomprehensible vocabulary. Spare yourself. If you're stumped after your first reading of the question and don't know the definitions of two or more words, skip the question and come back later or make a guess. You may get the answer by puzzling it through with the techniques in this chapter, but if you're at all in danger of running out time, your first priority should be questions where the main challenge is reasoning rather than vocabulary.

3. **Choose the most precise words.** If you're stuck between two equally plausible alternatives, the one that is more descriptive is generally right. In question 9 above, *controversial* may seem logical at first glance, but *iconoclastic*, a more precise word, is the best choice. To go a step further, distracters are often simple words while right answers are often more precise (and difficult) words.

4. **Near the end of a section, pick the most obscure word.** ETS loves to put a vocab zinger in the last question of a section—with words like *munificence*, *obstreperous*, and *synergistic*, *calumny*, to name a few we've seen. If you're at the end and torn between a word you don't know and a word you do know that doesn't sound exactly right, pick the former.

The Old SAT: Analogies

The farewell tour of the SAT analogies ends in January of 2005, and few students will mourn their passing. That is, unless you enjoy trying to think up relationships between weird words you've never heard of. Got a match for *cramming : analogies*? Our vote would be *disentangling : gobbledygook*—or better still, *shoveling : excrement*. The Class of 2006 can laugh all the way to their test. This section is for those lost souls graduating in 2005 who still must do battle with these quintessential SAT questions.

An obvious fact about the analogies is that you need to know the definition of twelve words to have the best chance of getting the question—two in the first analogy, and ten more in the answer choices. Without any context—like a sentence or paragraph—it is hard to figure out words that you don't know.

SAMPLE TEST

"I find that I can play around with numbers in a math problem until I come up with an answer, but if I don't know what a word means, I am pretty much stuck."

—680 V, 730 M

The obvious solution to the analogy questions is to create your own context in the form of a sentence to establish a relationship between the words. Call it the make-a-sentence strategy. In the words of one student who scored 800 V, 730 M, "I always tried to make a sentence relating the first two words, and then substituted the answer choices and tried to see which pair fit my sentence best. For instance, 'a crumb is a little piece of bread' and 'a splinter is a little piece of wood.'"

We think that the make-a-sentence strategy is the most important key to doing your best on the analogies. Let's give it a try:

Directions:
Each question below consists of a related pair of words or phrases, followed by five pairs of words or phrases labeled A through E. Select the pair that best expresses a relationship similar to that expressed in the original pair.

IDEOLOGUE : POLITICIAN ::

(A) pragmatist : theory
(B) negotiate : diplomat
(C) soprano : singer
(D) idea : philosopher
(E) dilettante : art

This one is simple if you follow the make-a-sentence strategy. An ideologue is a politician who believes strongly in theories and ideas. Therefore, "an ideologue is a kind of politician." Answer (A) is incorrect because a *pragmatist* (someone who is practical) is a kind of thinker, not a kind of theory. Answer (B) is no good because *negotiate* and *diplomat* are in the wrong order. As for (D) and (E), philosophers think of ideas, but ideas are not a kind of philosopher, and a dilettante is a kind of artist—not a kind of art. But a soprano is a kind of singer. Answer: (C)

Here's another problem that has a different kind of relationship between the words:

COAX : BROWBEAT ::

(A) delineate : information
(B) delight : disappoint
(C) cajole : persuasion
(D) bully : wheedle
(E) criticize : lambaste

To coax is to gently persuade. To browbeat is to bully. Therefore, "coax is a milder form of browbeat." Response (A) is incorrect because *delineate* (explain) and *information* have no obvious relationship relevant to the question, and (B) does not work because *delight* and *disappoint* are opposites. In (C) to *cajole* is to persuade, but *persuasion* is the noun form and therefore does not fit. In (D), *bully* is a stronger form of *wheedle*—which means to persuade by gentle urging—and therefore reverses the relationship between *coax* and *browbeat*. Since *criticize* is a milder form of *lambaste* (scold severely), the answer is (E).

Though the make-a-sentence strategy works most of the time, it is harder to execute on some questions than it is on others. Consider this:

MENDACIOUS : DISINGENUOUSNESS ::

(A) regretful : deleterious
(B) mendicant : poverty
(C) mortified : disturbed
(D) deluged : overflowing
(E) truthful : honesty

The primary complication is that *mendacious* (dishonest) and *disingenuousness* (the quality of being disingenuous or deceitful) are, respectively, an adjective and a noun. Since they are different parts of speech, it is harder to fit them into a sentence. On the plus side, you know that the answer to an adjective : noun analogy will in all likelihood be another adjective : noun pair. The sentence that best joins these two is, "a mendacious person shows disingenuousness." But even if you didn't know that, you could figure this one out. *Mendicant* (beggar) sounds like mendacious but means something different and is a fairly obvious distracter when paired with *poverty*. *Mortified* (embarrassed) and *disturbed* have no relevant relationship, and *deluged : overflowing* does not apply to people. The answer is (E), which is another adjective : noun pair. Does "a truthful person show honesty?" Yes, indeed.

What sort of tricks does ETS use to throw you off your game? A common one is to use a second definition of a word. For instance:

DOG : FOLLOW ::

(A) hound : shadow

(B) chase : detach

(C) stalk : watch

(D) canine : lead

(E) pursue : hassle

When you hear the word *dog*, what is the first word that pops into your head? Cat, of course. But this question uses a different meaning, as in "questions about ties to organized crime still dog the senator." To be "dogged" is to be pursued by something that can cause negative consequences. *Follow* is a more neutral word for *dog* that does not have the bad connotations. The make-a-sentence method can work here, though it is a bit awkward: "Dog is a bad way to follow." *Hound : shadow* is a distracter that plays on the dog theme, as does *canine : lead*. *Chase : detach* has no obvious relation to anything, and *pursue : hassle* reverses the logic of *dog : follow* by putting the negative word second. Answer: (C).

Another common ETS trick is to fill the answer choices with words that are similar to those in the first analogy pair but don't match its logic:

APPARITION : FEAR ::

(A) ghost : haunted

(B) ghoul : terrorize

(C) clown : mirth

(D) werewolf : sinister

(E) riddle : frustration

Assuming that you know an *apparition* is a ghostly figure, you may be tempted to choose (A), (B), or (D). Don't fall for it. The correct answer, (C), mirrors the relationship of *Apparition : Fear*, not the subject matter. An *apparition* causes fear. A *clown* causes *mirth* (glee or good humor). The only other answer that remotely makes sense is (E), but *riddles* don't necessarily cause *frustration* even though they can. Conclusion: focus on the relationship between the words in the first analogy, not their meaning.

But I've Never Seen These Words in My Life!

Hmm. This is a problem. In fact, this is one of the reasons why the test-makers are cutting the analogies—they cause too much emphasis on rote memorization. If you know the definitions of the words in the first analogy, relax. You'll still probably get the question right. If you see a logical answer, choose it. If not, the correct answer may be the response(s) in which you don't know one or more of the words. Don't make the mistake of choosing an answer simply because you know the words and they kind of, almost, fit.

If you don't know one of the words in the first analogy, you'll be in for a harder time. First, scan the answer choices. Do all of the pairs have a logical relationship? Probably not, and any of those that don't can be eliminated. Of those that do, make a sentence with them and then look back up at the initial analogy pair. Does the word you know in that pair seem to fit in with the sentence(s) you have made? Pick the answer for which the sentence you have made seems to make the best fit.

If you don't know either of the words in the first analogy, look at the answer choices and guess among those that do seem to have a logical, specific relationship. If you are at the beginning of the analogy questions, guess words that are relatively simple. If you are near the end, choose the logical pair that includes the two most advanced vocabulary words.

Above all, don't waste a lot of time on analogy questions in which you don't know the definition of one or both of the initial pair of words (unless you have finished everything else in the section). The reading comprehension questions give you more context to work with and are a better bet for spending time on if you're stuck.

> **❝Get a word-of-the-day email or calendar and try to incorporate new words into your vocabulary.❞**
>
> **—660 V, 690 M**

Reading Comprehension

Reading Comprehension passages are the black hole of the SAT. Too many students get sucked into them and are never seen or heard from again. (At least not with their sanity intact.)

The passages look reasonably benign. All you need to do is read. Easy, right? But the passages are long and so booooorrring. As paragraph after paragraph drones on about the cultural differences between Tadzhikistan and Uzbekistan, or about the shrinking habitat of the Peruvian three-toed newt, students inevitably lose their way. Concentration drops. Anxiety increases. The clock ticks. And suddenly you've at the end of a paragraph—and don't remember anything about what you've just read. Panic city. Game over. Goodbye Harvard, hello Fitchburg State.

Well, maybe it won't be quite that bad. But Reading Comprehension is an area where preparation can make a huge difference. Very few of the Reading Comprehension questions are exceptionally hard, at least when judged by the percentage of students who get them wrong. Students generally miss them because they get flustered by the process of reading the passage.

With the advent of the New SAT, reading comprehension will be divided into two types of questions: the traditional passages of 500-800 words, which may consist of two paired passages, and new 100-word passages called Paragraph-length Critical Reading.

The most important issue: how to manage your time and attention between the questions and the passages. Will you go to the passages first or the questions first? Will you read the whole passage or just relevant portions?

The choice is especially crucial for the longer passages because they take gobs of time. Since reading speed and efficiency tend to go down after the first hundred words, the long passages will have a multiplied effect on your time. The Reading Comprehension is not the hardest section on the SAT, but it is often the most stressful. "I was nervous, and it is very tough to concentrate on long passages when your mind is wandering and thinking about other things," says a student who scored 560 V, 650 M.

All the other multiple-choice sections have a similar rhythm: you may be nervous at the beginning, but then you answer the easy questions at the front and settle down. Many students can complete the first half of a typical section well before time is half gone. No longer worried about finishing, students can relax a little as they tackle the tough problems that tend to be concentrated at the end of the section, or as they revisit questions they may have skipped.

> **"It's hard to prepare for the vocab just because the English dictionary is so dang long. We prepped in English class and I studied flashcards, but very few of those words actually showed up."**
>
> **—770 V, 800 M**

Reading Comprehension does not work that way—at least not if you read the passage before answering the questions. On a typical long passage, a student must read for five or ten minutes before blackening any ovals. Although reading is a crucial part of answering the questions, it doesn't *feel* like answering the questions. High-strung students are always worried about the clock, and if the number of questions they have answered is not keeping pace with the time, anxiety can take hold. For this reason, we recommend that slow readers and high-strung test-takers consider a method that gets them answering questions before too much time has elapsed. Some students may prefer to do Reading Comprehension passages first— even if they come after the Sentence Completion questions in a given section. Others may want to do the long passages last. We recommend that you experiment.

Despite its stress-inducing format, the Reading Comprehension does cut students one major break: most questions refer only to particular lines in the passage, and those lines are noted. Some questions, called *Vocabulary-in-Context*, ask you to define a particular word. Others, called *Literal Comprehension* questions, ask you to explain what is meant by a particular line or lines. Both of these types can generally be answered without regard to the passage as a whole. A third type of question, which the College Board calls *Extended Reasoning*, does refer to the whole passage. These questions can relate to the tone or point of view of the speaker, the main idea of the passage, or some other big-picture issue. The secret to the long passages is to comprehend the main characteristics of the passage well enough to get the extended reasoning questions while wasting as little time as possible reading portions of the passage that are not directly relevant to any of the questions.

In the pages that follow, we offer examples of (1) a conventional long passage, (2) a paired selection of long passages, and (3) two paragraph-length passages.

Three Kinds of Passages

According to the College Board, every SAT includes at least one fiction passage, as well as nonfiction selections from the humanities, social sciences, and natural sciences. With such a vast array of possibilities, there is no way to predict the exact subjects you will see in the Reading Comprehension. Nor is there any point in trying. But by understanding the kind of reasoning in these sections, you can get a feel for the issues that are likely to be raised. Within the categories of long and paragraph-length passages, there are three basic types:

First Person and Fictional Passages

These include portions of diaries, memoirs, short stories, or novels. In compiling this book, we examined ten versions of the SAT administered between 1995 and 2002 in an edition of the College Board's *10 Real SATs*. Of the thirteen long passages of this sort, a majority were devoted to the experiences of women and minorities. Included were narratives from a Chinese American, a Haitian American, a Japanese American, a Mexican American, and a scholar offering personal reflections on the Navajo tribe. A common theme: the difficulty of balancing full participation in American life with loyalty to one's roots. The Chinese American wrote of her frustration at seeing her immigrant mother humiliated by a white woman. The Haitian American girl wrote about how her immigrant mother pushed her to become a doctor. A female poet explored a similar theme—her effort to balance the conflicting demands of motherhood and writing. Often, the passages address customs that are likely to be undervalued or misunderstood by white culture. The Japanese American explained the non-verbal way that Japanese families communicate when arranging marriages.

Third Person/Academic Passages

A majority of both the long and paragraph-length selections fall into this category. Most are written by scholars who are defending a particular point of view on, say, Black American fiction and the Romantic literary tradition (to use a real example). There is no way to generalize about the topics except to say that they include a healthy number with a minority and/or female focus. In a sample taken from a recent edition of *10 Real SATs*, historical figures who were referenced included Joan of Arc, Jane Austen, Frederick Douglass, W. E. B. DuBois, Marcus Garvey, George Orwell, Pablo Picasso, and Mark Twain. Social scientific topics included an anthropologist's analysis of cultural differences in the United States and an essay about the role of fences in suburban culture. Scientific topics included radio astronomy, genetics, and plastic surgery. Not all of these passages are academic. One passage in a recent SAT was taken from an essay by an animal trainer about how dogs perceive the world. The third-person passages have innumerable themes, but there is at least one to keep in the back of your mind: myth vs. reality. The test-makers like to find passages that take a new look at familiar topics.

Paired Passages

These selections crop up occasionally among the long passages. Combined, the two essays are generally about 800 words long. They are usually third-person/academic, though an occasional first-person essay may appear. Your task: establish a relationship between the passages. If one passage outlines a widely held historical theory, the other passage may attack that theory or revise it in light of new information. If one passage examines a big topic, the other may look at a particular facet of the issue. Sometimes, the passages focus on topics with common themes. An essay on Frederick Douglass was paired with an excerpt about literature written by nineteenth-century women, comparing the "imprisonment" of the female role in that era to slavery. Another passage, offering a largely positive analysis of the societal impact of broadcast media, references George Orwell and suggests that he was wrong in believing that mass media would become a tool of governmental oppression. A companion passage also suggests

Orwell was wrong, but for a different reason—that he failed to see the possibility that mass media could perpetrate mass deception even if the government were not in control of it. The paired passages are like puzzle pieces that do not always fit neatly together. Your job is to figure out how they connect.

Long Passages: Example #1

Each passage below is followed by questions based on its content. Answer the questions on the basis of what is stated and implied in each passage and in any introductory material that may be provided.

Questions 1–10 are based on the following passage.

The following selection is from a biography of Betty Shabazz, a college professor and civil rights activist who was best-known as the wife of Malcolm X, the famed African American leader who was assassinated in 1965.

After her heartrending death in the summer of 1997, journalists and friends eulogized Betty as a phenomenon of resilience—as one who had conquered
5 betrayal, violence, grief, and fear. "That she survived at all is miraculous," Angelou said. "And she survived whole." But whether they served on the battlefield or by the hearth, none of the black-
10 liberation struggle's veterans escaped undamaged. Nobody who drew close to Malcolm and survived—and none drew closer than Betty—escaped the vortex of his death and life. "There are a lot of
15 people who went back into the grave," said Jean Reynolds, one of Malcolm's former disciples, describing the despair that followed the minister's 1965 slaying. "People lost their minds, committed
20 suicide little by little every day."

In many ways, Betty not only survived in the postassassination years, but thrived. She fought with quiet conscience for education and human-rights causes,
25 exhausting herself in far too many campaigns for dignity, often on behalf of black women and children. She was not an ideologue. She never lifted Malcolm's sword to slash white supremacy. She pre-
30 ferred to think of herself as a moral booster for Black America. Some black nationalists dismissed her as a bourgeois integrationist. But throughout her life,

her defiance against the power structure's disposal of her husband surfaced in the subtle shades of resistance.

She believed in womanpower, yet she never considered herself a "libber," and often sent young women home to boyfriends and husbands after dispensing earthly advice about communicating with men and choosing the right lipstick. She was queenly and eruptive, aristocratic but touchable to the rootsy folk in Brooklyn or Harlem. She demanded respect and deference always, whether holding forth an international women's conference or bargain shopping. She was gracious and cantankerous, soulful and uncouth, fantastically generous and nosy. She was almost always disgracefully late. And she could cuss like twenty men, a genius she discovered after fielding too many threatening phone calls from her husband's enemies in the months before and after his death.

Betty was charming and coy, and knew just when and how to sling the javelins of her eyes. "That lady had the prettiest eyes," gushed a Harlem nationalist who had secretly served as her bodyguard in the late 1960s on behalf of her domineering sister-in-law and rival, Ella Collins. "Yeah, I know that was Malcolm's wife," he said, "but I still flirted with her." Her femininity, one friend said, "just oozed. And she knew it. And she enjoyed it." Betty was afflicted with neither fits of dullness nor brilliance. But she was divinely practical and sensible when discussing education, Malcolm, and other beloved topics. She saw through hypocrisy and pretension, and had no compunction about telling it like it was. Few of her comrades ever saw her crumble, not even when the men began throwing fistfuls of dirt on her husband's coffin. Royalty never weeps in the streets. Besides, Malcolm had warned that the salt in her tears would only embitter her.

To Niara Sudarkasa, a friend and former president of Lincoln University, the historically black school in Pennsylvania, Betty was "a tireless traveler and resolute voice on behalf of economic, political, and social justice for the dispossessed and downtrodden from Selma to Soweto." To an academic colleague, she was a "rock steady" homegirl. To a travel companion who helped nudge her relationship with Coretta Scott King from rivalry to tolerance to genuine affection, she was "a flawed, lovely human being." To her eldest daughter, she was a heroine who dwells "amongst the spirit of women."

Yet the widow's life was also an epic tragedy. In her latter twenty-five years, she shrugged off the nostalgic "Mrs. Malcolm X" cape and clad herself in a distinguished new identity. But she may never have fully come to terms with the past. In the end, she was no more indomitable than countless other long-suffering black women whose names history has ignored. She longed for the privilege of fragility as often as they surely did, but there was her children's survival to consider, and her own. Only in recent years has African America begun to properly recognize the women who stayed alive and upright through the convulsions of the black-liberation struggle. But to ignore the cost of their endurance is no less than abuse.

1. The author's primary objective in the passage is

   (A) to undermine the idea that Betty was primarily a civil rights activist
   (B) to call attention to the resilience of Betty and women like her
   (C) to suggest that Betty was a more important figure than historians previously realized
   (D) to assert that Betty's career after the assassination was more important than her earlier work
   (E) to discredit the idea that Betty did not contribute to Malcolm X's career

2. The primary function of the first paragraph is to emphasize

   (A) the tragedy of Betty's death in 1997
   (B) the nobility of the black-liberation struggle
   (C) the importance of remembering Malcolm X

   (D) the unity of Malcolm X's followers
   (E) the pain felt by those in the black-liberation struggle

3. In line 13, "vortex" is a metaphorical reference that calls to mind

   (A) an argument between enemies
   (B) a battle between armies
   (C) a collision of vehicles
   (D) a whirling mass of water or air
   (E) a robbery at gun-point

4. From lines 23–36, it may be inferred that in the years after the assassination, Betty

   (A) was less radical than some black leaders
   (B) was not an advocate for black rights
   (C) changed her views on white supremacy
   (D) became alienated from most black leaders
   (E) urged black nationalists to be more vigilant

5. In lines 46–48, the phrase "whether holding forth at an international women's conference or bargain shopping" is intended to illustrate that Betty

(A) enjoyed speaking at international women's conferences
(B) showed impatience when she felt slighted
(C) had the same personal style in a variety of settings
(D) had an active life and many interests
(E) could be both gracious and cantankerous

6. The purpose of the sentence beginning in line 48 ("She was gracious... generous and nosy.") is to show that Betty had

(A) an unstable mind
(B) diverse personality traits
(C) common mood swings
(D) difficulty staying focused
(E) a cerebral approach to life

7. In line 74, "compunction" most nearly means
(A) compulsion
(B) candor
(C) disdain
(D) dislike
(E) regret

8. By stating in line 105 that Betty "longed for the privilege of fragility," the author suggests that she

(A) disliked her image as a strong woman
(B) considered herself to be privileged
(C) thought that underprivileged people are fragile
(D) believed that she could not be fragile
(E) envied other long-suffering women

9. In context, "recognize" in line 110 most nearly means

(A) distinguish
(B) acquaint
(C) acknowledge
(D) welcome
(E) delight

10. Which of the following best describes the author's attitude toward Betty?

(A) skeptical
(B) dutiful
(C) admiring
(D) scrupulous
(E) noncommittal

We'll wager that without the time pressure of taking a real SAT, you found these questions relatively manageable—at least compared to the Sentence Completions and some of the brutal grammar questions in Chapter 4. The answers: 1.(B) 2.(E) 3.(D) 4.(A) 5.(C) 6.(B) 7.(E) 8.(D) 9.(C) 10.(C). The explanations:

1. **Getting the Main Idea**
Reading Comprehension questions often begin with an item asking you to identify something akin to the primary objective or main idea of the passage. These questions are generally on the easy side. Note that these questions typically ask for a response from the author's perspective rather than your perspective or someone else's. Your first job with any reading passage is to understand what the author intends to convey. In this one, the writer is at great pains to emphasize Betty's resilience in overcoming obstacles. Answer: (B).

2. **Feeling Their Pain**
This extending reasoning question asks you to relate the first paragraph to the passage as a whole. Response (A) is a distracter that plays on the fact that the first clause of the paragraph references Betty's death. But the point of the paragraph is to talk about Betty's struggles, and by extension the struggles of others in the black liberation movement. The emphasis is on pain endured by those in the movement rather than on their nobility, importance, or unity. Answer: (E).

3. **A Challenging Metaphor**
Among the changes in the New SAT is the addition of a few more literary terms such as *metaphor, simile, personification,* etc. A metaphorical reference explains one concept or situation in terms of another to suggest similarity. (Similes do much the same thing using *like* or *as*.) The key to this question is knowing that a *vortex* is a whirlpool, or a whirling mass of air. Answer: (D).

4. **Radicals and Moderates**
Some of the most challenging Reading Comprehension questions require you to make inferences. In other words, you've got to find the right answer from hints or incomplete information in the passage. In this question, the second paragraph includes a number of clues to the correct response. In line 23, the author refers to the fact that she *fought with quiet conscience,* and in line 36 the author notes Betty's *subtle shades of resistance.* Notable as well is the fact that Betty was accused of being a *bourgeois integrationist* by black nationalists. But most telling is the author's observation that Betty *never lifted Malcolm's sword to slash white*

supremacy. The paragraph makes no reference to any change in her views, and the fact that Betty was out of step with *some black nationalists* does not mean that she was alienated from *most black leaders*. But Betty was clearly less radical than some black leaders. Answer: (A).

5. Showing Betty's Style

This question is typical of those that require students to understand the function of a particular sentence or phrase. The relevant excerpt immediately follows *She demanded deference and respect always* and serves as a concrete illustration of the variety of settings in which she maintained this personal style. Answer: (C).

6. Diverse Adjectives Make a Point

The sentence in question shows the diversity of Betty's personality traits. Such traits would not be inconsistent with mood swings or even with an unstable mind, but the passage does not suggest that either is present. Answer: (B).

7. Compunction, Not Compulsion

This is a standard Vocabulary-in-Context question. *Compunction* means remorse or regret. *Compulsion*, a word that sounds like *compunction*, is a none-too-subtle distracter. Answer: (E).

8. A Different Kind of Privilege

This question is typical of the more difficult Extended Reasoning questions. *Longed for the privilege of fragility* is an oblique way of suggesting that Betty wished that she could let her guard down. But, according to the passage, because she had a central role in the black-liberation struggle, she believed that she needed to stay strong and therefore did not have the privilege of fragility. This is not the same thing as her disliking her image as a strong woman; the passage does not describe Betty's opinion of her image. Responses (B) and (C) use *privileged* and *underprivileged* as distracters, and there is no suggestion that Betty envied other women. Answer: (D)

9. Another Word with Two Meanings

A favorite stratagem of ETS is to build Vocabulary-in-Context questions around words that have more than one meaning. *Recognize* is not a hard word, but it has more than one definition, and synonyms are elusive. If you recognize a person, he or she is familiar and may be an acquaintance. But *recognize* can also mean recognition or acknowledgment. The correct response becomes clear with a simple restatement of the relevant line. Instead of *begun to properly recognize*, the passage could just as easily say *begun to grant proper recognition to.* To *recognize* a person's achievements is also to *acknowledge* them. Answer: (C).

10. **A Positive Tone**
    Although the author acknowledges Betty's faults, his portrait is unquestionably admiring.
    Answer: (C).

SAMPLE TEST

Questions 11–20 are based on the following passages.

The following passages discuss interactions between Native Americans and European settlers in the years preceding the American Revolution.

Passage 1

When the Puritans first landed in Massachusetts they discovered an Indian custom so curious they felt called upon to
Line find a name for it. In 1767, when
5 Thomas Hutchinson wrote his history of the colony, the term was already an old saying: "An Indian gift," he told his readers, "is a proverbial expression signifying a present for which an equivalent
10 return is expected." We still use this, of course, and in an even broader sense. If I am so uncivilized as to ask for the return of a gift I have given, they call me an "Indian giver."

15   Imagine a scene. The Englishman comes into the Indian lodge. He falls to admiring a clay pipe with feathers tied to the stem. The tribe passes this pipe around among themselves as a ritual gift.
20 It stays with a family for awhile, but sooner or later it is always given away again. So the Indian, as is only polite among his people, responds to the white man's interest by saying, "That's just
25 some stuff we don't need. Please take it.

It's a gift." The Englishman is tickled pink. What a nice thing to send back to the British Museum! He takes the pipe home and sets it on the mantelpiece.
30 The next day another Indian happens to visit him and sees the gift which was due to come into his lodge soon. He too is delighted. "Ah!" he says, "the gift!" and he sticks it in his pouch. In consterna-
35 tion the Englishman invents the phrase "Indian giver" to describe these people with such a low sense of private property. The opposite of this term would be something like "white-man-keeper," or,
40 as we say nowadays, "capitalist," that is, a person whose first reaction to property is to take it out of circulation, to put it in a warehouse or museum, or—more to the point for capitalism—to lay it aside
45 to be used for production.

      The Indian giver (the original ones, at any rate) understood a cardinal property of the gift: whatever we are given should be given away again, not kept. Or, if it is
50 kept, something of similar value should move on in its stead, the way a billiard ball may stop when it sends another scurrying across the felt, the momentum transferred. You may hold on to a Christ-
55 mas gift, but it will cease to be a gift in the true sense unless you have given something else away. When it is passed along, the gift may be given back to the original donor, but this is not essential.
60 In fact, it is better if the gift is not

returned, but is given instead to some new, third party. The only essential is this: *the gift must always move.*

Passage 2

The obvious contrast between the British treatment of Native American tribes and that of the French is fertile territory for modern-day revisionist critics. But the difference is due less to any political or moral imperative than to mere expediency. The French came to the New World less as colonizers than as traders. The supply of beaver pelts, the lifeblood of New France, depended on the good offices of the Algonquin, the Huron, and the Iroquois tribes. By the mid-1700s, the number of French in North America was scarcely more than 50,000 souls scattered in far-flung outposts from Lake Superior to Newfoundland. These settlements were overwhelmingly male, and, human nature being what it is, intermarriage with the native population was the inevitable result.

The British experience included no such need for interdependence. To be sure, most Anglo colonies weathered a tenuous period soon after their inception during which they gladly accepted any aid proffered by the Indians. But wave upon wave of emigrants bolstered their ranks, and, in places where disease had ravaged the first settlers, a second, hardier generation grew up to take their place. While the French settlers included a preponderance of lone-wolf males who were drawn to trading furs deep in Indian country, the Anglos were more likely to arrive in family units, especially in the New England colonies. The result was a stable, contiguous pattern of settlement that quickly became self-sustaining.

Where the French developed a symbiotic relationship with the native tribes, the British colonies had little use for them. Land, not pelts, was the commodity the Anglo emigrants sought in the New World, and the Indians were their primary obstacle to taking it. Among the Virginia settlers, the early years of uneasy coexistence with the natives gave way to a policy of removal and/or extermination, especially after the Indian uprising of 1622. The New Englanders were somewhat more conciliatory and experimented with the creation of "praying towns" to convert the Indians to Christianity. But after the so-called King Philip's War of 1675–76, the New Englanders, too, seemed to subscribe to the adage coined two centuries later that "the only good Indian is a dead Indian."

1. Passage 1 is best described as

(A) a response to a controversial question
(B) a parody of a humorous incident
(C) an explanation of a cultural difference
(D) a condemnation of an unjust situation
(E) an overview of an unfamiliar way of life

2. In Passage 1, the phrase "white-man-keeper" in line 39 serves to highlight the author's belief that

(A) the concept of Indian giver was a product of English perceptions
(B) early stereotypes of Native Americans were unfair
(C) English settlers were unlikely to exchange gifts with Native Americans
(D) English settlers were seeking to create a capitalist society
(E) the English were more generous than the Native Americans

3. In Passage 1, use of the phrase "Indian giver" in line 46 differs from the earlier usages in lines 14 and 36 because it refers to

(A) the fact that true gifts should be passed along to others
(B) the English custom of storing gifts in warehouses and museums
(C) the cardinal property of gift giving
(D) the English distaste for exchanging gifts with the Native Americans
(E) the Indian custom of gift giving rather than English perceptions of it

4. In line 47, "property" most nearly means

(A) characteristic
(B) location
(C) possession
(D) design
(E) product

5. In Passage 2, the author attempts to

(A) compare two conflicting views
(B) undermine a universal belief
(C) explain a difference in outcomes
(D) revise an outdated theory
(E) form a new hypothesis

6. The author uses the second sentence of the first paragraph to suggest that the differences in the way that French and British settlers treated the Native Americans were due to

(A) coincidence rather than intention
(B) design rather than expediency
(C) circumstance rather than principle
(D) experience rather than naïvete
(E) avoidance rather than desire

7. The author of Passage 2 cites the fact that the French came "less as colonizers than as traders" (line 8) in order to

(A) account for the nomadic lifestyle of the French settlers
(B) show that the French depended on the Native Americans
(C) highlight the French dependence on the trade in beaver pelts
(D) explain why the French were hostile to the Native Americans
(E) describe the French pattern of settlement in the Great Lakes region

8. Which of the following pairs best represents each author's approach to examining relations between the Native Americans and the European settlers?

	Passage 1	Passage 2
(A)	organized	moderate
(B)	analytical	detailed
(C)	cautious	controlled
(D)	anecdotal	comparative
(E)	methodical	scholarly

9. The author of Passage 1 might criticize Passage 2 because it

(A) glorifies the French at the expense of the British
(B) overlooks key details about the Virginia colony
(C) condones violence against the Native Americans
(D) places too much blame on the British settlers
(E) omits the point of view of Native Americans

10. Both passages are consistent with the idea that

(A) the British settlers had little understanding of the Native Americans
(B) the removal of the Native Americans from their lands could have been prevented
(C) the British settlers gave better treatment to the Native Americans than did the French
(D) more dialogue would have improved relations between the British and the Native Americans
(E) only a minority of the British settlers mistreated the Native Americans

These questions are a bit harder than those in the first set of questions. The two-passage format is more complicated because you need to deal with two authors. Sometimes the two passages are in basic agreement, sometimes they conflict, and sometimes, as in this case, their relationship is harder to define. The only thing for sure is that they present some sort of contrast. Every edition of the old SAT included one set of questions dealing with two passages. It remains to be seen how frequently this format will appear on the new version.

The answers: 1.(C) 2.(A) 3.(E) 4.(A) 5.(C) 6.(C) 7.(B) 8.(D) 9.(E) 10.(A). The explanations:

1. **Cross-Cultural Communication**
   This one is typical of Extended Reasoning questions that ask you to show an understanding of the passage beyond the particulars being discussed. The passage is about the English concept of Indian giver and how the English misunderstood the Native American custom. The difference was cultural; the English viewed gifts as private property while the Native Americans shared them. Answer: (C).

2. **A Statement Made for Effect**
   The phrase *white-man-keeper* gets our attention. Many people are familiar with the phrase *Indian giver*, a term created by the English settlers that reflects their perception of a Native custom. *White-man-keeper* would be a logical Native American perspective on English customs, and the phrase carries extra force because most readers will never have considered such a concept. *White-man-keeper* highlights the fact that Indian giver reflects English cultural assumptions. Answer: (A).

3. **Same Phrase, Different Meaning**
   This question is tricky because the author's third use of the phrase *Indian giver* conveys a different meaning than the first two. Those in lines 14 and 36 refer to the English perception of the Native American practice. But the author intends the reference in line 46 to connote gift-giving as the Native Americans practiced it. The author's intentions are made clear by a parenthetical reference "*(the original ones, at any rate),*" which suggests that the Native Americans practiced a true form of gift-giving before their contact with the English. The rest of the paragraph goes on describe this true Indian giving, in contrast to the stereotype of Indian giving created by the English. Answer: (E).

4. **Understanding Alternate Definitions**
   Like *recognize* in question 9 in the last section, *property* can have several meanings. Property can be a piece of real estate or a possession, but in this case

property refers to a characteristic of a gift. Answer: (A).

5. **Seeing the Main Objective**
   You might be tempted to choose (A) because the passage does describe two sequences of events that may be said to conflict, but it would not be accurate to call them *views*. Instead, the author is intent on explaining why the experience of the British differed from that of the French. The British treatment of Native Americans differed from that of the French because their respective colonies developed differently (e.g., the French depended on trade with the Indians while the British did not). The passage shows how these differences led to different outcomes with respect to the Native Americans. Answer: (C).

6. **Understanding Cause and Effect**
   The second sentence says that "the difference is due less to any political or moral imperative than to mere expediency." Response (B) includes the word *expediency* but wrongly states that *design rather than expediency* accounts for the difference. Response (A) is also a plausible choice, but coincidence is not the same thing as expediency. The British found it expedient to treat the Native Americans differently because of differing circumstances. While the French had incentives to interact with

and depend upon the Native Americans, the British had none. Answer: (C).

7. **How Trade Leads to Dependence**
   The fact that the French came as traders is crucial because it shows their dependence on the Native Americans. The tribes supplied the pelts that were *the lifeblood of New France*. Response (C) is incorrect because the real issue is not dependence on beaver pelts per se, but dependence on the tribes. In turn, this dependence caused the French to interact differently with the Native Americans. Answer: (B).

8. **A Funky-Looking Pair Problem**
   Problems like this have appeared occasionally through the years, so we thought we should throw one in. Passage 1 is built around a single anecdote, the story of the pipe that is offered as a gift. Passage 2 compares the experience of the British with that of the French to explain differing interactions with the Native Americans. Answer: (D).

9. **What the Authors Would Think**
   Some questions, typically near the end of a section, may ask you to infer what one author might think of another author's point of view. A major preoccupation of the author of Passage 1 is to describe how the English failed

to see things from the Native American perspective. The second passage, however, does not include any mention of the native perspective. It is reasonable to infer that the author of Passage 1 might take exception to this fact. You might be tempted to choose (C), but the second passage does not condone the treatment of the Native Americans even if it does describe it in a matter-of-fact way. Answer: (E).

10. The trick to this question is to understand the meaning of *consistent with the idea*. It does not mean that both passages must explicitly endorse the idea, but rather that they must merely be compatible with the idea. If you're stuck, try the process of elimination. Passage 2 seems to contradict response (B); Passage 2 states that the main objective of the British settlers, who came in overwhelming numbers, was to take land. The British did not treat the Native Americans better than the French treated them, and there is nothing in either passage to indicate that more dialogue between the sides would have changed anything. Neither passage suggests that only a minority of British settlers mistreated the Native Americans. However, both passages support the idea that the British settlers had little understanding of, and little incentive to understand, the Native Americans. Answer: (A).

Paragraph-Length Passages

Paragraph-Length Critical Reading is the only variety of question to be added to the New SAT that has not previously appeared on the SAT II: Writing Test. As a result, we will learn more about these questions as 2005 unfolds. In the meantime, the College Board says that the passages of about 100 words will be followed by one or two questions similar to those about the long passages. Two samples follow.

Before 1900, ambient light was a non-issue. When our ancestors gazed at the heavens, they saw a profusion of bright stars and planets, as well as the chalky outline of the Milky Way. Meteoroids streaked across the sky on a regular basis, and the constellations fired the imagination of everyone from poets and philosophers to common folk. Today's urbanite knows little of the allure that the night sky once held. The phrase "catch a falling star" has limited meaning for today's city dwellers; many have never even seen one.

1. From the passage, it is possible to infer that the "ambient light" described in line 1 is produced by

(A) bright stars and planets
(B) city lights
(C) meteoroids
(D) the Milky Way
(E) an extraterrestrial source

2. The passage implies that

(A) modern people are less interested in the night sky than were their ancestors
(B) meteoroids are less frequent today than in past centuries
(C) the phrase "catch a falling star" is not familiar to today's city dwellers
(D) ambient light has changed the look of the night sky
(E) the brightest stars and planets are in the Milky Way

History isn't usually the class that sends students bounding out of bed in the morning eager for another day of school.

Line
5
When Hollywood wants to conjure the image of boredom at school, history is the course that is chosen. And why not? History teachers everywhere have bought into the idea that they must cover all there is to know about any given era. As a result,
10
they cram in as many facts as possible, and students spend their time memorizing rather than thinking.

3. The rhetorical question "And why not?" (line 6) primarily serves to emphasize that

   (A) most students do not work hard in history class
   (B) history is a logical subject to illustrate boredom at school
   (C) Hollywood ought to be more truthful in its portrayals of history
   (D) many history teachers need to improve how they teach
   (E) there is no good reason why history class should be boring

4. It may be inferred from the passage that the author believes that

   (A) facts are not important to the study of history
   (B) Hollywood should stop making fun of history classes
   (C) history is inevitably a boring subject

   (D) history teachers of past generations were more effective
   (E) history classes should cover fewer facts

Answers: 1.(B) 2.(D) 3.(B) 4.(E). The explanations:

1. **What Is Ambient Light?**

   If you don't know what *ambient* (enveloping) means, the most important clue for this question occurs in the references to *urbanites* and *city dwellers* in the last two sentences. Nighttime ambient light—that which is given off by man-made sources and dims the night sky—is much more prevalent in cities. The fact that ambient light was not an issue before 1900 is because electric lights (first invented in 1879) were not prevalent outdoors at night before that time. Answer: (B).

2. **The Author's Main Point**

   The author uses the discussion of stars, planets, the Milky Way, and falling stars to illustrate how people today, especially those in cities, have a diminished ability to see the night sky. Response (C) may seem like a plausible choice, but the idea that "catch a falling star" has limited meaning to city dwellers does not necessarily imply that they are unfamiliar with the phrase. Answer: (D)

3. What Is a Rhetorical Question?

It is a device that accentuates emphasis. *And why not?* validates Hollywood's choice of history class to illustrate boredom by suggesting that there are no logical objections to doing so. Answer: (B).

4. What the Author Believes

The author is attacking the way that history is taught. The author suggests that history classes are boring because teachers *have bought into the idea that they must cover all there is to know about any given era* and therefore *cram in as many facts as possible*. This is not the same thing as suggesting that facts are not important. Rather, the passage simply implies that fewer facts should be covered. The idea that many students are bored by history class is consistent with the passage, but the author implies that more students would like history if it were taught better. Answer: (E).

Honing Your Strategy

We suggest that you develop a unique style for the Reading Comprehension passages. You may develop one approach for the long passages and a different style for the short ones, or you may approach both types the same way. Here are your options:

1. **Read the passage and then answer the questions.** Most people's first impulse is to do the straightforward thing and read the passage. Often, this is the WRONG approach—especially on the long passages. Reading an 800-word passage end to end will give you an interesting (or not-so-interesting) taste of a subject, but the questions will deal with only a fraction of this information. "Never read the whole thing thoroughly— you'll be too pressed for time," declares a student who scored 680 V, 740 M. "Read the questions first and then look for the answers. Carefully

A KEY TO READING COMPREHENSION

"Reading comprehension questions have answers that are meant to confuse you," says a particularly insightful 790 Verbal scorer. "If you're trying to decide between two interpretations of a passage in your mind, it's quite likely that there will be answer choices that match each interpretation in every question. I would recommend that you don't let your personal opinions get in the way. Try to become the author and use his or her point of view."

reading the complete passage is a waste of time," says a Davidson-bound student with 680 V, 730 M. In a typical 800-word passage, one of the questions applies directly to less than half the lines. Vocabulary-in-context and literal comprehension questions can be answered by going directly to the lines that are referenced. Extended Reasoning questions can be answered by reading strategic parts of the passage.

Students who should consider reading the longer passages in their entirety include those who are speedy readers and those whose train of thought will be disrupted by not reading everything. One 710 V scorer poured cold water on skimming. "My advice is to slow down and focus on the story," he says. We are more inclined to support this strategy on the shorter passages, where the potential drawbacks of reading the whole passage are much smaller. See what you think.

2. **Skim the passage or read only part of it, then tackle the questions.** This method will be most useful for the long passages. "A trick that works for me is reading the first and last paragraphs as well as the first sentence of each paragraph in between," says a 750 V, 720 M scorer. Another possibility is to read until

you understand the writer's point of view and then skim the rest. We recommend that you experiment with the balance between reading, skimming, and skipping. If you feel yourself constantly referring back to the passage, you may need to read more thoroughly. One trick: if you find yourself getting interested in the passage, that may be a signal that you understand the basic idea and should skip farther down. Strange as it may sound, getting interested in the passage may distract you from your real goal, which is answering the questions.

3. **Start by reading or skimming the questions, then read the passage, then answer the questions.** There was a lively debate among our survey respondents as to whether reading the questions before the passage was helpful. "Reading the questions before the passage helps you read for what you need," says a 740 V, 710 M scorer. A Brown admit who scored 770 V, 750 M advises that reading the questions first is "really helpful when the selection is boring." A Princeton-bound student with 720 V, 670 M advises that after first reading the questions, students should read the passage, formulate answers to the questions as they read, and then compare their

MARKING THE PASSAGE

Most students are not in the habit of writing in their books. In school, students are often required to hand in their textbooks at the end of the year. Marking them up is a no-no. Not so for your SAT test booklet. We strongly recommend that you write in it. Make your pencil an extension of your brain and write as you go. You'll see your thoughts on paper—a boon for visual learners—and your ideas will still be on the page twenty minutes later if you skip the problem and come back. Using the booklet for math computations is a no-brainer, but writing there can also pay dividends in Reading Comprehension. Testifies one student who scored 730 V, 690 M, "The passages are so dry, dull, and uninteresting that it is easy to lose concentration. I had to force myself to stay concentrated by underlining parts of the passage that seemed important, and by so doing, I had a brief summary of the passage underlined."

responses to the answers. Says a student who scored 640 V, 680 M, "The strategy I used was to read the questions and circle key words to look for, then go back and read the passage."

"I never read the questions before the passage because it breaks my concentration and prevents me from getting a full understanding of the passage," writes a student who scored 800 V, 720 M. A Princeton admit who scored 730 V, 770 M believes that reading the questions first "interrupts your understanding of the passage as a whole when you are watching out for specific information." A third student who scored 610 V, 690 M eschewed

reading the questions first because he forgot them by the time he was into the passage.

If you do decide to read the questions first, are you going to "glance" at them, or are you going to read them thoroughly? A glance may only give you a hint of what is to come but will take less time. We recommend that you experiment with reading the questions quickly, and then more thoroughly, and see which works best for you. If you do the latter, you'll definitely want to mark the passage at the spots addressed by the questions. Some students, after marking the passage, may then choose to read only the lines they have marked while

IS IT POSSIBLE TO THINK TOO MUCH?

Many students think so. "Focus on the concrete," says a student who scored 710 V, 650 M. Adds a second, "I tend to overanalyze and so I can create links between any words and find multiple answers to every question. Don't read too in-depth in the passage—read it at a surface level." This student has a nifty 750 V to back up her advice.

answering the questions, though this method will leave a few Extended Reasoning questions that must then be dealt with.

4. **Start with the questions, then glance over to the passage and mark it at the spots which are addressed by particular questions. Then read the passage until those spots and answer each question before moving on in the passage.** This method may work for students who have difficulty remembering the passage when they answer the questions. By going directly to the questions immediately after reading the relevant material, students can take the questions one at a time and then keep reading. This method may require students to skip questions that do not reference a particular line or lines. The downside is that students must jump back and forth between the passage and the questions.

5. **Answer the questions without having first read the passage. Use the questions to guide your reading.** For all students, this method is worth trying on the short passages. With only about ten lines to read, some students will find this an efficient way to pick out the answer. On the longer passages, a totally question-based approach may be helpful for slow readers or for those who have had difficulty with these kinds of questions. "I would suggest not reading the passage through, but looking for the context of the questions. By the end, you'll have read most if not all of it," advises one student who got a 750 Verbal but said she struggled with the Reading Comprehension. "Most of the time, you don't need to read the passage to answer the questions," chirps another student who scored 610 V, 680 M. "I'm a slow reader. I just tried to answer as many

questions as I could without reading the passage," says a student who managed a 690 V using this approach. The primary flaw in this method is that it gives students little basis for answering the Extended Reasoning questions that deal with the main themes of the passage. Students who generally run short of time in the Reading Comprehension may use this method to guarantee themselves a good shot at getting the questions that focus on particular lines in the passage.

Each of the five approaches has its advantages, and we recommend that you try at least several of them as a way of figuring out which one best suits your learning style.

Finding the Point of View

It is easy to figure out someone's point of view when you know the person. Take your mom, for instance. You know she'll be angling for you to go to bed earlier, do your homework sooner, and clean your room now. No surprise there. You've lived with her seventeen years, you know her point of view, and you can guess what she is going to say about ten seconds before she opens her mouth.

The trick to the Reading Comprehension passages is to figure out the point of view of someone you don't know—after only a few

hundred words on a printed page. Nothing is more important than mastering this skill.

Weak readers read everything as if it were an encyclopedia entry. They may understand the words on the page, but they don't hear the author's voice. Who is the writer and why did he or she write the passage? What beliefs or assumptions underlie the passage? Who are the writer's allies? Adversaries? What idea(s) is the writer defending? Attacking? Most passages won't spell out the answers to questions like these, but savvy readers will find plenty of evidence.

> **"My advice is to take difficult English courses and read as many classics as you can, such as *Wuthering Heights* and *Great Expectations.*"**
>
> **—670 V, 700 M**

In highlighting point of view, we include two additional concepts that are separate but closely related: tone and main idea. Tone is how the writer expresses himself: emotional, restrained, sarcastic, matter-of-fact, unequivocal, and circumspect are all examples of tone. And main idea? We won't insult your intelligence with an explanation of that, but suffice it to say that the main idea flows out of the writer's point of view.

Keys to Success

1. **Don't overlook the introduction.** Each long passage is preceded by one to five sentences of italicized text. Many students simply breeze past this material, but it can include crucial details. One student, who scored 620 V, 710 M, reports that she read the introduction and glanced immediately to the questions to see if she could answer any of them before proceeding to the passage itself. The introduction is especially important in paired passage questions because it will help you establish a relationship between the passages.

2. **Practice, practice, practice.** Only repetition will teach you the best way to approach Reading Comprehension. It doesn't matter which strategy you choose—as long as you find one that is right for you. "Reading comprehension requires focus to be able to get through efficiently and effectively, and focus will only come with practice," says a student who scored 710 V, 750 M. If you're uncertain how to approach the passages, our recommendation is to read until you get the point of view, then to skim the rest and to move to the questions. Whether you should read the questions before the passage depends on whether doing so breaks your concentration, and whether you can remember enough while reading the passage to do you any

good. If you do decide to read the questions first, be sure to experiment with marking the passage.

3. **Find answers that match the tone of the passage.** If the passage about F. Scott Fitzgerald is written in high-minded academic prose, don't choose *(C) Gatsby was a scumbag.* The answer is much more likely to be *(D) Gatsby was emblematic of a moral crisis in the America of the 1920s.* Stay away from answers that use less specific language in favor of those that express ideas with precision.

4. **Do the paired passages one at a time.** In other words, read the first passage and/or do the questions related to it; then, read the second passage and/or do the questions related to it; and lastly, do the questions relevant to both passages. Reading both passages before answering any questions would likely cause confusion and back-tracking. By finishing your work on questions relevant only to the first passage before moving on to those about the second, you will make yourself better prepared to understand the second passage.

5. **Remember that the answer may not be in the line referenced in the question.** Suppose a question informs you that line 14 is the place where the author refers to "a dark shadow on my

heart." If the question asks what this dark shadow might symbolize, you may not learn until line 19 whether the phrase is a reference to the death of her only child or a remembrance of her much-lamented pet guinea pig. If you use the questions to locate relevant lines in the passage, be prepared to read a little before and a little after the line number(s) quoted in the question.

6. **When in doubt, focus tightly on the meaning of the passage.** Even the best students get stuck on questions where more than one response seems right. Often, students delve beyond the obvious meaning of the passage or second-guess obvious answers. "I would recommend not reading too much into the questions and making sure you understand what the question is asking," writes a 1600 scorer bound for Princeton. Adds an 800 V, 770 M scorer, "Don't think so deeply—the test writer probably didn't." Keep in mind that as the College Board itself says, answers to Reading Comprehension questions can be both true and wrong. The correct response is not necessarily the one that reflects circumstances in the outside world, but rather the one that expresses the appropriate response to the passage.

7. **Stay calm.** The strategy that makes you feel the most relaxed is the one you should use. If it is any consolation, even the highest scorers get confused and frustrated by Reading Comprehension. Complains a 760 V scorer, "Questions such as 'What is the best title for this story?' are particularly frustrating; this is a matter of personal opinion...it doesn't make sense that there is just one correct answer." Alas, making sense is not always the number one priority of the folks who make the SAT. A 700 V scorer swears that "It often seems like there are two right answers." Adds this student, "Sometimes being lucky is the best option."

6

MATH

TOTAL TESTING TIME: 70 MINUTES

Sections:

▸ **2 of 25 minutes**
▸ **I of 20 minutes**

Question Types:

▸ **Standard Multiple Choice**
▸ **Student-Produced Response ("Grid-Ins")**

The new SAT Math section features one addition and one subtraction. Topics normally taught in Algebra II will be added, while quantitative comparisons will be subtracted. The biggest change with the coming of the New SAT: math will comprise only one-third of your SAT I score instead of one-half. Poets, rejoice. Engineers, gnash your teeth.

Here's the good news about the Math SAT: it's easier than the Verbal. At least it was for the Class of 2003—which had an average score of 507 on the Verbal but a robust 519 on the Math. Average Math scores have gone up 16 points in the past decade, apparently because students are taking more demanding math courses. That leads to more good news: most people agree that preparation often has a bigger impact on the Math than on the old Verbal SAT—the sections that now comprise Critical Reading on the New SAT. Nobody can predict which vocabulary words may pop up in Critical Reading, but the math problems stay reasonably consistent from test to test.

That said, we'll wager that not many of you are aiming for a 519, or for that matter a 520, as your math score. Getting a 620 or 720 may take some doing, especially because students often have more trouble finishing the Math than the Verbal. Throw in all those nasty ETS tricks—especially near the end of each section—and the Math SAT can become a stress-inducing, teeth-grinding, have-an-accident-in-your-pants kind of experience. And that's on a good day.

We got an ear-full about it on our surveys. "My biggest enemy was the clock. I never finished any of the math sections," complains one student who nevertheless was able to eke out a 690. A 710 scorer bemoans the fact that he was "pressed for time" and therefore "skipped over vital information." Adds a 730 V, 720 M scorer with rare eloquence: "It sucks to miss a question because you are going too fast and say 2 + 3 = 6." Along with the complaints about time pressure came strong frustration that low-level math could be so difficult. "I take really high math [multivariable calculus] and I still can't get an 800 on the math," fumes a second student who scored 690. This student and many others railed about questions that were misinterpreted, tricks that cheated them out of problems they knew how to get, and simple bonehead mistakes. With high-scorers like these in such a lather, imagine how average students feel.

It's Not about the Math

The fact that you may have gotten good grades in Algebra II and Geometry is a feather in your cap, but it doesn't guarantee that you'll get the score you want on the SAT Math. Relevant math skills are necessary but they're only part of the equation. Imagine if everybody who earned an A in ninth and tenth grade math courses were to get, say, a 700. The bell curve would be busted and ETS would have to go back to the drawing board. But that's exactly what would happen if the test were simply an assessment of geometry and algebra skills.

A sad irony about the SAT—and particularly the math—is that many students believe they have done extremely well immediately after taking the test, only to be disappointed later. This pattern, repeated over and over at high schools throughout the nation, is more proof that the math on the SAT Math is not the issue. When students do not understand a problem, they know their answer is wrong. On the SAT Math, students generally know how to do the problems and believe they have gotten them right, never suspecting that they have fallen for a well-disguised distracter.

> **"The most difficult part of the math section was knowing how to go about doing the problems. The actual computation was simple algebra and geometry."**
>
> **—800 V, 800 M**

But that is how the game is played. To create its desired mix of high scorers, low scorers, and medium scorers, ETS juices up many of the questions with unexpected twists and turns. Some have complicated directions intended to sow confusion; others steer students toward seemingly obvious answers that are wrong; still others build in a final step in the calculations that many students forget to do. The ability to spot these head-fakes is what ETS and the College Board refer to as "math reasoning"—and what separates average scorers from high scorers. After laying its traps, the test-makers add insult to injury by "speeding" the Math Section to make sure that some students do not have time to finish and others can do so only by rushing—thereby falling into the aforementioned traps.

As you begin your preparation, remember the principles of SAT-taking that we discussed in chapter 3. Here is a reminder of the two biggies:

- **Take timed practice tests.** Have we mentioned that practice tests are important? The best way to build test-taking savvy is to get tricked a few times. Are you missing questions because of math concepts or because of the ETS two-step? Practice tests will show where your vulnerabilities are.
- **Fine-tune your speed.** Your goal should be to move as fast as you can without losing accuracy. Finish a 25-minute section in 20 minutes and see how you do. Experiment with various skipping strategies. Discover how speed can help you relax by taking the pressure off.

As with Reading Comprehension, it may be necessary to unlearn some strategies your teachers have taught you. For instance, many math teachers require students to show their work and take off points if students skip steps. But the SAT test-makers are not interested in process—only the correct answer. It is absolutely crucial that you skip steps on the SAT when you can get the answer quickly, and you should write down only what helps you solve a problem. Are you one of those organized, meticulous students who prints every step in immaculate detail? If so, you may need lots of practice in forcing yourself to move faster, skip steps, and eyeball problems to figure out approximate answers when doing so will increase your speed.

Inside the Bag of Tricks

The following is an overview of the most common ways that the test-makers jerk your chain. The questions may seem easy in this context, but imagine encountering them in the middle of a headlong chase to finish the test before time is called.

Information Overload

Are you the kind of person who can remember a phone number without writing it down? Or are you the kind who forgets it while fumbling for a pen? The answer may mean a lot on the SAT. With its word problems full of zigzags and double-talk, the SAT puts enormous emphasis on what psychologists call short-term working memory. Though the computations behind the problems may be easy, the written scenarios are often confusing. Here is an example:

> A bread basket contains biscuits and muffins. There are half as many biscuits as muffins. The muffins are either blueberry or raisin, and three times as many muffins are blueberry as are raisin. If one piece of bread is to be drawn at random from the bread basket, what is the probability that the piece drawn will be a raisin muffin?

(A) $\frac{1}{12}$

(B) $\frac{1}{6}$

(C) $\frac{1}{4}$

(D) $\frac{2}{6}$

(E) $\frac{2}{3}$

Answer: (B). If you know a little probability, you can do the numbers easily: $\frac{2}{3} \times \frac{1}{4} = \frac{2}{12} = \frac{1}{6}$. The hard part is getting your brain around how to set it up. Because the problem does not reveal until the end what you are looking for—the probability of getting a raisin muffin—you'll need to read it at least twice. You'll need to translate "half" and "three times" to fractions, all the while keeping straight muffins vs. biscuits and blueberry muffins vs. raisin muffins. Half as many biscuits as muffins means that two of every three pieces of bread ($\frac{2}{3}$) are muffins. Three times as many blueberry muffins as raisin muffins means that one out of every four muffins ($\frac{1}{4}$) are raisin. The proportion of bread that is muffins times the proportion of muffins that is raisin yields the probability that the piece selected will be both muffin and raisin. Hence, $\frac{2}{3} \times \frac{1}{4} = \frac{2}{12} = \frac{1}{6}$. The calculation is easy—not-so-easy are the reading, inference, and short-term memory to keep it all straight.

KNOW YOUR CALCULATOR

Students have been allowed to use calculators on the SAT since 1994, but with the coming of the New SAT, calculators will take on added significance. College Board says that students will still be able to answer every question without a calculator, but common sense says that a calculator will be a big help for some. The most important rule: make sure your calculator has fresh batteries. If the screen goes blank after the third math problem, you're out of luck. Be familiar with all of your calculator's idiosyncrasies, including the location of the keys and their touch. Calculators have their own personalities; make sure you know yours well.

Tricky Sequences

The following is a simplified version of a time-honored SAT sucker punch. A Dartmouth professor we know calls this "the fence-post problem":

> A farmer wants to build a fence that is 100 feet long using posts that are 10 feet apart. How many posts will the farmer need to complete the fence?
>
> (A) 9
> (B) 10
> (C) 11
> (D) 12
> (E) 100

Did you say 10? That's the answer ETS and College Board want you to get, but the real answer is (C)11. (You need 11 posts because one will go at the beginning of the fence and one on the end.) Even if you got it right in this example, would you get a question like this if it were buried midway through a 3 hour and 45 minute test with a little camouflage? Let's try a slightly harder variation on the theme:

> The first number of a sequence is 4 and every number after the first is 4 more than the number immediately preceding it. What is the value of the 50th number?
>
> (A) 196
> (B) 200
> (C) 202
> (D) 204
> (E) 208

Shame on anyone who chose 204. The sequence starts with four—just as if the counting by 4s had begun from 0—and the 50th term is 200. Answer: (B). Is the ability to get questions like this really "reasoning"? Or is it simply the ability to spot a dirty trick? Your opinion may depend on whether you got the question right.

Less-Than and Greater-Than Gamesmanship

Though this concept is easy, the test-makers like to engender confusion with less-than and greater-than. Consider the following:

What is the least possible integer for which 60 percent of that integer is greater than 6?

(A) 8
(B) 9
(C) 10
(D) 11
(E) 12

There are two possible screw-ups here. First, you could forget the fact that you are doing a less-than/greater-than problem and chose 10, the number that 60 percent of which is 6. You might also mess up by choosing 9, which is the greatest possible integer that 60 percent of which is less than 6. The tricky part is that the question begins with the phrase "least possible," yet the answer, 11, must be greater than the number (10) that 60 percent of which is 6. The test-makers know that when students are in a hurry, they tend to miss information in the second or third sentence of a question as they rush to answer it. By changing the focus from "least possible" to "greater than," they transform a relatively easy question into a relatively hard one.

■ ■ ■

When the Solution Isn't the Answer

Some questions will ask for a solution that can only be found by computing the value of something else. There is no great secret to these except that sometimes students do the initial calculation and forget that they must perform one (or two) more operations before getting their answer.

For instance:

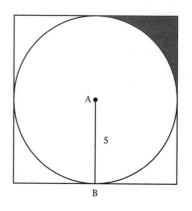

In the figure above, AB is the radius of the circle. What is the area of the shaded region?

(A) $100 - 25\pi$
(B) $25\pi - 100$
(C) $25 - \dfrac{25\pi}{4}$
(D) $5 - 20\pi$
(E) $25 - \dfrac{50\pi}{2}$

There's no way to figure out the area of the shaded region directly, but you can figure out the area of the non-shaped region and subtract. With the radius of the circle being 5, you know that the area of the circle is 25π. Subtract that from the area of the square, 100, to get $100 - 25\pi$, the area of the four regions inside the square but outside the circle. But don't forget the last step. You must divide by four to get the area of the shaded region Answer: (C). There are harder variations of this idea, but you'll get them so long as you remember what you're solving for.

■ ■ ■

The Deceptively Easy Problem

The test-makers love to stick these in at the end of sections to throw you for a loop. Check this out:

Points *A* and *B* are on line *L* in the figure above. How many different points on line *L* are half as far from Point *A* as from Point *B*?

(A) Four
(B) Three
(C) Two
(D) One
(E) None

The answer is (C): Two. This problem rests on a paradox. Though there is only one point on line *L* that is an equal distance from points *A* and *B*, there are two points that are half as far from *A* as from *B*. Most students will look to the left of point *A* for a point that is half the distance from *A* as it is from *B*, forgetting that there is a second point between *A* and *B* that is also half as far from *A*. This problem is a classic example of an end-of-the-section trick.

■ ■ ■

This Can't Be Right…

The test-makers love to play on your insecurities. On a multi-step problem, it is always unnerving to get to the second-to-last step and see a bizarre value. That's what they count on to mess you up. Like the following problem:

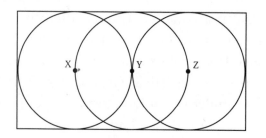

In the figure above, points X, Y, and Z are the centers of the three circles. If each circle has an area of 50, what is the area of the rectangle?

(A) $\dfrac{50}{\pi}$

(B) $50 - \dfrac{8}{\pi}$

(C) 50

(D) $\dfrac{200}{\pi}$

(E) $\dfrac{400}{\pi}$

In order to get this problem, you need to solve the formula for the area of a circle πr^2 backwards to get the radius of the circle. You know that the base of the rectangle is $4r$ and the height is $2r$. But solving $50 = \pi r^2$ for r gives you a nasty $r = \sqrt{\dfrac{50}{\pi}}$ —not the sort of value you are expecting, especially since there are no square roots in the answer choices. The test-makers hope you will bail out here and try another approach. But stick to your guns. By multiplying the base × height, you get rid of the radicals $4\sqrt{\dfrac{50}{\pi}} \times \sqrt{\dfrac{50}{\pi}}$ and your answer is $\underline{200}{}$, (D).

■ ■ ■

Optical Illusions

When you're moving fast, your eye tends to slide over crucial information. See if you can get this little stinker:

If $m = \dfrac{1}{a}$ and $n = \dfrac{1}{b}$ and if $a = 5$ and $b = 6$, what is the value of $\dfrac{1}{m} \times \dfrac{1}{n}$?

(A) $\dfrac{1}{30}$

(B) $\dfrac{1}{6}$

(C) $\dfrac{1}{5}$

(D) 6

(E) 30

Answer: (E) 30. This problem rates at medium difficulty, though probably 95 percent of the students who take the test know how to get it. The tough part is the confused wording. Since m and n are defined in terms of a and b, the most logical wording for this question would be, "If $a = 5$ and $b = 6$ and $m = \dfrac{1}{a}$ and $n = \dfrac{1}{b}$, what is the value of $\dfrac{1}{m} \times \dfrac{1}{n}$?" But instead, the question defines m and n first, then a and b, and then doubles back to asking "what is the value of $\dfrac{1}{m} \times \dfrac{1}{n}$." The obvious mistake, which many students will make, is to chose the answer that is equal to $\dfrac{1}{a} \times \dfrac{1}{b}$. Not coincidentally, that answer choice is (A)—the first one on the list. While distracters don't always appear in the (A) slot, they are particularly effective there because a student may move on without examining the other answers.

■ ■ ■

Confidence is good on the SAT Math, but overconfidence can be a killer. That's why even math whiz kids may need a refresher on basic algebra and geometry. "I am in AP Calculus this year and I guess I just took knowing algebra for granted," says a student who was disappointed not to get his math score above 690. "I should have spent more time reviewing some of the algebra and geometry concepts I haven't had to deal with in a few years," moans a 640 M scorer. How do you find out if you're in the same boat? Take some practice tests and see what you miss.

Playing with Percentages

This one is the toughest problem of the bunch. It uses percentages, a topic from middle school math, but the challenge comes in the way the question is formulated:

> A car dealership normally charges $18,000 for a certain type of car. This price is 20 percent more than the amount it costs the dealership to get the car from the factory. At a clearance sale, the dealership decides to sell all cars for 20 percent less than its cost from the factory. How much does this type of car cost at the clearance sale?

(A) $9,680
(B) $11,340
(C) $11,680
(D) $12,000
(E) $15,000

Did you say (C) $11,680? Oops. If you said (D) $12,000, bravo! This is a hard one, and it hinges on the fact that $18,000 is 20 percent more than another number. Therefore, you can't take 20 percent of $18,000—which most students do—but rather you must figure out what number plus 20 percent of itself equals $18,000. Hmm. You know you're looking for a round number. $16,000? That's $2,000 less than $18,000, but you know immediately that $2,000 is 20 percent of $10,000. Gotta be lower. How about...$15,000? Bingo. Twenty percent of 15 is 3 and 20 percent of $15,000 is $3,000. Subtract another 20 percent and your answer is $12,000.

Don't feel bad if you missed this one—not many will get it right.

■ ■ ■

When the Test-Makers Invent a Symbol

Talk about weird. Sometimes ETS goes off the deep end and say something like this: Let][be defined by A][B = BA². Every time you see an expression like 7][3, you know to translate it to 3(7²). That in itself is not hard, but generally there is a second or third wrinkle to the problem that makes everything run together. Since you're dealing with a new concept, these are particularly brutal on short term memory. An example:

> Let W∗X∗Y∗Z be defined for all numbers W, X, Y, and Z by W∗X∗Y∗Z = WY − XZ. If A = 5∗3∗4∗2, what is the value of A∗7∗2∗4?
>
> (A) −8
> (B) 0
> (C) 4
> (D) 8
> (E) 20

The answer to this question of medium difficulty is (B) 0. The only challenge is keeping the numbers straight in your head. By the formula W∗X∗Y∗Z, A = (5 × 4) − (3 × 2) = 14. In turn, 14∗7∗2∗4 = (14 × 2) − (7 × 4) = 0. If this problem gives you trouble, you may have some issues with short-term memory. Even if you didn't have any trouble with the problem just now, you're more likely to space out and lose your train of thought under time pressure.

Taking the Pressure Off

Small wonder that so many downtrodden souls feel used and abused by the Math SAT. We'll wager that most readers know every one of the formulas to solve the preceding questions. The traps are sneaky, but time pressure is what makes them work. If you're stressed, you'll get tricked. Relax and you won't be. Easier said than done? Sure. But there is one reliable way to take the pressure off: move quickly so that you are not fighting the clock. We're not talking about a headlong scramble, but rather about developing strategies that allow you to move quickly while staying under control. The following strategies will help:

Eyeball and Estimate

Every good SAT taker knows that half the time, you don't need to do any real calculations in order to get the right answer. By using round numbers, you can often estimate the answer in your head and then scan your choices for the right one. For example:

> A chain of department stores must reduce its inventory of shirts, which totals 7,200. For a three-day period, the chain will offer a deep discount on all its shirts with the goal of selling between 15% and 16% of its shirts. Which of the following is a number of shirts that the chain could sell to satisfy that goal?

(A) 1,026
(B) 1,086
(C) 1,221
(D) 1,411
(E) 1,662

This question should take ten to twenty seconds. At a glance you know that 10% of 7,200 is 720. Add half of 720, or 360, to get 15% of 7,200. That number is 1,080 and the answer is (B) 1,086—the response that is closest to 1,080 while still being greater.

Another example:

Suppose that a jogger runs from her home to a park at a pace of 8 miles per hour, and then immediately returns home along the same route at a pace of 7 miles per hour. If the total time she spent was 1 hour, how many minutes did it take her to jog from her house to the park?

(A) 34
(B) 30
(C) 28
(D) 24
(E) 20

This one can be solved as a ratio and proportion problem but you should only need a few seconds to get it by eyeballing and estimating. Look at the answers. Since the jogger was going faster on her way to the park than she was on the way home, (A) and (B) are obviously wrong. You know you're look-

ing for a number less than 30 but not a lot less. Response (D) 24 would mean that it took her 36 minutes on the way back. Common sense says that a one-eighth decrease in speed won't lead to a 50% increase in the amount of time needed to cover the distance. The answer must be closer to 30 minutes and therefore it is (C) 28. (If you're good, you realized that the ratio of time spent on the two distances, 32 minutes and 28 minutes, would be the same as the ratio of the speeds at which they were covered, 8 miles per hour and 7 miles per hour.)

Plug In the Answers

Sometimes, the quickest way to answer a problem is not to try to solve it in the conventional way. With all the answers staring you in the face, an alternative is to plug them into the question and see which one works. Also called working backwards, plugging in should be a core strategy for just about everyone. Some problems are particularly suited to plugging in, such as the following:

> If y and z are different positive integers and $11y + 12z = 237$, what is the greatest possible value of z?
>
> (A) 11
> (B) 15
> (C) 17
> (D) 19
> (E) 21

There is more than one way to solve this problem, but here is ours: You're looking for the greatest possible value of z that fits the equation, so multiply the answer choices by 12, moving from largest to smallest. Your goal is to find the largest one that produces a product with 12 that, when subtracted from 237, yields a sum divisible by 11. You can see immediately that 21 can't be right because $12 \times 21 = 252$. Next, try $12 \times 19 = 228$. That's 9 less than 237—obviously can't be right. Next: $12 \times 17 = 204$. $237 - 204 = 33$. Divisible by 11? Yes—problem solved. Answer: (C).

Some readers can probably see a few more shortcuts to getting this answer—the thought process moves faster than we can write it.

One final tip: if a problem has you stumped, go to the answers and plug in the middle value and see if you can solve it. Even if this answer does not prove to be the right one, you may be able to tell whether the correct answer is greater or less than the middle value, and thereby narrow the list of possible answers to two.

■ ■ ■

Draw Pictures

On a test that puts enormous pressure on your short-term memory, jotted notes and drawings can be a big help. Drawing as you read takes only a few seconds, and you may be surprised at how much time you will save from not having to reread or double-check your facts. (Heed the immortal words of Mark Twain: "Slow down, I'm in a hurry.") Be as free as possible with your pencil, using your test book as your scratch paper. If drawing does not come naturally to you, take a practice test and force yourself to do so.

There are certain situations when drawing is crucial. Geometry problems are an obvious example. The test-makers will often draw pictures to go with problems, but sometimes they don't. So hear this: **on any geometry problem without a picture, be sure to draw one yourself.** The fact that there is no picture may be a sign of some hanky-panky that a picture will clearly expose.

Let's try an experiment. Answer the following question without a diagram:

Four lines in the same plane intersect at point *T*. These lines form equal, non-overlapping angles. What is the measure of the angles?

(A) 45°
(B) 60°
(C) 90°
(D) 120°
(E) 140°

Without a diagram, your answer is probably 90 degrees. Now draw a point with four lines running through it. See your mistake? Four lines make 8 angles. Answer: (A) 45°.

Diagrams can also help on information overload questions:

The members of a certain health club have a choice of swimming or lifting weights. 54 of the members use the swimming pool and 47 members lift weights. If 13 of the members who use the swimming pool also lift weights, how many people are members of the health club?

(A) 78
(B) 88
(C) 101
(D) 113
(E) 114

The only potential issue with this moderately easy problem is keeping the information straight. A quickly jotted Venn Diagram showing the overlapping categories would help—see below—or some other visual prompt that helps you visualize the three categories of members. Answer: (B) 88

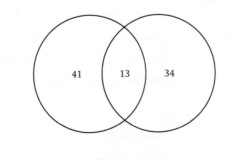

Grinning through the Grid-ins

Though the majority of questions on the SAT Math are multiple-choice, some are not. The Grid-ins were created in 1994 to give hapless students even more to lose sleep over. ETS was already an expert trickster before Grid-ins were invented, but there was one problem. Though students might be fooled into computing a wrong answer, they could be saved from getting the problem wrong if their incorrect response did not appear in the answer choices. And even if it did, students sometimes realized their mistake upon seeing the correct answer in the list of possible responses.

The Grid-ins are nasty because you can get the wrong answer and never have a clue. Fortunately, Grid-ins comprise only a relatively small percent of the math questions on the SAT. The questions themselves look very much like standard multiple choice:

If $a^2 + b^3 = 89$ and $a - b = 1$, what is the value of $\frac{b}{a}$?

But instead of five multiple-choice responses to choose from, students are confronted with a rectangle on their answer sheets that looks like this:

Students are asked to "grid in" the correct ovals while inserting a decimal point or fraction line where appropriate. Students have the option of writing their

answer in the top row of boxes but receive credit only if the ovals are filled in correctly. No questions have a negative answer.

But back to the equation at hand. At a glance, you know that b must be either 3 or 4 because 5^3 is equal to 125 and is too big. If b were 2, a would be 9, but that does not satisfy the $a - b = 1$ equation. If b were 3, a^2 would have to be 62—no good either. So b is 4, a is 5, $a - b = 1$, and $\frac{b}{a}$ = 4/5. The answer should be gridded in as follows:

or theoretically, you could also grid it in as:

Notice that this Grid-in problem has a

subtle trick. In the two equations at the beginning of the problem, $a^2 + b^3 = 89$ and $a - b$, a precedes b. Yet the problem asks for $\frac{b}{a}$ as the answer. To further throw you off, $\frac{a}{b}$ is an improper fraction while $\frac{b}{a}$ is not. Therefore, flipping the fraction to $\frac{b}{a}$ converts it to a conventional fraction—the opposite of what would seem to be logical.

The Grid-in problems are a haven for tricks like these. Without the safety net of multiple-choice answers, you'll need to be extra careful not to be hoodwinked.

The Old SAT: Quantitative Comparison Questions

These questions will get the ax as of March 2005 largely because nothing like them ever appears in school. But for the benefit of the Class of 2005, we offer the following overview of the Quantitative Comparisons and a few words of advice. Members of the Class of 2006 and beyond should skip this section in the interest of sanity.

"The quantitative comparison was the hardest because of the format; it doesn't test your ability to do math as much as to get in the swing of a strange questioning style."

—800 V, 730 M

DIRECTIONS FOR QUANTITATIVE COMPARISON QUESTIONS

The questions each consist of two quantities in boxes, one in Column A and one in Column B. You are to compare the two quantities and on the answer sheet fill in the correct oval.

        A if the quantity in Column A is greater;
        B if the quantity in Column B is greater;
        C if the two quantities are equal;
        D if the relationship cannot be determined from the information given.
        AN E RESPONSE WILL NOT BE SCORED.

Notes:

1. In some questions, information is given about one or both of the quantities to be compared. In such cases, the given information is centered above the two columns and is not boxed.
2. In a given question, a symbol that appears in both columns represents the same thing in Column A as it does in Column B.
3. Letters such as x, n, and k stand for real numbers

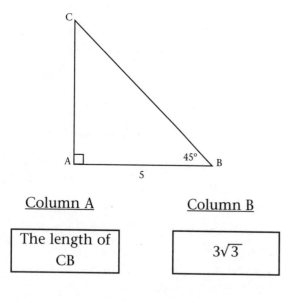

Column A	Column B
The length of CB	$3\sqrt{3}$

All that is necessary to solve this problem is the knowledge that the sides of a 45°–45°–90° right triangle are always in the ratio of $1:1:\sqrt{2}$. Therefore, the length of CB is $5\sqrt{2}$. You should know from memory that $\sqrt{2}$ is just less than 1.5—and therefore the length of CB is about 7. Since you know $\sqrt{3}$ is less than 2, $3\sqrt{3}$ must be less than 6. Answer: (A), the quantity in Column A is greater.

This one is slightly tougher:

$$(a + 1)^3 = 27$$
$$b^2 = 4$$

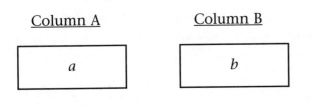

Column A	Column B
a	b

If the cube of $5a$ is divided by 5, the result is x.

$$a > 0$$

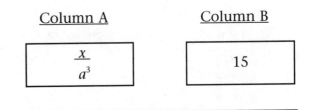

Column A	Column B
$\dfrac{x}{a^3}$	15

Believe it or not, this is one of the hardest quantitative comparisons you'll see. It looks easy on the surface. The term $(a + 1)$ must equal 3 because 3^3 is 27. Therefore, $a = 2$. And since $b^2 = 4$, b must also be equal to 2. Right?

Wrong. As hurried students are prone to forget, -2^2 also equals 4. The answer is (D), relationship cannot be determined. This highlights the most important rule for quantitative comparisons—watch those negative numbers. The test-makers rely on the fact that students are more accustomed to dealing with positive numbers than negative ones. Unless the problem tells you that all numbers are positive, you cannot assume it.

The following is another problem with a variation on this theme:

The first hint is $a > 0$. When the test-makers go out of their way to tell you that the numbers cannot be negative or zero, it usually means that (D) will not be the answer. Why? As we saw above, negative numbers can make the relationship between the quantities undeterminable. When the possibility of a negative number is taken away, the answer is more likely (A), (B), or (C).

Like so much of the SAT, this problem is dressed up to look harder than it is. The key is to substitute $\frac{(5a^3)}{5}$ for x. 5^3 is 125 and therefore $x = 25a^3$. Therefore, the answer is (A) because the quantity in Column A is greater.

If negative numbers are the biggest bugaboo on quantitative comparisons, fractions are a close second. A quick reality check: which is greater, $(\frac{1}{3})$ or $(\frac{1}{3})^2$? What about $(\frac{1}{3})^2$ vs. $(\frac{1}{3})^3$? You know this but you might miss it while rushing to beat the clock. **Positive fractions raised to a**

THE ART OF A GUESS

Distracters are a pain in the neck most of the time, but when you have no idea what the right answer is, they can be helpful. Since the correct answer is generally accompanied by at least one or two wrong answers that resemble it in one way or another, your best bet is to guess an answer that is similar to the other responses. Suppose you face a question with the following answers:

(A) 444
(B) 500
(C) 887
(D) 888
(E) 889

Without knowing the question, it is a good bet to eliminate (A) and (B) because they have the least in common with the other answers. Even if you pick randomly between (C), (D), and (E), your odds of answering correctly are now one in three rather than one in five. If you can eliminate two answers in a similar manner for every question that stumps you, the odds are good that you will raise your score. As a footnote, the responses above came from a question about an arithmetic sequence, and the answer was (E) 889.

---

higher power are always *less* than those raised to a lower power. A mistake like this is understandable, but you'd be amazed at how many students suffer a complete blackout and say something silly like $\frac{1}{6} > \frac{1}{5}$.

Another common screw-up: forgetting that **anything multiplied by 0 = 0.** Just a friendly reminder. If the question has not specified that the numbers are greater than zero, make sure that substituting 0 into your calculations won't change the answer.

Our final piece of advice is a theme we have repeated throughout the book. Beware the too-easy-looking problem that comes in the second half of the section. You'll find tricks lurking in the weeds. As with every other section of the SAT, the best way to get the feel of the Quantitative Comparisons is to practice them and learn from your mistakes.

Since there are only four possible responses to a Quantitative Comparison question, each wrong answer will cost you one-third of a point rather than one-quarter. As with every other section of the SAT, random guessing will not, on average, affect your score. But again, since few guesses are truly random, you should always guess.

Oh Yeah, the Math

Everybody has made a big deal about how the SAT is adding Algebra II. That's important news, but hold the phone. At least 80 percent of the test is still lower math that you learned for the first time in Algebra I, Geometry, or even before that. We won't waste your time with every topic that might appear on the test; you've studied it all in your previous math classes. But there are some topics that you should know without having to think twice. A quick refresher:

Prime Numbers

Memorize the first ten: 2, 3, 5, 7, 11, 13, 17, 19, 23, 29. The test-makers love to mess around with these.

Addition and Multiplication of Integers

Anybody can figure these out by thinking about it, but know them off the top of your head.

Even + Even = Even
Odd + Odd = Even
Odd + Even = Odd
Even × Even = Even
Odd × Odd = Odd
Odd × Even = Even
Negative × Positive = Negative
Negative × Negative = Positive

■ ■ ■

Squares, Cubes, and Square Roots

Know the square of every whole number from 1 to 15:

$1^2=1$	$2^2=4$	$3^2=9$	$4^2=16$	$5^2=25$
$6^2=36$	$7^2=49$	$8^2=64$	$9^2=81$	$10^2=100$
$11^2=121$	$12^2=144$	$13^2=169$	$14^2=196$	$15^2=225$

Know the cube of every whole number from 1 to 5:

$$1^3=1 \qquad 2^3=8 \qquad 3^3=27$$
$$4^3=64 \qquad 5^3=125$$

Know the approximate value of the following square roots:

$$\sqrt{1} = 1$$
$$\sqrt{2} \approx 1.4$$
$$\sqrt{3} \approx 1.7$$
$$\sqrt{4} = 2$$
$$\sqrt{5} \approx 2.25$$

Don't forget that fractions squared or cubed are smaller than the original fraction, and negative numbers squared are positive while negative numbers cubed are negative.

■ ■ ■

Mean, Median, and Mode

The mean is the arithmetic average of a set of numbers, the median is the middle value of the set, and the mode is the value that is most often repeated within the set. Of these, mean or average is probably the most important. It is amazing how many confusing ways that the test-makers can devise to ask you to average a set of numbers.

■ ■ ■

Ratio and Proportion

Definitely review the intricacies of this concept, and know all of the ways to express ratios:

$$\frac{1}{4} = 1:4 = .25 = 25\% = \frac{25}{100}$$

The ability to convert word problems into ratios and back again is a crucial skill.

■ ■ ■

Exponents

Think you know what $a^2 + a^3$ is? It equals a^5, right? Think again. You can't simplify $a^2 + a^3$ unless you also know the value of a. The same goes for $a^3 - a^2$. The rules for exponents are as follows:

Add the exponents when multiplying:

$$a^3 \times a^2 = a^5$$

Subtract the exponents when dividing:

$$a^3 \div a^2 = a \ \text{ or } \ \frac{a^3}{a^2} = a$$

Multiply the exponents when raising to a power:

$$(a^3)^2 = a^6$$

■ ■ ■

Probability and Combinations

Too many students have been stumped by the tiny bit of probability that appears on the SAT. There are two rules to know. First, when all possible outcomes are equally likely, the probability of a particular set of outcomes is equal to the number of those outcomes divided by the number of all possible outcomes. For instance, suppose 12 playing cards are placed face-down on a table. If three are diamonds and nine are spades, the likelihood of getting a diamond from a random draw is 3/12 or 1/4.

> **❝I felt unprepared to answer these bizarre probability questions.❞**
>
> **—760 V, 640 M**

Combinations problems are a touch harder. For instance: In a cafeteria, children may choose one vegetable and one meat. The vegetables include corn, beans, peas, tomatoes, and lettuce. The meats include chicken, steak, beef, and fish. How many possible combinations of vegetables and meats can a child choose? All it takes is knowing the formula. Simply multiply the 5 vegetable choices times the 4 meat choices. 4 × 5 = 20 combinations.

■ ■ ■

Triangles

No math topic is more important than triangles. You need to know their basic properties off the top of your head—regardless of whether relevant formulas and diagrams are printed in the front of the section. (You shouldn't waste time looking.) **The first rule of triangles is that every single one of them contains three angles that measure a total of 180°.** Here are some special triangles you should know:

Equilateral Triangle – all sides equal length

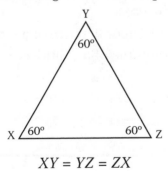

$$XY = YZ = ZX$$

Isosceles Triangle – two sides equal length

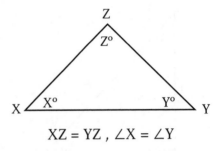

$$XZ = YZ, \angle X = \angle Y$$

Right Triangle – one angle of 90°

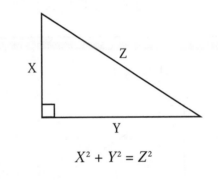

$$X^2 + Y^2 = Z^2$$

30° – 60° – 90° Right Triangle

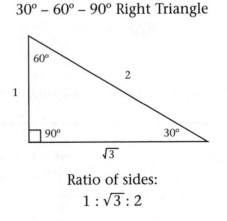

Ratio of sides:
$$1 : \sqrt{3} : 2$$

45° – 45° – 90° Right Triangle

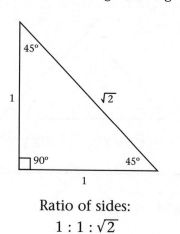

Ratio of sides:
$$1 : 1 : \sqrt{2}$$

3–4–5 Right Triangle

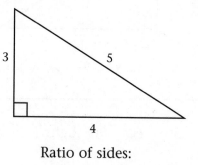

Ratio of sides:
$$3 : 4 : 5$$

Other common ratios: 5:12:13 and 7:24:25

Perhaps the most important formula related to triangles: area = $1/2(bh)$ where b = base and h = height.

■ ■ ■

Parallel Lines

More common-sense rules to know cold:

1) $A° = E° = D° = H°$
2) $B° = F° = G° = C°$

Any angle from 1) + Any angle from 2) = 180°

■ ■ ■

And Finally

A few formulas related to circles that should be etched indelibly in your brain:

πr^2 = area of a circle
πd, $2\pi r$ = circumference of a circle
$\pi r^2 h$ = volume of a cylinder

where $\pi \approx 3.14$, d = diameter, r = radius, h = height.

Practice Problems

To help you brush up, try these practice problems. Solutions and explanations follow.

1. If p and r are different prime numbers greater than 2, then $(p \times r) + 2$ must be

   (A) an even integer
   (B) an odd integer
   (C) prime
   (D) divisible by 2
   (E) divisible by 3

2. If a and b are integers > 0 and $a \times b = 8a + 3$, which of the following must be true?

   I. a is even
   II. $a > b$
   III. $a + b$ is even

   (A) None
   (B) I only
   (C) II only
   (D) III only
   (E) I, II, and III

3. If a and b are positive integers, the expression $\dfrac{7a^{(b+3)}}{3a}$ is equal to which of the following?

   (A) $4a^{(b+3)}$

   (B) $7^{(b+3)}$

   (C) $21^{(b+4)}$

   (D) $\dfrac{7}{3}$

   (E) $\dfrac{7a^{(b+2)}}{3}$

4. In a supermarket, a can of beans costs one-fifth less than a jar of peaches. If the can of beans costs $2.00, how much does the jar of peaches cost?

   (A) $2.20
   (B) $2.40
   (C) $2.50
   (D) $2.60
   (E) $3.00

5. If a student scores 92 on each of her first three quizzes, and then gets grades of 86, 90, and 76 on subsequent quizzes, what is the average of her quiz grades?

   (A) 86
   (B) 88
   (C) 89
   (D) 90
   (E) 91

6. At a particular school, the day is divided into 7 periods. Students must take a class during at least 6 of those periods. No class is offered during more than 1 period. If students may choose from 5 different classes during each of the 7 periods, how many different schedules are possible?

   (A) 28
   (B) 35
   (C) 36
   (D) 42
   (E) 49

7. On a flat surface, a man walks 30 feet, then turns at a 90° angle and walks 40 feet. He stops and digs a hole 20 feet deep. How many feet is the bottom of the hole from the spot where he started?

(A) 35
(B) 40
(C) 50
(D) $\sqrt{70}$
(E) $\sqrt{2900}$

8. The area of polygon ABCDEF is 15. If BC = CD, what is the area of the shaded region?

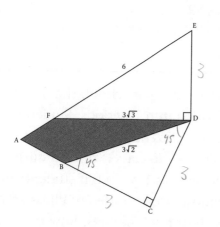

Note: Figure not drawn to scale

(A) $10.5 - 4.5\sqrt{3}$
(B) $15 - 4.5\sqrt{3}$
(C) $15 - 4.5\sqrt{2}$
(D) $12\sqrt{2}$
(E) $12 + 9\sqrt{3}$

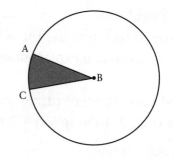

9. The circle above has a diameter of 12. If point B is at the center of the circle and the measure of ∠ABC is 30°, what is the area of the shaded region?

(A) 3π
(B) 12π
(C) 18π
(D) 24π
(E) 30π

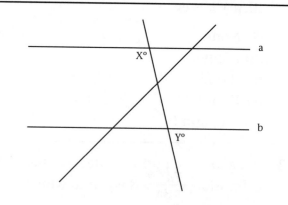

Note: Figure not drawn to scale

10. In the figure above, a ∥ b. If x = 100, what is the value of y?

(A) 80
(B) 90
(C) 100
(D) 110
(E) 120

The answers: 1.(B) 2.(D) 3.(E) 4.(C) 5.(B) 6.(D) 7.(E) 8.(A) 9.(A) 10.(A)

We rate these questions medium to hard. Explanations:

1. Priming the Pump

Prime numbers and even/odd counting come together in this one. You know that p and r are odd because all primes greater than 2 are odd. Their product must also be odd, as must $(p \times r) + 2$. The answer is (B).

2. Understanding Even and Odd

This one is slightly harder than question 1. Since $8 \times$ any number will be even, $8a + 3$ must also be odd. Therefore, $a \times b$ must also be odd and both a and b must be odd. The proposition that $a > b$ is also false. For instance, if $a = 1$, $b = 11$. Since both a and b are odd, $a + b$ is even and (D) is correct.

3. The Agony of Exponents

The key on this one is simply that when you divide exponential expressions with the same base, the exponents are subtracted. The 7/3 stays and $(b + 3) - 1 = b + 2$. Answer: (E).

4. More Playing With Percentages

We thought you were due for another nasty ratio and proportion problem. The natural tendency is to compute one-fifth of $2.00—40—and make your answer $2.40. But the right way to solve is to say that $2.00 is $\frac{4}{5}$ of x. Therefore, multiply $2.00 by $\frac{5}{4}$ to get $2.50. Answer: (C).

5. Weighing Weighted Averages

This moderately easy problem has a small wrinkle. If you compute the average of 92, 86, 90, and 76, you get (A) 86. But you're not that gullible (we hope). The student got a 92 on her first three quizzes, therefore the 92 must be counted three times to get the average of all 6 values—making the answer (B) 88.

6. The Right Combination

The students can take one of 5 classes during 7 periods. Therefore, $5 \times 7 = 35$ choices. The twist: Since they can also opt not to take a class, there are actually 6 options during every period. Answer: (D) 42.

7. A New Use For Right Triangles

Don't fret if you were stumped by this one—it may be the hardest of this bunch. To get it, you need to envision two perpendicular planes, one going along the ground and the other perpendicular to the ground. Each plane has a right triangle in it. The first has sides of 30 and 40 feet—and therefore you know that the hypotenuse is 50 feet because of the 3-4-5 rule. The side that is 50 feet is also the first side of a triangle perpendicular to the ground, which extends 20 feet down into the hole. Now that you know that two sides are 50 and 20, you can use the Pythagorean Theorem to compute the hypotenuse of the second triangle, which is also the distance from the bottom of the hole to the beginning point. Answer: (E) $\sqrt{2900}$.

8. **Calculating Area By Inference**

   The two triangles in this figure are, respectively, a 1-$\sqrt{3}$-2 right triangle and a 1-1-$\sqrt{2}$ right triangle. Since $BD = 3\sqrt{2}$, both BC and $CD = 3$. By similar reasoning, $ED = 3$. Therefore, the area of BCD is $\frac{1}{2}(3 \times 3)$ while the area of DEF is $\frac{1}{2}(3 \times 3\sqrt{3})$. Subtracting these from 15 yields the answer, (A) $10.5 - 4.5\sqrt{3}$.

9. **Circular Reasoning**

   A few easy calculations are all you need for this one. The question gives you the diameter of the circle, 12, which makes the area 36π. With $360°$ in a circle, a $30°$ slice is $\frac{1}{12}$th of the area. Answer: (A) 3π.

10. **Angles and Parallel Lines**

    This one is either hard or extremely easy. Since $\angle x$ and $\angle y$ are adjacent to the same line that cuts two parallel lines, $x° + y° = 180$. If $x = 100$, $y = 80$ and the answer is (A).

The SAT's New Math

For all the hullabaloo about the addition of higher-level math, the truth is that only 15–20 percent of the math questions will cover new topics. You will have learned most of this material in your Algebra II class. And get this straight: the addition of new math will not necessarily make the test harder. On the old SAT, the math itself was never the issue; the test-makers were merely playing tricks with simple material. Expect more of the same on the New SAT, but the odds are good that the questions dealing with higher math will be more straightforward. Fewer mind games and more emphasis on the math is a good deal for students who work hard in school and know the formulas.

The following is an overview of the most significant new topics. We assume you have seen them in Geometry or Algebra II. If you're rusty, the following pages will jog your memory. But if you have difficulty following the examples—or if you have never encountered one or more of the topics—you may want to dust off your algebra textbook.

Algebraic Equations and Inequalities

This is a catch-all phrase that covers a lot of territory. In algebra, the goal is to solve for an unknown variable. Some equations have only one variable; others have several. With a one-variable equation, it is possible to solve for that variable, as in

$$8x - 5 = 27$$
$$8x = 32$$
$$x = 4.$$

With two variables, the best you can do is to simplify the equation, or solve for one variable in terms of the other. For instance, you might encounter a question such as:

What is the *y*-intercept of the line determined by the equation

$$4x - 4 = 3y + 3?$$

(A) 7

(B) -7

(C) -7/3

(D) 3/7

(E) 1/7

To solve this problem, you need to be familiar with the formula for a line: $y = mx + b$, where m is the slope of the line and b is the *y*-intercept. The long way to solve is to labor through the algebra until you get to $y = 4/3x - 7/3$. A quicker way is simply to subtract 3 from both sides to isolate the $3y$, then divide -7 by 3 to get the value for the intercept. Answer: (C).

In addition to this sort of problem—a "linear equation" in algebra jargon—you will also see equations that include exponential terms. A special case of these, quadratic equations, is discussed below.

One possibility would be an equation like this:

$$\frac{-4x(y^2 + 2) + 8x}{-xy^2}$$

(A) −4

(B) 4

(C) $\frac{4}{xy^2}$

(D) 8

(E) 16

The key to this problem is to recognize that if you *distribute* -4x, you can create like terms that can be consolidated and dealt with. That is, if you multiply -4x by all the terms inside the parentheses, you get

$$\frac{-4xy^2 - 8x + 8x}{-xy^2}$$

From there, you can get rid of the 8x's and divide to get your answer: (B) 4.

In addition to equations, you may also encounter inequalities that involve quantities that are *less than*, *less than or equal to*, *greater than*, or *greater than or equal to* (respectively, <, ≤, >, and ≥) other quantities.

A variation on this theme is a domain and range problem such as the following:

If $f(x) = 6x^2 + 5$ for $-2 \leq x \leq 4$, then which of the following gives the range of f?

(A) $\{y: -12 \leq y \leq 20\}$
(B) $\{y: -29 \leq y \leq 20\}$
(C) $\{y: -8 \leq y \leq 9\}$
(D) $\{y: 4 \leq y \leq 20\}$
(E) $\{y: 29 \leq y \leq 101\}$

In case you have forgotten, the domain of a function is the set of values for which the function is defined, in this case $-2 \leq x \leq 4$. The range is the set of values that are the output—the value you must solve for. If you know how to do the problem, the computation is simple. Plug -2 and 4 into $6x^2 + 5$. Keep in mind that when you square -2, the product is 4 and not -4. Therefore, $6(-2)^2 + 5 = 29$ and $6(4)^2 + 5 = 101$. Answer: (E).

■ ■ ■

Radical Equations

For reasons not entirely clear to us, equations with roots in them are called *radical*. (For good measure, the number under the root is called the *radicand*.) But we digress. Like exponents, roots have their own special protocol. You can add them, as long as they have the same *index* (the little number that tells you the power of the root) and radicand. Thus,

$$3\sqrt{4} + 5\sqrt{4} = 8\sqrt{4}$$
and
$$7(\sqrt[5]{128}) - 5(\sqrt[5]{128}) = 2(\sqrt[5]{128})$$

By the same token, numbers under a radical sign with the same index can be multiplied and divided just like regular numbers. For instance,

$$\sqrt{9} \times \sqrt{5} = \sqrt{45}$$
and
$$\sqrt[3]{30} \div \sqrt[3]{6} = \sqrt[3]{5}.$$

Quadratic Equations

A quadratic equation is defined by the fact that a) it consists of more than one term joined by a plus or minus sign b) it has only one variable and c) its largest exponent is 2. Quadratic equations are noteworthy because you can *factor* them in interesting ways. Factoring is the opposite operation of distributing. To factor an equation, you pull out a number, as in:

$$6x^2 + 8 = 2(3x^2 + 4)$$

Since 2 is a factor of both $6x^2$ and 8, it is possible to pull it out. (Whether you should distribute a number *in* or factor it *out* depends on what you are trying to do—both come in handy depending on the situation.)

But it does get harder. The "general form" of a quadratic equation is

$$ax^2 + bx + c = 0$$
or to use numbers
$$2x^2 + 10x + 12.$$

For the purposes of the SAT, the most important kind of quadratic equations are the ones, like $2x^2 + 10x + 12$ that have roots that are integers. These can be put together and taken apart with relative ease. In other words:

$$2x^2 + 10x + 12 = (2x + 4)(x + 3)$$

Is this ringing a bell? Are you experiencing déjà vu Algebra II? You should be. If you can't factor a quadratic equation such as this by eyeballing it, get an algebra book and refresh your memory. You know that $2x^2$ will separate into $2x$ and x. To factor out the 10x, you know that one of the integers plus 2 times the other integer equals 10; and lastly, you know that one integer times the other equals 12. The only integers that satisfy these criteria are 3 and 4, yielding $(2x + 4)(x + 3)$.

To put it back together, you can use the trusty FOIL method: multiply the First two terms ($2x$ and x), then multiply the Outside terms ($2x$ and 3); then multiply the Inside terms (x and 4); and finally, multiply the Last two terms (4 and 3). That spells FOIL and you're back to $2x^2 + 10x + 12$.

This allows you to do some amazing sleight-of-hand, such as the following:

If
$$\frac{3x^2 + 15x + 18}{3x + 6} = 0$$

what is the value of x?

(A) 3
(B) –3
(C) 6
(D) –6
(E) –2

The first key to this question is to see the similarity between the numerator and the denominator of this expression. Whenever you have a denominator that looks like a factor of the numerator—in this case, the multiples of 3 are a dead giveaway—the odds are good that you can simplify the expression by factoring and canceling like terms. Think of it this way:

$$(3x + 6) \times (\underline{\quad\quad}) = 3x^2 + 15x + 18$$

Can you figure this one out by looking? What number multiplied by 6 equals 18? Did you get x + 3? Ok, back to the original equation. Let's re-write it this way:

$$\frac{(3x + 6)\,(x + 3)}{3x + 6} = 0$$

Now you've got it—simply cancel out the $(3x + 6)$'s to get $x + 3 = 0$. Answer: (B) –3.

Most of the quadratic equations that you will see on the SAT will be factorable in this way. As with special right triangles, there are a few special cases that are particularly likely to show up. Memorize these:

$$(x - y)^2 = x^2 - 2xy + y^2$$
$$(x + y)^2 = x^2 + 2xy + y^2$$
$$(x + y)(x - y) = x^2 - y^2$$

Some quadratic equations don't factor evenly, and to solve those you need a nasty-looking equation:

$$y = \frac{-b \pm \sqrt{b^2 - 4ac}}{2a}$$

This monstrosity is called the quadratic formula—you probably knew that already—and you should get reacquainted with it if your memory is fuzzy.

■ ■ ■

Trigonometry as an "Alternative Method of Solution"

The prospect of trig on the SAT has created a buzz, but the reality is a lot less intimidating than the hype. Trig will appear only as an alternative method of solution for questions dealing with 30-60-90 triangles or 45-45-90 triangles. (See pages 189–190.) The odds are good that you'll be able to do everything in your head without resorting to trig, but you may want to remind yourself of a few basic concepts. Trigonometry describes the relationships between the sides of right triangles. These relationships are dictated by the measures of the angles. *Sin* 30° will always equal $\frac{1}{2}$ no matter what the length of each side. The values for the sine (*sin*), cosine (*cos*), and tangent (*tan*) of any angle are available from your calculator at the touch of a key. All you need to know is this:

$$\text{sine} = \frac{\text{opposite}}{\text{hypotenuse}}$$

$$\text{cosine} = \frac{\text{adjacent}}{\text{hypotenuse}}$$

$$\text{tangent} = \frac{\text{opposite}}{\text{adjacent}}$$

Here is what a problem might look like:

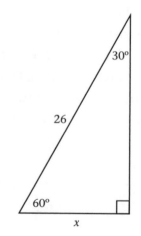

In the figure above, what is the value of x?

(A) 10
(B) 12
(C) 13
(D) 26
(E) 30

This problem can be solved in one of two ways. First, you can simply remember that the ratios of the sides of a 30-60-90 triangle are $1-\sqrt{3}-2$. Or, you can whip out your calculator and hit *sin* 30 or *cos* 60. Either way, the side of a 30-60-90 that is opposite the 30° angle is one-half as long as the side opposite the 90° angle. Answer: (C) 13.

■ ■ ■

Negative and Fractional Exponents

The old SAT included only exponents that were positive integers. The new one will have a few extra twists. Consider an expression such as $4^{3/4}$. Pretty funky. With fractional exponents, you treat the top half like a regular exponent and then use the bottom number to take the root, i.e. $4^{3/4} = \sqrt[4]{4^3}$. From there, you get $\sqrt[4]{64} = 2$.

You may also see some negative exponents, such as 5^{-2}. Simply take the reciprocal, $\frac{1}{5^2}$, and solve.

■ ■ ■

Functions and Function Notation

The old SAT dealt with functions, but now you will be required to recognize and use proper notation. It isn't necessarily hard:

If $f(x) = 3(x) + 3^x$, you might be asked to solve for $f(4)$. Therefore, $f(4) = 3(4) + 3^4$. Answer: 93.

But things could also get more complicated. Suppose you face a question such as: If

$$f(g(x)) = 8x + 4$$

and

$$g(x) = 16x + 8$$

which of the following is $f(x)$?

(A) 2
(B) $\frac{1}{4}$
(C) $\frac{1}{2}x$
(D) $2(8x + 4)$
(E) $2(g(x))$

In this problem, function f is a function of g. If $g(x) = 16x + 8$, and f turns $g(x)$ into $8x + 4$, what is $f(x)$?

You can tell by eye-balling it: $\frac{1}{2} \times (16x + 8) = 8x + 4$. Therefore, $f(x) = \frac{1}{2}x$ and the answer is (C).

Absolute value is another concept that you will see in combination with function notation or on its own. Can you compute $|f(x)|$ if $f(x) = x^3 - 3$ knowing that $x = -3$? Probably. You know that $-3^3 = -27$, and that $-27 - 3 = -30$. But the absolute value of a number is its distance from the origin—a positive value—and therefore the solution is 30.

The test may also include questions dealing with direct and inverse variation. When two variables show direct variation, if one increases then the other also increases. A function such as $f(x) = 10x$ is an example of direct variation. If x increases, so too does $f(x)$. An example of an inverse variation would be $f(x) = \frac{5}{x}$. As x gets larger, the value of $f(x)$ gets smaller.

To take it a step further, you also must be able to recognize the shape of functions—direct, inverse, and otherwise—in data that is modeled on real world situations. For instance, suppose you encounter the following:

Price of Candy Bars ($)	Number Sold (Per Day)
.50	100
.60	80
.70	65
.80	57
.90	52
1.00	50

A convenience store is considering how much to charge for candy bars. The chart above shows the number of candy bars per day that the store expects to sell at each price. If the price of the candy bars is plotted on the y axis and the number expected to be sold per day is plotted on the x axis, which of the following graphs most nearly reflects the shape of the curve?

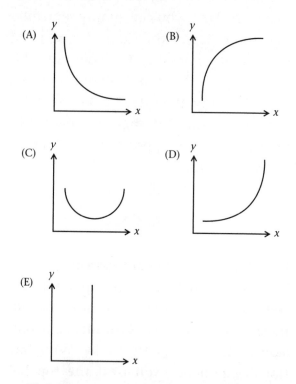

This question is a lot easier than it looks. From the data, you should immediately recognize an inverse variation. When price goes up, the number sold goes down. To put it another way, when the x variable goes up, the y variable goes down—and vice versa. That means a curve that is downward sloping to the right. Answer: (A).

Geometry and Measurement

While algebra will account for most of the new math, the test will also include some harder geometry. First, there will be more geometric notation, as in

$\overleftrightarrow{AB}$ → line AB

$\overline{AB}$ → line segment AB

$\overrightarrow{AB}$ → ray from A through B

AB → distance between A and B

$\overline{AB} \cong \overline{CD}$ → line segment AB is *congruent* to line segment CD

Nothing too difficult there. You'll also need to know, as you may already, that a line tangent to a circle is perpendicular to a radius drawn to the point of contact, as below.

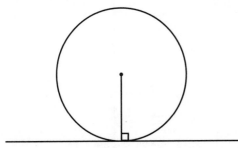

Perhaps the most significant additions to the geometry topics will be problems concerning the midpoint and distance formulas. Consider $\overline{AB}$. Suppose that A has coordinates (x_1, y_1) and B has coordinates (x_2, y_2). The midpoint of $\overline{AB}$ will have coordinates $(\frac{x_1 + x_2}{2}, \frac{y_1 + y_2}{2})$, and the distance AB will be $\sqrt{(x_1 - x_2)^2 + (y_1 - y_2)^2}$.

Our guess is that the midpoint formula won't cause your synapses to misfire, but the distance formula? Think $a^2 + b^2 = c^2$. In case your memory is shaky, that's the Pythagorean Theorem. When you find the distance between two points, all you're doing is finding the hypotenuse of a triangle. Let's do an example using a right triangle for simplicity. Suppose we need to find the distance of $\overline{PQ}$ that goes from point (1, 2) to point (4, 6):

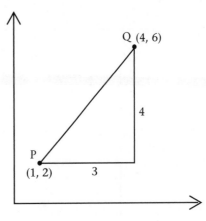

By plugging the coordinates of $\overline{PQ}$'s end points into the distance formula, we get

$$\sqrt{(4 - 1)^2 + (6 - 2)^2}$$
$$= \sqrt{3^2 + 4^2}$$
$$= \sqrt{25}$$
$$= 5$$

The difference between the values of the x coordinates (4 and 1) is 3, the length of the base. The difference between the values of the y coordinates (6 and 2) is 4, the length of the height. Using the distance formula, $3^2 + 4^2 = 25$, the square of the distance between the points. $\sqrt{25} = 5$ and there you have it.

We should hasten to add that the numbers rarely work out this cleanly—most square roots will be funky-looking decimals. But armed with your trusty calculator, you should not have a problem.

To help you get your juices going for the new math, here are some sample problems with answers below.

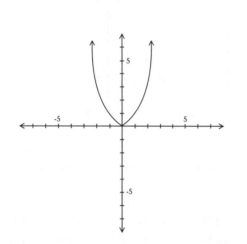

1. In the figure above, $f(x) = x^2$. Which of the following represents $f(x) = x^2 + 3$?

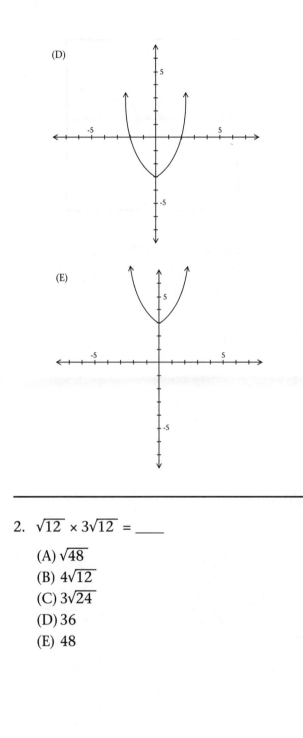

(D)

(E)

2. $\sqrt{12} \times 3\sqrt{12} =$ _____

   (A) $\sqrt{48}$

   (B) $4\sqrt{12}$

   (C) $3\sqrt{24}$

   (D) 36

   (E) 48

3. If

   $x - y = 4$

   and

   $x^2 - y^2 = 48$

   then which of the following is the value of y?

   (A) -8

   (B) -4

   (C) 2

   (D) 4

   (E) 8

4. $7^{-5/2} =$

   (A) $-\sqrt{7^5}$

   (B) -14^5

   (C) $\dfrac{1}{\sqrt[5]{7^2}}$

   (D) $\dfrac{1}{\sqrt{7^5}}$

   (E) $7^{-2/5}$

5. Suppose that ABC is a right triangle that has two congruent angles. The side opposite the right angle, BC, measures 12 inches. Which of the following most nearly approximates the length of AB?

   (A) 6

   (B) 6.5

   (C) 8

   (D) 8.5

   (E) $2\sqrt{12}$

6. Suppose that the population of a particular city is projected to double every 7 years. If the city's population is currently 23,000, which of the following may be used to express the city's projected population after 12 years?

(A) 23,000 (2^{12})
(B) 46,000
(C) 23,000 $(2^{12/7})$
(D) 552,000
(E) 23,000 (7^{2})

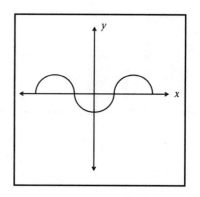

7. The figure above is the graph of $y = f(x)$. Which of the following is the graph of $|f(x)|$?

(A)

(B)

(C)

(D)

(E)

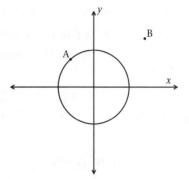

8. In the figure above, a circle that includes point A has its center at the origin. Point B is twice as far from the origin as point A. If the coordinates of point B are (6, 5), which of the following is the closest approximation of the circumference of the circle?

(A) 5π
(B) 6π
(C) 11π
(D) 30π
(E) $(\sqrt{61})\pi$

9. If
$$x^{-2} = \frac{9}{27\,(-2x - 3)}$$
then $x = ?$

(A) -3
(B) $\frac{1}{3}$
(C) 3
(D) 9
(E) 27

Number of books sold last week		
Book A	Book B	Book C
Store P 12	16	24
Store Q 16	20	20

Price of Books	
Hardback	Paperback
Book A $29	$16
Book B $22	$12
Book C $21	$9

10. Store P and Store Q are tracking the weekly sales of three best-selling books. Each of the books is available in both hardback and paperback. Both stores sell three times as many of the paperback editions of each book as they do of the hardback editions. What is the total cost of the hardback editions sold at Store P last week?

(A) $150
(B) $175
(C) $301
(D) $394
(E) $903

This batch of questions reflects the range of new topics that will appear in the math section. **The answers:** 1.(E) 2.(D) 3.(D) 4.(D) 5.(D) 6.(C) 7.(B) 8.(E) 9.(A) 10.(C). You may notice that ques-

tions 3–5 feature a run of three (D)'s in a row. We point this out because some so-called experts tell you to be leery of choosing the same letter three times in a row. Hogwash. Though it is true that strings of three are relatively unusual, you never know when you'll see one. Most versions of the SAT have several sequences of three in a row; we found one old SAT that had three such strings in a single verbal section. If you think you have the right answer, don't trouble yourself worrying if it happens to be the third (D) in a row. Focus on the content of the questions, not the pattern of letters on your answer sheet.

Now that we've gotten that off our chests, here are the explanations:

1. **Transformation**
   The main key to this problem is simply knowing that $f(x) = x^2$ means the same thing as $y = x^2$. The value of y gets big faster than the value of x because of the squaring, which yields the familiar u-shaped graph. Adding 3, or any new value that changes the graph of a function, is called a *transformation*. In this case, the transformation is to increase the value of y by 3 at every level of x. The answer choices include various nonsense along with the correct answer, (E), which shows the function shifted up by 3.

2. **Radical Thinking**

   This one is easy if you remember the rule for multiplying square roots. If the roots have the same index and radicand, as they do in this case, multiply them. $\sqrt{12} \times \sqrt{12} = 12$, and 3 x 12 = 36, (D).

3. **The Difference of Squares**

   This old chestnut is a special kind of quadratic equation known as the difference of squares. Any time you see $x^2 - y^2$, you can translate to $(x + y)(x - y)$.
   If $(x + y)(x - y) = 48$
   and $(x - y) = 4$,
   then $(x + y) = 12$.

There are quite a few combinations of numbers that would satisfy $(x - y) = 4$, but only one that will also satisfy $(x + y) = 12$. Answer: (D).

4. **Exponents Get Messier**

   A negative, fractional exponent problem will tie you in knots if you can't remember the rules for solving—but it should be easy if you can. A negative exponent means that you put the term in the denominator rather than the numerator, as in $x^{-2} = \frac{1}{x^2}$

With a fraction, you raise the number to the power of the numerator but put it under the root of the denominator, as in $x^{3/4} = \sqrt[4]{x^3}$. A negative, fractional exponent requires both of these operations. Answer: (D).

5. **Right Triangle Reasoning**

   A little trig anyone? This problem features a right triangle with two congruent angles—making it a 45-45-90. You probably know that the sides of a triangle like this are in the ratio of 1-1-$\sqrt{2}$. Hence, you could simply divide 12 (the length of the side opposite the 90° angle, and therefore the longest side) by $\sqrt{2}$ to get your answer. But the College Board and ETS want you to know that you can also use trig to solve this problem. You can use either Sine or Cosine. Let's take

$$\text{sine} = \frac{\text{opposite}}{\text{hypotenuse}}$$

The hypotenuse is 12 because it is opposite the biggest angle. So
$$\sin 45 = \frac{x}{12}$$
As the *sin* key on your calculator will tell you, *sin* 45 = .7071. Next, .7071(12) = 8.49. Answer: (D).

6. **Population Explosion**

The College Board and ETS say that the SAT will have more problems requiring students to apply numbers to real-world situations. This particular one is an example of an exponential sequence. We know that the initial population is 23,000, and that it will double every 7 years. After 7 years, the population will be 23,000(2). After 14 years, it will be 23,000(2^2). But the question asks for the population after 12 years. Here's a hint: $2 = 2^{7/7}$, and $2^2 = 2^{14/7}$. Got it now? The population after 12 years will be 23,000($2^{12/7}$). Answer: (C).

7. **Absolute Value With a Twist**

This question requires students to apply the concept of absolute value to a graph. As in question 1 above, the first key is to understand that $f(x)$ is the same thing as y. If we're taking $|f(x)|$, that means no y coordinate on the graph can be negative. For every point on the function where y has a negative value—that is, where the function dips below the x axis—we must flip it to make y positive. Let's say that a point on the function is (2,–1). Taking the absolute value of the function makes that point (2, 1). The correct answer is (B) because the middle part of the function has

been flipped over the x axis, and all the values of y are ≥ 0. Answer: (B)

8. **Going Around in Circles**

The formula for the circumference of a circle is πd where d is the circle's diameter. Since point A is on the circle, we know that the distance from A to the origin is the radius of the circle. Therefore, if point B is twice as far from the origin as point A, then the distance from point B to the origin is the circle's diameter. From here, the question boils down to applying the distance formula,

$$\sqrt{(x_1 - x_2)^2 + (y_1 - y_2)^2}$$

yielding $\sqrt{(6 - 0)^2 + (5 - 0)^2}$

or $\sqrt{61}$.

Answer: (E), $(\sqrt{61})\pi$.

9. **A Quadratic Equation in Disguise**

You should have recognized immediately that this problem is a scrambled quadratic equation. Your goal is to get everything on the same side of the equal marks so that you can factor it. First, remember that $x^{-2} = \frac{1}{x^2}$. Since both sides of the equation have more stuff on the bottom than the top, the easiest way to work is to flip both sides, yielding

$$x^2 = \frac{27(-2x - 3)}{9}.$$

Next, divide 27 by 9 to get

$$x^2 = 3(-2x - 3).$$

From there, distribute the 3 to get

$$x^2 = -6x - 9$$

and then

$$x^2 + 6x + 9 = 0.$$

Factoring yields $(x + 3)(x + 3) = 0$.
Answer: (A) –3.

10. **Digging Through Data**
The College Board calls this a "data interpretation" problem. The selection of data laid out in columns and rows is suggestive of matrix algebra, but all problems such as this can be solved with simple calculations. The question asks for the total cost of the hardbacks sold at Store P, and the crucial piece of information is that hardbacks account for 1/4 of all sales. Therefore, the number of hardbacks sold at Store P is: Book A, 3; Book B, 4; and Book C, 6. Next multiply these by the price of the hardbacks: $3(\$29) + 4(\$22) + 6(\$21) = \$301$
Answer: (C).

Keys to Success

1. **Find Your Approach.** We sympathize with the 590 M, 720 M scorer who writes, "Eventually I just didn't really know how to approach the SAT anymore because my teachers and my tutor would suggest contradicting methods." The moral: Don't fill your head with strategies from someone else. Our hope is that you will experiment with the approaches in this book, use those that work and discard those that don't.

2. **Balance Speed and Accuracy.** A famous basketball coach once said, "Be quick, but don't hurry." Practice tests are where you should push your speed to the limit. It may seem uncomfortable at first, but that means you're stretching yourself. Once test day nears, your priority should shift to finding a comfortable groove where you can relax and be efficient.

3. **Exercise Your Memory.** Short-term memory is half the battle on the math SAT. You may feel hopelessly absent-minded—at the ripe old age of 17—but the fact is that you can improve your short-term memory with practice. Many students are simply not in the habit of focusing because they rarely read and always

have distractions while studying. So...turn off the radio, get away from the TV, and really focus when you work. Practice doing problems in your head to build your capacity. If you're really serious, try memorizing strings of random numbers. If you work on your memory, it will improve.

4. **Trust Yourself and Move On**. Have you ever been on the verge of dropping a letter in a mail slot, only to find yourself ripping it open to double-check on something you meant to include? The chances are good that everything was there—but you just couldn't trust yourself. Some people are like that on the SAT, especially on the math. Trusting yourself is about more than merely saving time. It is a state of mind that says you are confident of success. So relax. Do your best and then move on.

7 WORD FOR WORD
QUOTES FROM THE STUDENTS ABOUT THE PREP COURSES

A major thrust of this book is that SAT coaching courses are often a waste of money. Chapter 2 offers an overview of the evidence behind this finding, but we suspect that some people will still need convincing. In the pages that follow, we offer a selection of quotes from students who received coaching from Princeton Review or Kaplan. We include quotes from every one of the 32 such students who got a combined score of over 1400, and we also include a selection of quotes from students who scored lower. In addition, we offer a sample of quotes from students who received one-on-one tutoring from other sources.

We recommend that you browse the quotes. Similar themes will be repeated, but you may glean additional insight from hearing many different voices. There are several reasons why we chose to quote every 1400 scorer who took a Princeton Review or Kaplan course. We wanted to include quotes from all students in a specified interval to demonstrate that we were not quoting selectively. If the point of taking a prep course is to do well on the test, we thought it only natural to hear from students who did just that. As a group, the 1400+ scorers were by far the most insightful and articulate of any cohort. Having reached the Holy Grail of standardized testing, they speak with special authority.

The statements that follow were made in response to items on our survey. Where the context is unclear, we have inserted text in brackets to help clarify it, and in a few cases, we have repeated our survey question in italics.

Students Who Took a Princeton Review Course

"I would not take this course again. The benefits were most definitely not worth the costs.... The course moved too slowly and was not challenging enough. It did not help me raise my score 100 points as it promised it would. Students who have below 500 on either subject would probably benefit greatly from the course.... I would recommend that students prepare on their own with books and software because these can provide more help than some of the instructors at prep courses.... Making educated guesses and finding a Joe Bloggs answer does not help improve scores that much on the higher end of the scale."

—800 Verbal, 750 Math

"[The prep course] was a waste of time. Completely. The only benefit was getting a vocab book and I made cards of all the words I didn't know...."

—750 V, 790 M

"I could have gotten just as much from simply purchasing the workbooks. We went over a lot of information I already knew and did not benefit from learning it again.... Parents forcing does not work. It has to be your decision.... I could have accomplished the majority of what we did in class from working in books, and at my own pace."

—750 V, 770 M

"[A prep course is worthwhile] because it forces you to prepare. Without the course, I wouldn't have spent as much time studying."

—730 V, 760 M

"[The course] raised my score significantly.... I would recommend it.... All students should prep as it gives anyone an edge. Strategies learned through explanation and working specifically on weaknesses is crucial."

—720 V, 730 M

"I was skeptical at first, but the course taught me to think like those who design the test, a factor I largely attribute my SAT success to.... Understanding the test and how it works is easily half the battle.... The drawbacks were sessions that didn't teach me anything. For example, vocab classes that reviewed words I could easily handle...."

—800 V, 700 M

"[The course] didn't do anything. Maybe if my test scores had started out lower.... [*Would you advise other students to take an SAT prep course?*] Yes, [if you're] too lazy to do it on [your] own [or] need encouragement/help if you don't know [the] answer!"

—710 V, 770 M

"[The course offered] familiarity with the test and basic test-taking strategy. I would recommend it to everyone."

—740 V, 740 M

"[A prep course is worthwhile] if you are willing to pay, because it is more motivating because you have to go to class."

—660 V, 800 M

"Princeton Review was a waste. Do 1-on-1 tutoring."

—700 V, 690 M

"I would not take the course again, nor would I recommend it. The teacher was awful."

—780 V, 660 M

"I didn't feel like [the course] gave me any advantage I couldn't have gained by practicing on my own. I was also at the top of the class, so it was not a challenging experience for me.... I became familiar with the test and thus was not as intimidated by it as I would have been otherwise.... My score was not raised very much.... [A prep course] forces you to do something instead of putting off doing it on your own."

—710 V, 710 M

"[It was definitely worth the cost]—it went over everything! All should take classroom prep @ Princeton Review."

—730 V, 670 M

"The actual class was not important. It was all the practice that helped.... [The class] was too long and spent too much time attending to the individuals with the poorest score, leaving me very bored. People who have no determination should take the classroom prep, people looking to improve a moderate score should take one-on-one, and driven individuals should prepare on their own."

—710 V, 710 M

"The least helpful strategy was finding the Joe Bloggs answer because I had a hard time identifying those answers."

—650 V 640 M

"[The course] was invaluable.... Flexibility, small classes, good instruction...I improved by 100 points.... Only motivated students should take prep courses—otherwise it's a waste of time."

—710 V, 710 M

"If you are disciplined enough to work thru a prep book, then this class is a waste.... It forced me to do the work on a weekly basis, learn tricks, etc.—very repetitive!!"

—690 V, 720 M

"It really helped. Everything was great, I would recommend it."

—700 V, 720 M

"The benefits were not worth the cost and I would not take this course again.... Perhaps the structure of the course was not meant for my learning style.... I don't think it was helpful to be learning with other students at different levels.... For me, working by myself helped me more than a prep course."

—740 V, 660 M

"I would take the course again. Not only did it improve my ability, it also made me more confident.... The only drawback was the time it took but the results paid off....The one-on-one tutoring is an excellent option for students with learning disabilities because it allows the student to develop a strategy specifically for their style."

—680 V, 720 M

"I think the SAT is a ridiculous, unfair system. Although I felt that I was acquiring an unfair advantage because my family could afford to pay for the course, the course was effective."

—710 V, 650 M

"They shouldn't guarantee points. Going up depends on how much time one spends on the work outside class on the test in a specific day."

—650 V, 690 M

"It did everything it said it would. I do recommend this course to others. I think people should take a class-room course and prepare on their own.... If you don't understand something, a book or computer program can't explain it to you."

—700 V, 700 M

"I learned a lot of great strategies but did not improve my score by the 100 points that were guaranteed. I would still recommend it to other students because I know that it can be very helpful for many students."

—650 V, 550 M

"I wouldn't recommend it to others because I don't know anyone whose score greatly improved."

—600 V, 620 M

"The prep course was too long, too many consecutive hours taking practice tests and exercises in the workbooks.... Students with time should take the prep course in order to ensure that they are practicing. Students with a lot of personal drive and discipline need not take a prep course so long as they are willing to put effort into studying."

—630 V, 630 M

"It was a very helpful course that put me on the right track for studying for the test. The strategies I learned helped me approach the test wisely."

—630 V, 600 M

"It didn't help me any."

—390 V, 490 M

"It took too much of my time, and it wasn't worth it. It raised my score only 10 points.... One word: overrated."

—510 V, 650 M

"The teacher was very helpful and my classmates were very nice. A good book and atmosphere to learn in."

—450 V, 490 M

"The course was very long (3 hours each session). I couldn't concentrate for that long so it was a drawback. Princeton Review did not keep its word about private tutoring if I didn't go up 100 points from my first practice test—I had to find a tutor on my own."

—640 V, 590 M

"My teacher at Princeton Review was really intelligent and had a great sense of humor. She really got me through the class learning a lot and having fun, which can be a challenging duality.... The biggest drawback for me was that there were a lot of students in the class who never did their work and didn't care at all."

—650 V, 530 M

Students Who Took a Kaplan Course

"It was time- and money-consuming. People in course had different needs and different goals. Hard to make course meet requirements of individuals.... I would suggest the classroom, or one-on-one tutoring if you are unable to work on your own. If you will procrastinate and only study a week or less before...books are just as helpful [as a prep course] if you take the time to use them."

—780 V, 780 M

"The classes did not help at all. The only reason I liked the program was for the access to old SAT exams.... I did not learn from the classes. Sometimes I knew more than the teacher and I had to explain problems to the class.... Students with fairly bright to very high scores should not take classes."

—750 V, 800 M

"I would recommend the company [Kaplan]. Some of the teachers were too laid back and did not know their subjects extremely well—it was college kids teaching us.... Students who do generally well but want the extra push should take a classroom course. Those who need a vast improvement should be in one-on-one tutoring because they need more personalized help."

—750 V, 730 M

"[The Kaplan course] motivated me to prepare on my own. The teachers did a really good job. The most important element of the prep course is working one-on-one with a teacher.... the prep course read from its book. The teachers explained things from the answer key. Kaplan was OK I guess. It got me motivated to prepare."

—700 V, 760 M

"I am very busy and have a lot of homework, so if I had not 'scheduled' time to study by taking the class, it would have been very hard to motivate myself to study on my own. I would advise others to take a class because you need to be prepared for the SAT and most high school students do not have the time, energy, or motivation to study on their own."

—710 V, 750 M

"Kaplan really dissects the SAT I for students and stresses all of the right strategies. We met once a week for three hours, covering one unit a week. We had weekly homework and vocab exercises. I loved the little dose of preparation we got each week, the way the course was designed. Practice tests scattered throughout the course gave confidence as we could see our scores improve. I would advise students to take a course because it is better to have a live person there to break down the test for you and coach you through your mistakes than to do it all on your own."

—710 V, 750 M

"I paid for the course but I only went once. Instead, I used the practice books they gave me the first day.... If you are able to figure out the problem by reading the explanations in the back of the book, then the three hours every Sunday is useless.... They tried to teach us how the test-maker thinks. However, you can go to Borders and get the same advice for free."

—750 V, 700 M

"I would have studied the books on my own (cheaper) and asked a guidance counselor my questions (free)."

—1360 V&M

"[The course] helped me to narrow in on my weaknesses and gave clues about taking the test. HOWEVER, the classes didn't help, it was taking the test twice that made a difference.... Didn't help that much because I need to practice the questions more."

—700 V, 730 M

"I would never take this course again. They rip people off. The only thing that they teach is how to do problems during the first few classes. Then they do problems with the whole class. I could have done the same thing at home."

—720 V, 690 M

❝I felt that I was barely helped at all.... The prep course was taught by a college student who wasn't very helpful. No, I wouldn't recommend it.... Everyone should prepare on their own. If someone is struggling they should get one-on-one. No one should take the classroom prep course.❞

—690 V, 710 M

"My scores went up before the prep course. The course only steadied my scores...I already knew most of the techniques taught. I would recommend it."

—690 V, 710 M

"My teachers didn't take the course seriously, so it was hard to actually learn anything. I don't blame the Kaplan course, I blame my teachers."

—660 V, 690 M

"Kaplan I would not recommend. What was taught in the classroom was the exact same thing printed in the Kaplan book I bought from the bookstore."

—740 V, 690 M

"It was very repetitive but I'm sure it could help others. I just hit a ceiling."

—660 V, 700 M

Based on your experience, what sort of students should take a classroom prep course?

"Ones that can't read because they read the book to you verbatim."

—650 V, 660 M

"Don't try to learn every vocab word or every math formula—you'll go crazy."

—600 V, 550 M

"I think it is more worthwhile to just buy a practice test book and do it on your own."

—610 V, 610 M

"Ones who want to waste time and money. Save a grand and buy the books."

—620 V, 660 M

"I would take this course again because it helped me feel more confident when taking the SATs."

—610 V, 640 M

"The drawbacks of the prep course were that it was very slow and boring and much of the stuff that we focused on were not what I need help with."

—610 V, 680 M

"All I needed was practice, and I could have gotten that from a book rather than paying the extra hundreds of dollars."

—690 V, 580 M

"My instructors were clear and they were there for me when I needed help.... I would advise students to take prep courses so that the instructors will guide the students personally on how to prepare."

—370 V, 470 M

One-on-One Tutoring

The following is a selection of quotes from students who took one-on-one tutoring from sources other than Princeton Review or Kaplan.

❝I think that practice makes the most dramatic effect on your score, but having a tutor kept me disciplined and focused, which I could not have done on my own.... A good program has one central feature, which is practice.❞

—770 V, 720 M

"Practice tests are the most useful thing ever because of their ability to help you understand the nature of the test and its questions, which relaxes you and lets you know what to expect. Tutor, however, is a great help in showing you how to approach the problems.... The good thing about tutoring is you can focus on one area. I was fine in math so I could just do English work."

—680 V, 800 M

"The actual course did not help that much.... The vocabulary sheets and the opportunity to familiarize myself with the test were the positive aspects of my prep program.... The tricks they taught, in some cases, took longer than figuring out the problem on your own.... I would recommend one-on-one tutoring to students who really need help and to those who do not need that much help. People who are extremely smart naturally do not need any tutoring."

—720 V, 720, M

"People should take tutoring if they have money to burn.... Prepare on your own."

—760 V, 690 M

"I felt that it was useless... There was a lot of wasted time.... People who have never taken standardized tests need help. I learn on my own more."

—670 V, 750 M

"Although the prices are getting rather extravagant, it is extremely helpful to have this one-on-one attention.... I would recommend this company, but there is always a chance of getting a tutor you don't like."

—690 V, 750 M

"[The positive aspects of my course included] learning your strengths and weaknesses, and learning strategies to save time and think clearly even when questions are unclear.... It was sometimes hard because it was one-on-one, so I felt put on the spot when I didn't know the answer to a question. Other than that, it was great.... If you are diligent enough, you can probably prepare on your own with good results."

—720 V, 710 M

"[Tutoring] brought my score from 1200 to 1340. You can't put a price on that. [I recommend] one-on-one instead of a class. It focuses on your individual needs."

—630 V, 710 M

"I think that what I got out of my prep course was stronger vocab and experiences from taking practice tests. If I had bought a good vocab book and made my own schedule, I think that I could have been just as effective. The positive aspects were that there was someone who served as a figure to keep me on task. As well, the tutor was helpful in reviewing my mistakes and giving test-taking strategies based on trends in the test."

—610 V, 800 M

"My tutor made me do the work on the tests. If he hadn't forced me to do it, I probably wouldn't have done it.... Lazy students who have parents that can afford it should get one-on-one tutoring.... I think most students should prepare on their own."

—690 V, 710 M

"[Students] that are nervous about the test should take one-on-one. It's mentally beneficial. Do not prepare on your own if you are nervous."

—670 M, 690 V

"I am not the most motivated person, but actually having to meet with someone forced me to do the homework and practice for the SATs.... Students who need someone to watch them do the work or need the extra attention/explanation should get a one-on-one tutor."

—540 M, 630 V

Acknowledgments

We are grateful to all those who assisted in the preparation of this book. We owe our greatest debt to the college counselors in our Advisory Group, and to the hundreds of students who gave us their insight about taking the SAT.

Alice Perry, chair of the English Department at Sandia Preparatory School, made timely corrections in the chapters about the Writing and Critical Reading Sections. Steve Beamish, math teacher at Sandia Prep, generously edited the chapter about the Math section.

We are grateful to our families for their support and encouragement through the many months we worked on this book.

We are indebted to our editors at Sourcebooks, including Todd Stocke, Peter Lynch, and Samantha Raue, whose support for our books is unwavering.

We appreciate the efforts of all, but responsibility for the final product is ours alone.

College Counselors Advisory Group

Marilyn Albarelli, Moravian Academy (PA)
Scott Anderson, Mercersburg Academy (PA)
Caroline Van Antwerp, Colorado Springs School (CO)
Christine Asmussen, St. Andrew's-Sewanee School (TN)
Bruce Bailey, Lakeside School (WA)
Samuel Barnett, SchoolFutures (VA)
Amy E. Belstra, Cherry Creek H.S. (CO)
Greg Birk, Kinkaid School (TX)
Susan T. Bisson, Advocates for Human Potential (MA)
Robin Boren, Dakota Ridge H.S. (CO)
Clarice Boring, Cody H.S. (WY)
John B. Boshoven, Community High School &
Jewish Academy of Metro Detroit (MI)
Mimi Bradley, St. Andrew's Episcopal School (MS)
Nancy Bryan, Pace Academy (GA)
Claire Cafaro, Ridgewood H.S. (NJ)
Nancy Caine, St. Augustine H.S. (CA)
Mary Calhoun, St. Cecilia Academy (TN)
Mary Chapman, St. Catherine's School (VA)
Nedra A. Clark, Montclair High School (NJ)
Anthony L. Clay, Carolina Friends School (NC)
Kathy Cleaver, Durham Academy (NC)
Alison Cotten, Cypress Falls H.S. (TX)
Alice Cotti, Polytechnic School (CA)
Rod Cox, St. Johns Country Day School (FL)
Carroll K. Davis, North Central H.S. (IN)
Renee C. Davis, Rocky River H.S. (OH)
Mary Jo Dawson, Academy of the Sacred Heart (MI)
Christy Dillon, Crystal Springs Uplands School (CA)
Walta Sue Dodd, Bryan H.S. (NE)
Tara A. Dowling, Saint Stephen's Episcopal School (FL)
Dan Feldhaus, Iolani School (HI)
Ralph S. Figueroa, Albuquerque Academy (NM)
Emily E. FitzHugh, The Gunnery (CT)
Larry Fletcher, Salesianum School (DE)
Nancy Fomby, Episcopal School of Dallas (TX)
Daniel Franklin, Eaglecrest High School (CO)
Laura Johnson Frey, Vermont Academy (VT)
Phyllis Gill, Providence Day School (NC)
H. Scotte Gordon, Moses Brown School (RI)
Freida Gottsegen, Pace Academy (GA)
Molly Gotwals, Suffield Academy (CT)
Kathleen Barnes Grant, The Catlin Gabel School (OR)
Madelyn Gray, John Burroughs School (MO)
Amy Grieger, Northfield Mount Hermon School (MA)

Elizabeth Hall, Education Consulting Services (TX)
Andrea L. Hays, Hathaway Brown School (OH)
Rob Herald, Cairo American College (Egypt)
Darnell Heywood, Columbus School for Girls (OH)
Bruce Hunter, Rowland Hall-St. Mark's School (UT)
Deanna L. Hunter, Shawnee Mission East H.S. (KS)
John Keyes, The Catlin Gabel School (OR)
Sharon Koenings, Brookfield Academy (WI)
Joan Jacobson, Shawnee Mission South H.S. (KS)
Gerimae Kleinman, Shaker Heights H.S. (OH)
Laurie Leftwich, Brother Martin High School (LA)
Mary Jane London, Los Angeles Center for Enriched
Studies (CA)
Martha Lyman, Deerfield Academy (MA)
Brad MacGowan, Newton North H.S. (MA)
Robert S. MacLellan, Jr., The Pingry School (NJ)
Margaret M. Man, La Pietra-Hawaii School for Girls (HI)
Susan Marrs, The Seven Hills School (OH)
Karen A. Mason, Wyoming Seminary (PA)
Lisa Micele, University of Illinois Laboratory H.S. (IL)
Corky Miller-Strong, Alexander Dawson School (CO)
Janet Miranda, Trinity Christian Academy (TX)
Richard Morey, Dwight-Englewood School (NJ)
Joyce Vining Morgan, Putney School (VT)
Daniel Murphy, The Urban School of San Francisco
(CA)
Judith Nash, Highland High School (ID)
Arlene L. Prince, University Preparatory Academy (WA)
Deborah Robinson, Mandarin H.S. (FL)
Julie Rollins, Episcopal H.S. (TX)
William C. Rowe, Thomas Jefferson School (MO)
Bruce Scher, Barrington H.S. (IL)
David Schindel, Vail Mountain School (CO)
Kathy Z. Schmidt, St. Mary's Hall (TX)
Joe Stehno, Bishop Brady H.S. (NH)
Bruce Stempien, Weston H.S. (CT)
Paul M. Stoneham, The Key School (MD)
Audrey Threlkeld, Forest Ridge School of the Sacred
Heart (WA)
Vincent S. Travaglione, La Jolla Country Day School
(CA)
Ted de Villafranca, Peddie School (NJ)
Scott White, Montclair H.S. (NJ)
Linda Zimring, Los Angeles Unified School District
(CA)

About the Authors

In 1980, when he was education editor of the *New York Times*, Edward B. Fiske sensed that college-bound students and their families needed better information on which to base their educational choices. Thus was born *The Fiske Guide to Colleges*. A graduate of Wesleyan University, Ted did graduate work at Columbia University and assorted other bastions of higher learning. He left the *Times* in 1991 to pursue a variety of educational and journalistic interests, including a book on school reform, *Smart Schools, Smart Kids*. When not visiting colleges, he can be found playing tennis, sailing, or doing research on the educational problems of Third World countries for UNESCO and other international organizations. Ted lives in Durham, North Carolina, near the campus of Duke University, where his wife is a member of the faculty. They are coauthors of *When Schools Compete: A Cautionary Tale* and *Elusive Equality: Education Reform in Post-Apartheid South Africa*.

Since entering Yale in the early 1980s, Bruce G. Hammond has devoted much of his time to counseling for college. At Yale, Bruce was editor-in-chief of *The Insider's Guide to the Colleges*. He subsequently served as managing editor of *The Fiske Guide to Colleges*. He is also the author of *Discounts and Deals at the Nation's 360 Best Colleges*. He has been quoted in numerous national publications, including the *New York Times*, the *Wall Street Journal*, *USA Today*, the *Washington Post*, *U.S.News & World Report*, *Business Week*, *Money Magazine*, and *Good Housekeeping*. Bruce lives in Albuquerque, New Mexico, with his wife and step-sons and is director of college counseling at Sandia Preparatory School.